Dave Gallaher

THE ORIGINAL ALL BLACK CAPTAIN

Matt Elliott

 HarperCollins*Publishers*

To my brother Joseph Carlaw Elliott, for whom there are three things in life: family, faith and football.

HarperCollins*Publishers*

First published in 2012
Reprinted 2012
by HarperCollins*Publishers* (New Zealand) Limited
PO Box 1, Shortland Street, Auckland 1140

Copyright © Matt Elliott 2012

HarperCollins*Publishers*
31 View Road, Glenfield, Auckland 0627, New Zealand
Level 13, 201 Elizabeth Street, Sydney, NSW 2000, Australia
A 53, Sector 57, Noida, UP, India
77–85 Fulham Palace Road, London W6 8JB, United Kingdom
2 Bloor Street East, 20th floor, Toronto, Ontario M4W 1A8, Canada
10 East 53rd Street, New York, NY 10022, USA

National Library of New Zealand Cataloguing-in-Publication Data

Elliott, Matt.
Dave Gallaher : the original All Black captain / Matt Elliott.
ISBN 978-1-86950-968-2
1. Gallaher, D. (David), 1873-1917. 2. Rugby Union football captains—New Zealand—Biography. 3. Rugby Union football—New Zealand—History. 4. Soldiers—New Zealand—Biography.
I. Title.
796.333092—dc 23

ISBN: 978 1 86950 968 2

Design and typesetting by Springfield West
Cover design by Jane Waterhouse, HarperCollins Design Studio
Front cover image courtesy of New Zealand Rugby Museum. Back cover image used courtesy of the family of Sergeant Joseph Cecil Thompson, of Childers, Queensland. Background images by shutterstock.com

Printed and bound in Great Britain by Clays Ltd, St Ives plc

Contents

Introduction

Travel through small towns in New Zealand and you will invariably see two things. The first is a war memorial statue or column erected in the years after the First World War, remembering those from the local community who did not come back. Most of these memorials feature the names of brothers, fathers and sons who made the ultimate sacrifice. It left these little communities with a sadness that is almost palpable even today when one reads the inscribed names.

The other sight is a field with a set of rugby goalposts on it. These big, white Hs have also stood for years; another memorial to those men from the town who looked forward to a Saturday afternoon 'chasing the oval', being part of local rivalries that have a fierce intensity for 80 minutes, perhaps once a year. In many instances, at the entrances to these grounds are memorial gates of stone or wrought iron, combining the remembrance of the sacrifice made by local men with that of their local passion. Boys grew into men on these fields. They grew up wanting to be All Blacks, to wear the black jersey, to represent their country at 'our' game. While being the toast of the country for winning on the football field against arch rivals has its own importance, the real heroes have been those boys and men who have fought for their country. They are the ones who really knew what it was like to experience 'trench warfare', to reach the 'do or die' moments, to find themselves under 'a bomb', to 'put their bodies on the line' when the coach rolls out 'the big guns' — all the phrases that are now such a part of sporting parlance, but which have a deeper, much more sombre resonance when one really thinks about them.

Mention of Dave Gallaher reminds us of the early glory days of New Zealand football, and the important foundation stones which he played a part in laying, on which one of sport's most revered and successful teams would be built. When the All Blacks perform the haka before matches in the United Kingdom and Ireland, we see a tradition that is as old as our encounters with those traditional foes. The haka has changed, but so has the game and all that revolves around it. As much as some writers regularly object to its presence in oft-repeated, pre-match wind-ups, when taking a broader view of the history of the game the All Black haka is a unique piece of cultural and sporting theatre. It was used as an entertainment, an offering of something unique 'from Maoriland', to opposing players and spectators. It still is, but the national rugby team no longer says merely that 'our identity is that of Maorilanders'. The haka also says that in New Zealand not only the game but also the *history* of the game and those who have worn that black jersey with the silver fern on the breast are inseparable parts of our love of the sport.

Gallaher's name also reminds us of the tragedy of war, and — particularly pertaining to New Zealand — of that place called Passchendaele, where so many men represented their country with pride, in something bigger than sport, where they didn't want to let down their mates and where their lives were cruelly ended. Thousands are honoured in graves which extend plot after plot, row after row, in war cemeteries near the battlefield where they died. Many remain 'Known only unto God'.

We can only wonder what the future contributions by Gallaher to his community and football could have been were he to have returned from the war, but even in death his influence and legacy are enduring.

Rugby has a wonderful oral tradition built from the retelling of stories over bar-leaners, kitchen tables, and sideline pickets. Players become 'legends', as do their accomplishments. Many of us have grown up hearing those oft-told stories, so it is exciting for the writer when research throws up confirmations of old tales or additional information on the lives of those who feature in them. One of the unexpected surprises during the two years of research for this book was, while looking up the medical records of Dave's mother, coming across an entry for Dave as a boy. I was also fortunate to come across a scrapbook that was compiled by Charles Stitchbury, who was a stalwart of the Ponsonby club as a player and a committee member, and also manager of the Auckland team during Gallaher's years as selector/coach. This provided a wonderful snapshot of activities of the Ponsonby club on and off the field 11 decades ago. I hope that some of the findings within add to the rich history of the game, be it through adding new insight into our past or starting new debates, but also by giving a fuller picture of one of the most important figures in New Zealand rugby history.

I have no hesitation in acknowledging the decade-long Gallaher family research done by Kay Carter, granddaughter of Dave's brother Oswald. Her work, while reassuringly confirming aspects of my own research, also gave me a more definite picture of the wider Gallaher family relationships. It was a real pleasure to meet up with her when she and her husband Bill were in Katikati presenting her family history to relations.

Gallaher's direct descendants are private, humble people. They, like Dave, see him as but one part of a now much larger group of men: the All Blacks. They also know that there was more to him than just being a footballer. Special thanks to Adrienne Tubbs, a great-granddaughter of Gallaher, for the time she gave me.

For ease of description I have referred to New Zealand rugby teams as the All Blacks in all instances, and also use the moniker 'The Originals' for the 1905 tourists. There is not space in this book to offer a play-by-play description of each match on the 1905 tour of Great Britain and Ireland. Besides, in commemoration of the centenary of that tour, three books were published in New Zealand doing just that. They are recommended to those wanting to focus on the detail of the tour, as they range from the strictly historical 'scrapbook' record of Bob Howitt and Dianne Haworth's *1905 Originals* and Christopher Tobin's album, *The Original All Blacks 1905–06*, to John McCrystal's superb, interpretive account of the tour, *The Originals: 1905 All Black Rugby Odyssey*. I owe a debt of gratitude to rugby writers and historians such as Neville McMillan, Rod Chester, TP McLean, Ron Palenski and Lindsay Knight (to name just five) who have kept the vibrant history of the game alive.

Thanks are due also to: Max Cryer; Tony Johnson for his thoughts on Gallaher and his 1905 teammates; Brian Finn and Charlotte Wilson at the New Zealand Rugby Union; Dave Syms, Auckland Rugby Union; Bryan Williams, Ponsonby Rugby Club; George and Ina Hermes, www.ramelton.net; Paul Paton, archivist at Auckland Grammar School; Robert Love; staff of Birkenhead Public Library; Keith Giles, Photographic Librarian, and Auckland Public Library's Sir George Grey Special Collections staff; Archives New Zealand (Auckland and Wellington); Jocelyn Chalmers, Alexander Turnbull Library; Martin Collett, Auckland Museum Library; Grant Little; Alison Brook, Vicki Marsdon, Eva Chan, Kate Stone and Anna Bowbyes (HarperCollins).

More personal thanks to Mel for her support, suggestions and map creation, and to Murray for his ongoing interest.

'Their impact on the game has earned the first All Blacks a unique place in any history of the Rugby Union. Everything which followed was comparatively straightforward, even ordinary, compared with the explosive originality and dazzling combination of Gallaher and his men.'

— OL Owen, *History of the Rugby Football Union*, 1955

'Happy is the man who, when his football days are over and his part is merely that of a watcher from the stand, or of the critic in the committee room, knows that it is said of him that it was he who made a certain famous team of long ago, and that it was he who inspired fourteen other men to deeds of which, without him, they were quite incapable. They will speak of it as his team, and to have his name thus linked with that famous combination as its master and its leader is the greatest honour that can ever come the way of the Rugby footballer.'

— D Gallaher and WJ Stead, *The Complete Rugby Footballer on the New Zealand System*, 1906

'I found in war-time that there was a considerable virtue in men who had played games like professionals to win, and not, like public-school boys and amateurs, for exercise. ... New Zealanders, when they went to war, found it easier to get down to the moral plane of a German soldier, and were even capable of thinking a ruse or two ahead in the game of total war. Englishmen spent some time and casualties in finding war ungentlemanly before they tossed the rules overboard and moved in on the same basis. I don't know that the cunning and professionalism of my fellow countrymen is to be commended on abstract grounds, but these are comfortable qualities to have about in war-time. ... It was only that they looked on war as a game, and a game to New Zealanders is something that they play to win, against the other side and the referee, if necessary.'

— John Mulgan, *Report on Experience*, 1947

Ramelton

The Gallaghers' prospects were poor.

At the 2011 Rugby World Cup in New Zealand, thousands of fans going to and from Eden Park for matches stopped to admire the recently erected statue of David Gallaher, captain of the 1905 All Blacks. Those who knew their rugby history admired the depiction of the famous footballer. Others read the legend bearing an outline of his career and his contribution to football in New Zealand. Some stood in front of the statue to be photographed, while others (who may have imbibed liberally of one of the tournament's chief sponsors' product) posed comically, trying to tackle the bronze figure. Generally, there was a sense of reverence towards the statue that, as an initiative of the Ponsonby Rugby Club, had taken 15 years to have made and placed, in time for the World Cup, on the outskirts of one of world rugby's most famous grounds.

It was with noticeable surprise that those unfamiliar with Gallaher read that his life began, not in a small wooden cottage in the back-blocks of New Zealand or a nondescript suburb in one of the main centres, but thousands of miles away on the other side of the world.

David Gallagher was born on 30 October 1873, in the town of Ramelton, which lies in the county of Donegal, 90 miles north-west of Belfast in the northernmost tip of Ireland. While the town had a recorded history that went back six centuries, it had been formally established 300 years earlier. A land-owner by the name of William Stewart had purchased a large parcel of land and brought out hundreds of families from Scotland to settle in the area. The stone buildings they built were the basis for the town that sits where the River Lennon meets the south-western arm of Lough Swilly.

Gallagher's father was 61-year-old local merchant James Henry Gallagher, and his mother was 29-year-old Anna Maria Hardy Gallagher (née McCloskie), a qualified teacher originally from Belfast. David — baptized Presbyterian two months later in the town's First Ramelton Meeting House — was the couple's seventh child, following Joseph (1867), Maria (known as Molly; 1870), and Thomas (1872). Three died in infancy: Isabella (born 1868), James (1869), and Jane (1871). James and Maria had married seven years before David's birth. A widower, James already had two sons from his first marriage. He remarried a year after his wife of 22 years had died. A draper of some three decades' standing, his shop was prominently placed in the town at Market Cross. Following David, three further children were born in Ramelton to the couple: William (1875), Oswald (1876), and James Patrick (1878), who was named after both his father and the deceased third Gallagher child.

Life was not easy for the large family, who lived in quarters above James's shop. Ireland was still recovering from the devastating famine of 1846–51, which had seen the country's population drop by 20 per cent due to death on a large scale and rampant emigration. James was in his sixties and not always possessed of the energy required of a shopkeeper. While his drapery business had been successful for some years, it was now on the wane. The fault for this was not entirely his own. With competition from Victorian industrialization in England, demand lessened for the linen products that had made Ramelton well known and prosperous. As the local economy slowly wilted, it is believed James had a short-lived business partner who was rich with promises to improve the shop's fortunes but not much else. The supposed saviour turned the shop's books even further into the red. James resorted to selling an assortment of wares; anything to bring in what little money he could for his family. Meanwhile, Maria carried much of the burden of raising the children. The Gallaghers' prospects were poor.

Ramelton. The Gallaghers lived above the shop later sporting the name Corry's. RAMELTON.NET

Then the silver-tongued entrepreneur George Vesey Stewart arrived back in the north of Ireland. Originally from the neighbouring district of County Tyrone, he had purchased 10,000 acres of land in the eastern Bay of Plenty from the New Zealand government. His vision had been to establish a little piece of Ulster on the other side of the world. He promoted his settlement in a vast number of Orange and Presbyterian halls throughout the north of Ireland. A self-confident, convincing orator, he had with him a lengthy booklet outlining the process of emigration, the costs involved, and the prospects for those who invested in his idea once they had arrived in New Zealand. The booklet boasted statements such as:

To secure success and to live with ease and comfort, no person should join my party with a capital less than £3 to £5 per acre, according to the amount of land for which he may apply; that is, £3 per acre for the practical working agriculturalist, his bone representing £2 and £5 per acre for the employer of labour.

The first party of his (largely moneyed) settlers had been transported out to Maoriland in 1875. Vesey Stewart set his own family up on one of the settlement's choicest sites, building a homestead that still stands at Athenree, just south of Waihi.

The instant population slowly established itself as the town of Katikati; struggling to live somewhat, due to its isolation, because as yet there was no road connecting it with Tauranga. The businesses that had been set up needed a greater population to service. And more workers were needed for the farms and fields that had been broken in and were becoming productive. So, two years after the first party landed, Vesey Stewart was looking to repeat his entrepreneurial success and at the same time bolster the numbers of customers or manual labourers available to those already in Katikati.

From here, the Gallagher family history muddies somewhat. To have a place among those travelling to New Zealand was not a cheap exercise. For James Gallagher, his family's passage alone cost nearly £80. Then money was required not only to purchase a block of land, but also to develop it. It took months before families would begin to be self-sufficient, so money was needed to feed his wife and young children, plus pay for other expenses in the interim. James had grown up on a farm but had not worked one during his adult years, and money was not something he had a lot of. So why did he undertake such a dramatic relocation and how did he pay for it?

One possible answer lies in the return to Ramelton of a man called Martin Corry, who had left the town for the American goldfields and returned a self-made man. James, in his twilight years, may have intended to try to establish a better life for his family before his passing. It is conceivable that Corry bought James's struggling business, which was in a good location, and then used the premises for another enterprise. With money from the sale, the family could afford to emigrate. New Zealand was a new colony, a promised land of sorts. Economically, it was advertised as about to spring to life in the same way that plantings in its fresh and fertile soil would. But for James to suddenly commit to becoming a farmer when he was of an age and a physical state not at all suited to hard, manual labour seems a strange decision.

However, a *Bay of Plenty Times* article from 1887 on the subject of Maria reported that, in Ramelton:

> *... she for many years enjoyed the friendship and patronage of the celebrated Irish philanthropists, Lord and Lady George Hill. It was with a view of carrying out a plan of Lord George's for the benefit of the Donegal peasantry that [the family] first came to Katikati, it being intended that a depot for the Donegal Knitting Company should have*

been established at Katikati, but, unfortunately, the noble founder died within six months of the arrival of Mrs Gallagher in the colony, and his kindly scheme was not carried on by his heir.

Lord Hill had owned an estate for 40 years at a place called Gweedore, a little over 20 miles west of Ramelton. His land had hundreds of tenant farmers working it. To this day historians debate whether his methods as landlord were of benefit to the local people or not. Certainly, he built stores and improved infrastructure such as roads and bridges. He tried to lessen the reliance on illicit liquor by purchasing grain from farmers. As a way of attracting tourists, he built a hotel and had a model farm operating around it. But some historians claim that the changes he made to land holdings on his property were financially detrimental to those who worked the land.

Hill did hold ambitions to develop a woollen industry, supplying wool (not of exceptional quality, it must be said) to a branch of a London firm that sold woollen items. Thus, when Vesey Stewart was making his way through the north, he might have gone calling on Lord Hill, who then proposed an Antipodean outpost and advertised, or spread the word, for someone to manage the enterprise. It would make sense to have an experienced draper such as James become the agent for the Donegal Knitting Company.

It could have been with some financial backing from Lord Hill that the family made the move. If Maria did enjoy their 'friendship and patronage', the Hills might have taken pity on the plight of the family or seen James as someone in a position that made him willing to leave Ireland and establish the business venture.

So, the family signed up for Vesey Stewart's venture and prepared to farewell Ramelton. They sold most of their possessions, taking with them what they could. Two things were left behind. The first was small and fragile. The youngest child, eight-week-old James Patrick, was a sickly infant, so much so that he was considered of too weak a constitution to survive three months at sea. He was left in Ramelton, to be cared for by friends of the family. As hard as it was for the family to leave their home and head off into the unknown, it must have been inordinately painful for Maria to part with a child she had given birth to only weeks before.

The second item left behind appears to be the spelling of their surname. In Ireland, Gallagher was pronounced with the second 'g' being silent. So, to avoid confusion over spelling and pronunciation in their new homeland, the surname was truncated to 'Gallaher'. It was all part of a new beginning.

From Belfast to Auckland

*For James Gallaher there began to build
unease about the final leg of their journey.*

The *Lady Jocelyn* was a 4,000-tonne iron clipper, described as 'the fastest and finest of Messrs. Shaw, Saville and Co's. fleet'. Her large sail area and sleek bow meant she could, in favourable conditions, travel up to 300 miles in a day. She was an uninviting, dark shape at anchor in Carrickfergus Harbour when the tired Gallahers arrived at the Belfast quay. The journey from Ramelton to Belfast — by ferry and trains — had been an arduous one, particularly with small children in tow. Torrential rain hadn't made things any easier.

As the family entered the public departures shed, the scene was a chaotic one. All around four-and-a-half-year-old David and his family groups of people and trolleys of luggage were passing, being readied for transport to the clipper. Over the din of disorganization, names were being called. A steam-tug, the *Shamrock*, was busy loading and ferrying passengers across the grey, windswept, rain-pocked lough to the larger vessel. That trip alone took an hour. Not all of the passengers were loaded as scheduled, so they had to wait out a frustrating night ashore before travelling to the ship the following day. It was a situation that caused more anxiety to those who were already beginning to question whether emigration was the right thing to be doing.

A writer for the ship's newspaper, the *Lady Jocelyn Herald*, recorded:

On arrival at the ship, the scene on board was still more interesting than that at the depot. What a change from the comfortable homes were the narrow berths allotted to us! Paterfamilias appeared almost dumb-founded as he watched every gaze of his better half, and he would almost cringe at her first effort at speech-making. The curtain lecture at home had been bitter enough, but what was that to what was now expected? 'Where am I to put the children?' 'We can't live here.' 'You had no business to destroy our home; take us back again; we shall never live through the voyage; if we do a very fine life we shall have' were some of the mildest utterances.

The Gallahers, with two adults and six children, were one of the largest family groups aboard. Their £77 fare saw them allocated the Second Cabin on the Intermediate level of the ship, with Steerage (for the lowest fare-paying passengers) below them. They began to familiarize themselves with the layout of the ship, their travelling companions, and the best way to manoeuvre around their cramped quarters without cracking shins or heads. Prior to departure, there was a final medical inspection of passengers by doctors and of their tickets by government officials. With nothing untoward being recorded on their visit, the ship's captain was informed that he could set sail.

On 17 May 1878, the Gallahers farewelled Erin's Own as the *Lady Jocelyn*'s anchor rose and she slowly made her way out of the harbour. Tears were shed and emotional passengers stayed at the stern of the ship, their eyes fixed on their former homeland until the grey silhouette of Ireland could be seen no more.

In rolling blue-water seas, the travellers quickly discovered which items were best not left unsecured, with numerous crockery and glass articles early casualties of the journey. There was great initial excitement among the children, who had much to explore, running around decks, climbing up and down ladders and even the ship's rigging.

As the 378 passengers settled into their time on the briny, a number of committees were established for entertainment and for more serious purposes, including the appointment of watches. The *Lady Jocelyn Herald* informed all the men that they were expected to participate. One of the most important was the night watch, in which 'The duties of the watch is to see that [there is] no smoking between decks, prevent the spread of fires, and, in short, to guard the lives and property of the passengers.'

Four years earlier, in one of New Zealand's worst maritime disasters, a blaze aboard the *Cospatrick* had taken the lives of 470 people who were travelling to Auckland from Gravesend. It is thought that the fire began in one of the ship's holds when straw caught fire. How it was set alight is uncertain, although it has been surmised that a less-than-honest crew member with an open flame might have been rummaging through the dark hold in which the ship's cargo was stored. Thus, smoking was prohibited below decks on the *Lady Jocelyn*, and vigilance asked for when it came to extinguishing candlewicks and matches.

For the general good health of those on board, passengers were also encouraged to keep their berths clean and dry. Despite a clean bill of health for all before sailing, there was a medical scare when two mild cases of smallpox were discovered by the ship's doctor, Dr Grinders. A regimen of disinfecting all berths was instigated, and camphor bags were made, which were then hung around the neck as a supposed way of warding off possible infection. Fortunately, good weather meant that Grinders could treat patients in the fresh air of the top decks. He also had to deliver a baby, as well as attend the sad death of a 13-month-old who had suffered from whooping cough and bronchitis. The child was buried at sea. Grinders was also kept busy tending the numerous sprains and scrapes of those who had trouble negotiating their way around the ship in heavy seas.

To keep the passengers entertained there were athletic contests, singing and amateur dramatic performances, chess and draughts playing. A lending library was set up. One afternoon, a large crowd gathered on deck to watch Mr Frederick Douglas attempt to walk five miles in one hour. Under the watchful eye of two time-keepers and an umpire, he began his task, walking back and forth over a distance of 15 yards. Unfortunately, his attempt was unsuccessful, as he finished in 63 minutes and 40 seconds.

At the end of the first month's sailing, a day school was set up for children, with Maria Gallaher volunteering to be one of the eight teachers taking classes.

The crossing of the Equator saw the usual seafarer's toasting of Neptune, with men being given whisky and brandy while the women enjoyed champagne and sherry. When they reached the Tropic of Cancer, the scene was described in the *Lady Jocelyn Herald* as one where:

The ship was surrounded by dolphins sporting themselves in the blue water, and a few samples of the 'Portuguese man-of-war' might be seen floating on the surface and occasionally unfolding their gelatinous and many coloured sails to whatever wind there might be. … In five or six different points of the horizon we could see ships sporting all their sails, but spell-bound like ourselves, and reminding one of the ancient mariner's expressions — 'Like painted ships upon a painted ocean.'

The spouts from pods of whales were frequently seen, as well as flying fish. Whale birds, Cape pigeons, albatrosses and others wafted along behind the ship. A Cape pigeon was reportedly caught and 'had its life sacrificed to the advancement of science, or more probably to the decoration of a lady's hat'.

As the ship steadily progressed south, its newspaper began publishing pieces of encouragement and advice to the new settlers:

Of the success of the settlement we have not the slightest doubt. We have before us the evidence of the first party — those plucky pioneers — who will receive us with open arms and a Cead mille Failthe [sic]. At the same time we must impress on our readers not to expect too much at the onset and not to be discouraged if the first season's crop should not come up to their expectations.

However, further reading showed that there should be no reason for the first crop to fail:

No time should be lost in planting potatoes. An acre of fern land can be cleared in one day by a man, when the land is ready for the plough. Potatoes are planted either in drills as at home, with one light ploughing, or else by dropping the seed into every third furrow of the plough. The ridges, or lazy bed system, we do not recommend, unless in swampy ground. … Potatoes will yield double crop on such soil, and can be planted either with the plough or the fern hook. We recommend our settlers to purchase in Auckland for their first potato crop four cwt per acre of guano or bone dust, or both in equal proportions.

Eighty-six days after leaving Ireland, the *Lady Jocelyn* made her way into Auckland's Waitemata Harbour. In anticipation of the day, one of the passengers wrote a poem, published in the ship's paper:

The guilded [sic] youth of Auckland town
Will ne'er forget the day
That brings the Lady Jocelyn boys
To anchor in her bay
For she has maidens grave and gay
And maidens young and fair
To make them wives to plague their lives
So let them all beware.

The Auckland that was spread out before the *Lady Jocelyn* passengers was still a fledgling city. Buildings made of wood, rather than the more familiar stone, lined many of the dirt streets. The lean timber structures bore none of the signs of age or permanence that the squat, sturdy buildings of their former home did. Barely 40 years since European settlement, Auckland looked like a hastily assembled, dirty town.

Samuel Macauley was a passenger who kept notes of the trip and compiled it into a diary a year after arriving. He wrote:

The first thing that impressed us was the fine wharf which Auckland can boast of having. It was a gloriously fine day and the sun was shining. For the first time we had the pleasure of seeing the fine weather that we are told is so in this island.

The new arrivals were advised on where to go and what to see. The Thames Hotel, directly across from the wharf, offered a three-course dinner for a shilling. British newspapers could be read at the Mechanics Institute. The Supreme Court House — Government House and its delightful grounds on the ridge above the city — offered views of the harbour. Further afield, a walk up Mt Eden was a good way to stretch the legs and take some solid exercise after the confinements of the ship, and the views from the summit were 'most rewarding'. For the commercially minded, there was the Market House at the top end of Queen Street, which was 'a neat covered building, and the scene here on a Saturday night — the vast confusion of tongues — the haggling and the shouting — is one never to be forgotten — an earthly pandemonium'. Those who were intending to purchase livestock were notified of weekly sales of sheep and cattle — in Remuera on Tuesdays, and Newmarket on Thursdays — as a good way to get a gauge on prices they could expect to pay. Mail from home could be collected at the Central Post Office, where gun licences could also be bought.

While the weather may have been a pleasant tonic for those shaking off a sluggishness brought on by weeks at sea, for James Gallaher there began to build unease about the final leg of their journey and their ultimate destination. In Queen Street he came across the shop of another former Ramelton resident, a baker by the name of Charles Canning. When Canning learned of the Gallaher family's plans, he did his best to dissuade James from travelling any further. Canning had heard that the going was tough in the so-called Bay of Plenty. He had heard of disquiet about conditions there among some of the first group of settlers. The ageing, bearded Irishman he saw standing before him was not a man of the land. When had he ever spent a day tending the soil, planting or attending to livestock? His physical frailties were all too obvious. His sons were not of an age to take on the back-breaking duties of a functioning farm, let alone one that did not yet exist. To Canning, James and his young family would be better off remaining in Auckland, trying to establish themselves there. The more Canning spoke, the less certain James was about carrying on to Katikati.

Walking around town, James saw Vesey Stewart, and began to recount to him what he had heard from Canning, and admitted an intention to stay in Auckland. But the man he was talking to was an entrepreneur, a businessman, and, in his own mind, a visionary. Vesey Stewart had to make sure that James's hesitation did not spread to the other families he had corralled this far. He would have none of the hearsay. Assurances and proclamations of the prospects available to new arrivals once in Katikati flowed from the ebullient organizer. They were nearly there. Arriving in a new country could be an overwhelming experience, but this was not the time for second thoughts. The land that awaited them was even better than that allotted to the first party. There were people waiting to meet them and help them get settled. The sales pitch went on and on, until the somewhat beaten James Gallaher was convinced to carry on to Tauranga.

A steamer — the *Hinemoa* — took the Gallahers and other Vesey Stewart settlers down the east coast from Auckland to Tauranga. How James's heart must have sunk when, once there, so close to Katikati, there were again those who urged him not to partake in the venture. Rumours could be explained away up in Auckland, but not in Tauranga where people knew exactly what the state of the Ulster settlement was. A number of the first settlement group had seen the parlous state of their allocations and abandoned them, opting to try their luck in Tauranga. As doubt further enshrouded James Gallaher, Vesey Stewart reappeared and assured the elderly man that there would always be one or two dissatisfied people, but that their word was not worth listening to. They were but a step away from a new and exciting life. The steamer *Staffa* would transport them and other families to Katikati. They would land not far from Vesey Stewart's own home, where they could see for themselves what could be made of the land. What's more, he would make sure they were all met on their arrival.

Twenty-four hours later, James and Maria apprehensively boarded the boat to take them and their six children to Katikati. It was the day of reckoning.

Katikati

'It was a barren prospect and they scarcely knew which way to turn.'

The *Staffa* coasted into a tiny harbour and settled at a landing where the various families could easily disembark, carrying with them what few possessions they had. As they stepped ashore they saw the detritus from other such landings, items that had sunk into the muddy sand, never to be recovered. There was no welcoming party. No escort to temporary lodgings. If ever James felt he had been conned by Vesey Stewart it was surely now, as he stood with his wife and young family on a beach in an unfamiliar land. Ahead of them lay an undulating landscape, slowly rising to dark hills. Samuel Macauley described the landscape as 'like a basket of eggs — it is so hilly'. As other settlers slowly dispersed, the Gallahers disconsolately made their way up from the beach to higher ground, but the vista from the new vantage point provided no new promise. Their new life began, not in a spirit of excitement and optimism, but on the verge of complete demoralization.

In an interview some years later with researcher Edith Mary Story, for the purposes of recording the experiences of settlers in a manuscript entitled 'Our fathers have told us' (lodged at the Alexander Turnbull Library), eldest son Joseph Gallaher, who was 11 years old at the time, recalled:

We strolled to the top of the adjoining hills, and looked around us. All was desolation. There was nothing to encourage my parents; it was a barren prospect and they scarcely knew which way to turn, or whether to turn at all. In vain they looked for the promised help, they felt mocked by the memory of the flowery words of the Vesey Stewart pamphlet.

Fortunately, and absolutely by chance, their luck did change temporarily. They came across another Ramelton family — the Wylies — who invited them to stay with them for a couple of weeks. During those days when they were the recipients of a wonderful beneficence, James Gallaher's 69 acres of land were allocated. While they waited for their farmhouse to be built, the Gallahers lived in a basic whare (or hut) with a dirt floor. It was an experience familiar to thousands of immigrants in the late nineteenth and early twentieth centuries. (Another of the Katikati families was the Mulgans. Descendant John was famous for his novel *Man Alone* and his war memoirs.)

The first party of Ulster arrivals had been able to choose land from a more attractive block than the second. Many were close to the coast and had easy access to water, with streams running through their properties. The parcels of land available to this second settlement were less picturesque and bore no resemblance to the countryside their new owners had left behind. The prospective land was not land that had been ploughed or farmed for a couple of centuries, and was merely overgrown or with stones — the bones of the earth — rising to the top with each tilling of the soil; it was land that had never been disturbed by Maori or European, and for good reason. Ground cover — such as the dominating fern — couldn't simply be pulled from the soil like a solitary weed, or tipped over into the dirt with a small blade on a horse-drawn plough. Below ground was a matted mass of roots, reluctant to leave their bed.

So, the Gallahers had their land, but it was a long way from becoming a farm. A house took some weeks to build. Clearing an acre a day to the point of it being nearly suitable for planting, as the *Lady Jocelyn Herald* had trumpeted, was an absolute impossibility. There was cutting and felling to be done before any blade could attempt to disturb the almost impenetrable mattress of fern roots. If the fern root wasn't thoroughly removed, it would take its toll on whatever crops were sown, reclaiming valuable space and nutrients intended for crops of oats or potatoes. Burning the fern looked to have achieved good results for some farmers, and the first crop sown in the ash-topped soil produced bountiful crops, but such success was not to be repeated in the following seasons.

While, like Ireland, the new country possessed no poisonous insects and snakes (only the rarely seen katipo spider), the new, wild land posed other hazards to small town children. In a November 1878 item titled 'A Child Attacked by an Entire Horse', the *Bay of Plenty Times* reported that:

On Tuesday a child of Mr Gallaher was attacked by an entire horse belonging to the Maoris, which had been roaming for some time about

*the Block. The little fellow was discovered by his mother insensible
with the brute standing over him.*

A neighbour was nearby and ran over to take control of the horse,
while Mrs Gallaher, shocked by the cuts to the young boy's face,
carried him inside the house and attended to him. Just which of the
Gallaher boys this was is unknown.

Soul-destroying news kept coming for James and Maria. Lord Hill
died. His son and heir, Captain Arthur Hill, abandoned the plans for
a southern outpost of the knitting company. The Gallahers were well
and truly on their own. The family could not simply get back on a ship
and return to Ireland. The continued deflation of the family's prospects
took their effect on Maria, and it is believed she suffered something
akin to a breakdown.

James had to have his land gradually broken in and try to make the
best of a dire situation. According to Joseph Gallaher:

*This hiring of plough and labour and the purchase of necessaries
soon got rid of the little money my parents had brought, and their
predicament was great. The land never yielded any harvest, as
it required treatment before it could grow anything. My father,
moreover, was not a farmer by occupation, but a tradesman, when
at home. All this trouble did not conduce to health and prosperity. By
this time the bills were running up.*

Barely two months after the second party had arrived in Katikati,
there was discontent among many of the settlers. All was not as
Vesey Stewart had led them to believe it would be, and once more the
businessman, mobilizing supporters to a meeting, had to quell unrest.

Finally, though, there was some good fortune for the Gallahers. Maria applied to teach at the new No. 2 School. She was granted the position with a valuable £2 a week wage. More importantly, the family could reside in the teacher's house. They moved once more, with James putting his land up for lease. It was a measure of how little James could do with the land that he planted what he could in fruit trees, themselves not maturing to produce fruit for a number of seasons. Eventually, he defaulted on his mortgage and lost ownership of his land, something he had never really had anyway.

Although there was a period of some stability, the financial burden continued to increase as the number of mouths to feed grew. Four more children were born to James and Maria in Katikati: George (1879), twins Henry and Charles (1881), and Douglas (1883). (Maria's great-granddaughter, Kay Carter, in researching an extensive family history, discovered in 2005 that James Patrick, the baby boy left behind in Ramelton, sadly only lived to the age of two.) David and the other school-age children accompanied Maria to the classroom each morning while James cared for the babies.

When it came to winter recreation, the focus in the town was firmly on football. The Katikati football club was established in 1880, and its strip was a black jersey and black knickerbockers. Teams representing Tauranga and Katikati clashed several times each season, and a combined side played Auckland most years, alternating between home and away. Joe Warbrick, a member of the 1884 All Blacks, and — along with four brothers — part of the 1888–89 Native team to Australia and Great Britain, was the local star. On occasion, Auckland players even represented Katikati. Tim O'Connor, the Australasian shot-put and hammer-throw champion, as well as noted footballer for the 1884 All Black, Auckland and Ponsonby teams, donned the Katikati colours along with three other city ring-ins following an Auckland visit to the Bay of Plenty. There was great excitement in the town at playing host to the burly football star, who had been born in County Tyrone in the north of Ireland.

James Gallaher pottered around the small area of land that surrounded the teacher's residence, and the *Bay of Plenty Times* reported in March 1885:

We have seen a sample of the hops grown at Katikati by Mr Gallaher. These hops are a good colour, and possess a fine aroma, and should be an encouragement to our settlers to select good rich flats and follow up this branch of husbandry. This enterprise of Mr Gallaher's is, we believe, the first attempt in this district on any scale, and the result seems to be quite up to expectation.

Hops were not just an ingredient for those wanting to make their own ale. They were also crucial to early recipes for bread, with the hops being used as a starter in home-made yeasts. Plus, they were very easily grown. In the summer months the vines could grow up to a foot in length per day, provided the root cuttings were planted in healthy soil and well watered.

Young David would join other local lads who gathered on the paddock of a farmer called Lockington to toe a football around, chase it as a pack, and scrag each other onto the ground. While he undoubtedly developed his football skills, this was also a time when he required some tenacity to even participate in the play. For Auckland Hospital patient records show that on 7 January 1886 David was admitted to Auckland Hospital to be treated for 'Contraction of left leg' and 'Spinal curvature'. (His age was listed as 11, although by this time he was in fact 14 months older.) The stunted muscles in his left leg, from which he had suffered for roughly eight years, had affected his posture and he had developed a degree of scoliosis. This meant that, as opposed to the natural spine curvature we all have running down the spine, David's spine was suffering a deformity that had it curving towards one side of his body. Following an operation on his leg, he was discharged on 14 January 1886. He was recorded as having 'Recovered'. Exercise was recommended by doctors as a recipe for good health, and fitness became a focus for David for the rest of his life.

On 10 June 1886, settlers felt and saw the central North Island volcanic plateau's fury when Mt Tarawera erupted, destroying the famous Pink and White Terraces. Two earthquakes in the dark of night badly frightened those who had never experienced such ground movement before. As dawn broke, providing some comfort to those who had not been able to return to slumber out of fear for what else the night might hold, the ground rumbled once more. Shortly thereafter, another subterranean roar and the ground shook again. Then, in what seemed like a matter of minutes, the sun disappeared behind heavy cloud. Many stood outside watching the sky's sudden change. They felt what they initially thought was rain; only it wasn't — it was volcanic ash from the erupting volcano some 75 miles away, and accompanying it was the strong smell of sulphur.

For a day the ash fell, causing great confusion to many who had no idea what the source of it was until word spread — confirmed later by the local newspaper — that Mt Tarawera had erupted. News that 40 people had been killed was as much of a shock as the preceding earthquakes. From a number of homesteads the volcanic eruptions could be seen, which drew a steady stream of visitors.

Maria had been very successful as a teacher when it came to her pupils passing examinations and progressing through the school, but in August 1886 the school committee was dealing with the fact that Maria was unwell, reportedly with 'inflammation of the bowels'. The Board of Education was informed and contingencies made for periods of absence. There was a complete lack of sympathy from some parents of children at the school, however. Maria had been combining motherhood with teaching, and now she was absenting herself through illness. This did not appear to be to the detriment of the children. A recent visit by a school inspector had concluded that, while he wanted to see more attention in some areas, 'I am satisfied with the results of this year's work.'

The positive appraisal did not placate the agitators, who began to press for a male teacher to take Maria's place. They made an approach to the Board of Education to have Maria removed from her position. When this was acted upon, another group countered it by petitioning that Maria be kept on. This resulted in great tension among parents at the school and throughout the small community, culminating in an escalation in intent to see Maria leave the school.

'We are informed,' wrote the *Bay of Plenty Times* in May 1887:

> ... *that the anonymous letter sent to Mrs Gallaher was of a most heartless and disgraceful nature. Too much opprobrium cannot be attached to the writer for so cruel and cowardly an act. Mrs Gallaher has been for a considerable time dangerously ill with brain fever, and had she seen the letter in question it is impossible to say how disastrous the consequences may have been. We trust we shall never have to chronicle again an action of so peculiarly dastardly a nature from Katikati or anywhere else in this district.*

Thirteen-year-old David and his family watched as Maria's health deteriorated. Their mother was in constant pain and often immobile. The older children, particularly Molly, carried more of the burden of tending to their young siblings. Joseph was contributing from his wages to the upkeep of the family. Thomas had left Katikati, looking for work. David left school and began working for the local stock and station agent, spending a lot of time riding through the district on horseback. He gave what money he could to his parents.

As Maria's condition worsened, and the task became too great for her family to care for her and try to provide her with some relief, she was moved up to Auckland Hospital. Her departure was distressing for all. She was admitted on 31 August 1887, terminally ill with cancer of the peritoneum and ovaries. Ten days later, she died, aged only 42.

A contributed obituary for Maria ran in the *Bay of Plenty Times* on 16 September 1887. It began, 'It is with deep regret we have to chronicle the death of a most esteemed member of our community' and described her family's journey from Ramelton 'where she was esteemed and respected by all classes' to Katikati. 'We offer our deep sympathy to the family and would remind them that the noble example of the self-sacrificing life "lost awhile" is for them a goodly heritage, and a bright example to follow.'

Maria was buried at the newly opened Waikumete Cemetery in West Auckland. The site had been developed to replace central Auckland's Symonds Street cemetery which had reached capacity. (Today Waikumete is New Zealand's largest cemetery.)

The loss to the family, particularly to the smaller children of whom the youngest was only four, would have been immeasurable. James, now in his seventies, had outlived his second wife. While there was an emotional toll, there were financial repercussions, too.

The money from Joseph's and David's wages could not support the family. The situation was desperate. Taking pity on the family, the school committee allowed them to remain in the teacher's house and approached the Board of Education to see if they could reimburse James for work he had done around the teacher's residence.

Joseph left Katikati for Auckland. James wrote to the Charitable Aid Board seeking assistance. He received a pittance and the advice that it would be best if the youngest children were put into an orphanage. Kay Carter believes it was Joseph, Molly and David who railed against the family being split up. (It was a situation that appears to have deeply affected David; Carter discovered that he later became a strong supporter of the Auckland Orphans' Club.) In 1889 William remained in Katikati, while James, Molly, 16-year-old David, Oswald, George, Henry, Charles and Douglas gave up their tenuous existence in the Bay of Plenty and moved north to join Joseph in Auckland.

The Wing-Forward and
Rugby Football in the 1890s

'On the ball! On the ball! On the ball!'

By the start of the 1890s, 700 football clubs (some short-lived) had been established in New Zealand. As interest in the game grew and provincial unions came into being, teams looked for competition, be it local, national or international.

Uniformity of interpreting the laws of the game as written by the Rugby Football Union (RFU) in England was lacking. Even the scoring system could be a matter of dispute between rivals. Ernest Hoben, who had been secretary of the Hawke's Bay union, saw the need for a governing body to administer the game in New Zealand. In 1891, he made his way around the provinces proposing the idea of a national body. Otago (later joined by Southland and Canterbury) initially opposed the concept. The agreeable provincial unions met in November

1891, to argue the case for a national union and draft its constitution. The following April, the New Zealand Rugby Football Union (NZRFU) was formed. Officers were elected and a Management Committee was chosen to deal with the day-to-day running of the game. Canterbury and Southland joined the body in 1894, although Southland later withdrew. Otago (facing a backlash from players) finally relented in 1895 and joined, with Southland being readmitted to the fold.

There was an almost annual tinkering with the points scoring system. In 1890 a try was only worth 1 point, and a goal following a try (what we now call a conversion) was worth 4 points. The emphasis, thus, was more on the goal than the try. The scoring of the latter gave teams the opportunity to *try* for the former.

As the decade progressed, it was settled that points could be scored in the following ways:

a try was worth 3 points
a goal following a try, 2 points
a dropped goal, 4 points
a goal from a mark or penalty kick, 3 points

The referee became the sole judge of play. Previously, players had been able to appeal to the umpires running the sideline for adjudication. They would raise their flags and play would stop if the referee agreed with the appeal.

The wing-forward position is one which hasn't been seen in a New Zealand team, at any level, since changes to scrum laws which saw a compulsory three-man front row introduced in the early 1930s. Obviously, there would be few alive now who have ever seen it. As such, it requires some explanation.

The best way to describe it is as an extra halfback. A wing-forward could feed the ball into a scrum and then, with his hand on the scrum, stand his ground in line with the front rows and do his best (within reason) to prevent the opposing halfback from following the ball as it passed through the scrum. When the other side fed the ball to the scrum, the wing-forward would advance close to the scrum and pressure the halfback, hopefully preventing him from running himself.

The scrum then was not the one that we know today. New Zealand teams favoured a seven-man scrum consisting of two front-rankers (hookers), a pivot (lock) in between two side-row forwards, and two back-row forwards. The pivots, anchoring the centre of the scrum, were men of similar physique to today's props.

Credit for the wing-forward position has been widely given to player and administrator Thomas (Tom) Rangiwahia Ellison. He holds a special place in All Black history. When the New Zealand Rugby Football Union was formed, Ellison proposed the motion that 'the New Zealand Representative colours should be Black Jersey with Silver Fernleaf, Black Cap with Silver Monogram, White Knickerbockers and Black Stockings'.

He was a member of the Native team which toured Australia and the United Kingdom in 1888–89, during which he played in an amazing 83 of 107 matches. The Natives had encountered teams who played with up to nine forwards, but mostly eight; this consisted of a front row of two, a second row of three, a third row of two, and then an eighth player locking in between the last two. Ellison noted that the Natives forwards matched the opposing scrums with only seven forwards. He then apparently mulled over the fact that the extra player could be put to better use. The only question was: where on the field?

Over the next two years, according to Ellison in his book *The Art of*

Rugby Football, he looked for a solution. He found it on the fields of Wellington club rugby:

> *In 1892, the three halves system, which had been adopted by the Poneke Football Club, was superseded by the wing game, which was devised by me as the result of personal experiences by me behind the scrum, as half-back for the club during the previous season, where I found it impossible for the smartest of referees to detect and amply penalize off-side interferences of opponents bent on spoiling my passes — impossible of detection because he could not have his eyes on both sides of the scrum at once; and impossible, of amply penalising, when detected, as it often paid a side better to play off-side, and incur the penalty of a free kick, than to permit an almost certain try to be scored against them.*

It is unclear if the wing-forward was used by the New Zealand team that Ellison captained to New South Wales and Queensland in 1893.

There is a line of thinking that the Alhambra football club in Dunedin had introduced wing-forwards a season or two earlier than Ellison, but some argue that these 'wing' players appear to be halves from the backline who were moved forward to wide of the scrum. Thus their roles were slightly different, as was one 'wing' adopted by the Westport club in 1886.

Further confusing the origin of the position is the credit Gallaher gave to Ponsonby and Auckland player John Arneil's playing style as a wing-forward in influencing his own play. (Arneil finished playing rep football in 1887, before Gallaher arrived in Auckland from Katikati. One presumes that if Gallaher did see Arneil play, it must have been when an Auckland team visited Waihi, Tauranga or Katikati for a match.

Although the most likely influence is a spoken one, with Arneil holding officer positions at the Auckland Rugby Union and Ponsonby club.)

Newspaper reports of matches in which Arneil took part include one of a match in Thames between that town's Wanderer's club and a visiting Ponsonby team. It specifically mentions his play as a wing-forward. Player lists for the 1887 match between Auckland and Canterbury have the blue-and-white hoops with one fullback, two three-quarters, three halves, seven forwards, and two wing men. Opposing them, the Canterbury team had no wings listed, but that is not to say they didn't play them.

A season earlier, when Sydney visited Auckland for a match at Newmarket's Dilworth Paddock, both sides had players listed as wing-forwards. A correspondent by pen-name of 'Spectator' wrote to the *Auckland Star* with his picks for the Auckland side and opined that: 'In wing men we are certainly very weak, as it is not only men that can dribble that we want on the edge of the scrum, but those who are fast and can collar, as well as being able to dribble.'

Going back even further, in 1883, the very year that the Auckland Rugby Union Football Association (ARFU) was formed, the *Otago Witness* ran a piece from the *Observer* newspaper appraising the skills and failings of the Auckland players who were about to take part in a match between the two provincial sides. Among them was a player by the name of Sims who apparently 'was a splendid wing man last season. ... Dribbles excellently and follows up well, but picks up far too much for a forward.' Gallaher also makes mention of Mr WW Robinson captaining Auckland in 1876 and employing two wing-forwards.

So, while Ellison's creation may not quite have been that 'new', he certainly wrote with great definition on the wing-forward's roles. He saw the position 'as one that was so physically demanding' that even experienced footballers such as Bob Oliphant, who had been an All Black and was an amateur sprinter of note:

> ... *required two months hard drilling at the gymnasium before they established their ability to hold the position and to perform its duties with absolute fairness and freedom from roughness. ... In advancing, receding or shielding, a wing-forward should not use his hands or elbows. Such practices are not pretty nor effective.*

Rugby was, after all, a gentlemen's game!

For Ellison, the skills and role of the wing-forward included that the players:

> ... *should be big, fast, active, and strong men. They should be good dribblers, good passers, good tacklers, and, above all, they should know how to shield their half back without being offside from the encroachments of the opposing backs or wings.*

The wing-forward was all the more visible in matches of the time because the scrum was arguably the most prominent feature of matches. Many referees whistled for scrums to restart play whenever a player was tackled, rather than allowing the player to place the ball on the ground in front of him, as per the rules, and allow competition for possession.

In the 1890s, the most prominent wing-forward was Wairarapa's Will McKenzie, known as 'Off-side Mac'. He played 20 matches for the All Blacks, and gained notoriety not just for his wing-forward play, but also for being ordered from the field in the 1893 match against New South Wales in Sydney. One of five brothers, and a bit of a character, McKenzie put on a fake limp as he made his way to the sideline after the referee dispatched him. Spectators thought he was retiring due to injury and sympathetic applause accompanied his walk across the chalk.

By 1901, local referees were unhappy with the role and play of wing-forwards, and at their annual meeting passed a motion they hoped would be adopted by the NZRFU that 'an effort should be made to abolish wing-forward play'. The union's Management Committee reply put the onus back on the referees, declaring that they were 'of the opinion that if Referees would strictly enforce the rules of the game it would abolish the objectionable features of wing-forward play'. The pertinent rules were those regarding players wilfully holding an opponent who has not got the ball, and charging or obstructing an opponent who is not holding the ball.

Rugby football had its roots in soccer, and the connection was still an obvious one in the 1890s with the ball being kept on the toe where possible. The poor condition of many grounds in the middle of winter and the players' rudimentary boots also dictated the way the game was played. A heavy, hand-stitched leather ball resembling a large walnut that had soaked up a lot of water and was covered in mud was easier to kick along the ground than it was to pick up, pass or hold onto. Thus, dribbling was a feature of the game and 'forward rushes' delighted crowds who would yell 'On the ball!' as the big men of the side charged downfield with the ball at their feet. It took a fearless defender to approach the stampeding herd and stop the flow of play. This was done by an opposing player kicking the ball away or, in a style that developed in New Zealand, a defender scooping up the ball and turning away from the rampaging pack.

Stopping forward rushes was dangerous, and dozens of injuries occurred from such play. The author's great-grandfather, James Carlaw, played for a Ponsonby football club called Native Rose. In May 1890, newspapers reported that he had been involved in a serious accident when he broke his leg in two places below the knee in a match against Athletic. Carlaw and another player both kicked at the ball at the same time, and the collision of legs resulted in the nasty accident. It was two years before he could take the field again.

In New Zealand there is an old rugby song, which had been popular throughout the country, called 'On the Ball' which described play of the day (along with some Victorian Christian themes):

Oh, some talk of Cricket and some of Lacrosse,
Some long for the Huntsman's loud call.
But where can be found such a musical sound,
As the old Rugby cry 'On The Ball!'

(Chorus)
'On the ball! On the ball! On the ball!'
Thro' scrummage, three quarters and all
Sticking together we keep on the leather,
And shout as we go 'On The Ball!'

On a cold wintry day, when the ball is away,
Let sluggards at home then remain
We'll kick and we'll follow, we'll run pass and collar;
As we shout the same merry refrain:

This life's but a scrummage we cannot get through,
But with many a kick and a blow

And then in the end, tho' we dodge and we fend,
Still that sure collar 'Death' takes us low:

But although brought down, there remains still a chance,
to pass, if we play the right game,
And the poor weary soul may at last win that goal,
Which is ev'ry true footballer's aim:

Remember then boys, as we journey through life,
There's a Goal to be reached bye and bye
And he who runs true why he's bound to get through,
And perhaps kick a Goal from his try

The song was written by a Palmerston North accountant, EW Secker, who was captain of the 1885 Manawatu rugby side which had a horror year. Not only could they not win an inter-union game, they couldn't even score a point. Two years later, Secker wrote the song (based on the tune of an English fox-hunt chorus) and had the Manawatu team sing it on their journey to play Wanganui. After he had finalized the music, and with interest from a publishing house, the song became a hit.

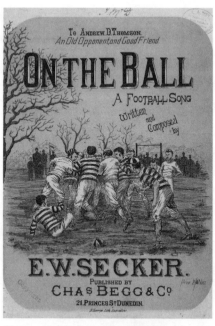

Sheet music of the popular New Zealand football song 'On the Ball'.
ALISTAIR GILKINSON, ARCHIVE OF NEW ZEALAND SHEET MUSIC

A major change to the game in Great Britain came in the middle of the 1890s, brought about by off-field activities. Football was a strictly enforced game for amateurs. In the industrial north of England, players were not happy at having to forgo wages by absenting themselves from work to play the game. They wanted a form of compensation, but this would render them professionals, and the RFU would not tolerate such payments. On 29 August 1895, at the George Hotel in Huddersfield, members of Northern football clubs had met and resolved that 'the clubs here represented decide to form a Northern Rugby Football Union and pledge themselves to push forward, without delay, its establishment on the principle of payment for broken-time only'.

Once the principle of amateurism versus professionalism had driven a wedge between clubs and the Northern Union had established itself, it then made changes to the rules of play. The changes were made with a view to making the game more attractive to spectators. The scrum was eliminated as a means to restart play, although not entirely. It remained but, instead of the ball being fed through rows of feet to the halfback, the ball was played back by one foot to a waiting player who could then play the ball. The final change and point of difference was the removal of two players from a team (two forwards), with Northern Union teams fielding only 13 players.

This sporting schism (as it is often referred to) had an impact on playing numbers and the strength of football teams in the north of England, but it would be some years before it had any major impact on football in New Zealand. In the meantime, football in the burgeoning city of Auckland was flourishing.

Auckland Beginnings

As long as the ball was in play, he was unbending.

James, Molly and the boys joined Joseph, who was residing in Garfield Street, Parnell. With a father of an age and physical deterioration which made him more akin to a grandfather, David looked to his brother Joseph (Joe) for guidance. In some ways Joe became Gallaher's father figure, the leader of the household. His example as a determined businessman, and, once settled in Auckland, as an enthusiastic member of local community organizations, was one which David followed as he matured.

Joe kept a keen eye on David and secured a job for the 17-year-old as a hand where he worked, at the Northern Roller Mills Company. The company was in its infancy, having taken over two city mills: one on the quay, and the other two streets away. The former was known for its extraordinary American-made machinery, whereas the latter's equipment was British. Combined, both sites could produce over

60 tonnes of flour per day from 2,500 bushels of wheat. For David, with much of the milling process being mechanized, it was a hot, dusty, noisy place to work, as the rollers, brushers, scourers and other machines rattled, clanged and clattered, producing flour without interruption all day long.

It wasn't long before Gallaher's name was regularly mentioned in newspaper sporting columns, although not in connection with his deeds on the wet and muddy fields where 30 men 'chased the oval', but rather as part of a team playing *on* an oval. Northern Roller Mills workers had a 'junior' cricket team (with players aged roughly in their late teens and early twenties) that, like those from other large businesses and even churches, played in the Auckland club competition. The then 19-year-old Gallaher earned his place in the side as a bowler, regularly capturing bags of wickets throughout the 1892 season. His pace was not express — he was described as a 'trundler' — but a feature of his bowling was his accuracy.

In one match, in December 1893 — where saying the batsmen did not excel would be a gross understatement — the Roller Mills side was dismissed by a side from the long-forgotten club Gordon for only 60 runs. (Gordon was something of a powerhouse in Auckland sport during the two decades before the end of the nineteenth century. It was an organization concerned with the well-being — both physical and mental — of 'working boys'. It fielded a large number of teams in most sporting competitions.) Gordon's batsmen fared even worse in being dismissed for 26, giving Gallaher's side a first innings lead of 34. However, the following Saturday, on one of the Auckland Domain wickets that was of marginal condition following heavy rain, Gallaher was the toast of the team. With Gordon following on, he bowled five 'destructive' overs, taking eight second-innings wickets for just four runs. Gordon was dismissed for a mere eight runs.

As for the winter code, from 1891 Auckland club-rugby eligibility had been based on the 'District Scheme' residential criteria. On 1 May each year, a player new to a club had to have been living in that club's zone for four months. Failing that, he had to play out the season for his previous club. The 16-week period was to discourage players from moving residence just for the football season. The scheme came into being due to dissatisfaction from clubs who felt their stand-out players were being induced to play for the more powerful clubs such as Ponsonby. Thus, in an effort to introduce some fairness to the competition and its results, players had to register with the clubs whose zone they lived within.

Gallaher initially joined the Parnell rugby club, playing Junior (Second XV) rugby for them as a hooker. The Parnell district was the largest geographically, encompassing Auckland's eastern suburbs, from the city fringe of Stanley Street and one side of the Auckland Domain, south to Onehunga and the Manukau Harbour, then east as far as the Tamaki River, and back along the foreshore to the city. The club wore maroon jerseys, with white knickerbockers and maroon socks. Their best-known footballer was WC 'Mother' Elliott, who had played for Auckland since 1887 and also excelled as a cricketer.

In 1894, Joseph Gallaher married Nell Burchell. The change in Joe's status meant that James and his children moved house again, settling across the city in George Street (now Georgina Street), Freemans Bay. It was a suburb that was starting to change from one that had an air of spaciousness, thanks to a mix of housing and fields, to a highly populated area full of small, wooden homes and encroaching industry. The street itself was a steep, narrow one that ran into a gully. Small workers' cottages sat as far forward as they could on their sections. On one side of the street, the small bedrooms at the front of the houses were dark, sunless and cold. On the opposite side, fires were kept lit in the kitchens at the dull rear of the houses to try to create some warmth. With help from David, Molly tirelessly and selflessly cared for James and the boys.

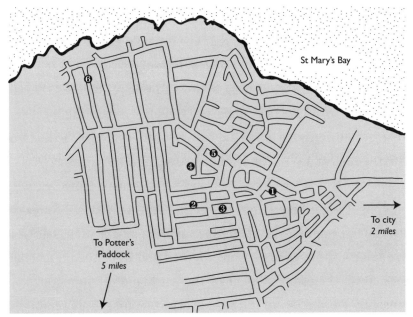

Gallaher's Ponsonby: ❶ George Street. ❷ Church Street. ❸ All Saints Church. ❹ Ponsonby District Football Club. ❺ Ponsonby Hall. ❻ Lawrence Street.

At the top of the hill was the more affluent suburb of Ponsonby. A recent local history, *Urban Village*, described the suburb at the time the Gallahers arrived as one where the:

> … *Catholic presence attracted many Irish working-class immigrants to the area. Most were manual labourers but some were skilled artisans and tradesmen. Wealthy business and professional people also built fine spacious homes on elevated sunny sections with sweeping harbour views. Shops and trades sprang up to service the expanding population.*

On 30 November 1894, James Gallaher passed away. The *Auckland Star's* death notice listed his age as 82. He was buried next to his wife, Maria, at Waikumete Cemetery. The family could not afford a headstone for the plot, which was not uncommon. To this day the Gallaher plot remains unmarked, and one wonders if it was a place much visited by family members, given that at the time it would have virtually been a day trip to travel out west and then back to the city.

As a result of the change of address to one inside the Ponsonby District Football Club's boundaries, Gallaher joined the local club, pulling on the famous black-and-blue hooped jersey for the first time in the winter of 1895. The club had come into existence in 1874. Its original colours were to be black-and-white stripes. However, when a couple of Englishmen, the Harvey brothers, arrived in the area two years later, bringing with them their old school jerseys of black-and-blue hoops, those colours were adopted and have been unchanged since. With the establishment of the Auckland union in 1883, and Ponsonby's affiliation to it, the club won the first three senior club championships and six in the first decade. It was the envy of other clubs, who couldn't attract players in the way Ponsonby could. The club, from its very beginnings, had a membership at committee level which included businesspeople of renown.

James Stitchbury had been an early settler when the suburb was first opened up. He later served as a city councillor, and his son Charles was a club stalwart. Thomas Masefield was an entrepreneur. Among his business endeavours was a relatively short-lived ferry service between Ponsonby and Northcote. They could, and did, entice players to the club with the prospect of job opportunities that did not exist elsewhere. Along with them, men such as (previously mentioned) businessman John Arneil and lawyer Albert Devore were not merely interested in the well-being of their men in black-and-blue. Both men were to be faithful servants of both the Auckland and New Zealand rugby unions, and summer sports players and committee members. Arneil, for example, had played cricket and rugby for Auckland, while Devore served as mayor of Auckland and was the ARFU chairman for 26 years.

Noticeably, the club's success diminished with the introduction of the District Scheme — which some critics of the club said was deserved. Gallaher's former team, Parnell, became the club to beat. Other long since disbanded clubs — such as Gordon, City, Grafton, and Newton — also claimed titles.

Ponsonby, like many clubs of the time, did not have its own home ground. Suitable, sizeable, affordable flat space was not easy to find along the ridges or through the sloping streets and gullies of the suburb. The Ponsonby Hall around the corner in Jervois Road and The Ponsonby Club Hotel up the road on the corner of Jervois and Ponsonby roads were the venues for many of the club's social activities. At this intersection stood a triumvirate of gas lamps, giving the area the nickname 'Three Lamps'. (They can be seen to this day, no longer standing in the middle of the intersection, but atop a building on the roadside.)

The home of Auckland rugby was Potter's Paddock, Epsom. (It is now the celebrated trotting venue — Alexandra Park — and the Epsom Showgrounds.) At the end of the nineteenth century, a portion of the land (roughly where the track and grandstand are today) was owned by the Tramways Company. It charged the rugby union between 5 and 15 per cent of gate takings for use of the venue, depending on the fixture. A large wooden grandstand dominated the southern touchline of the main ground. Alongside it was a large parcel of land which had been donated by early settler and local farmer William Potter. As many as a dozen fields hosted club matches on Saturdays. Players would assemble at their training sheds and then be transported to the ground by horse-drawn carriage — known as 'brakes' — at the cost of a shilling per player. Club games also took place across the harbour at Devonport, meaning an occasional ferry trip for teams.

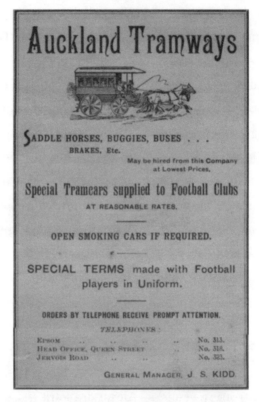

An 1896 advertisement for the brakes that would transport footballers to Potter's Paddock. AUCKLAND RUGBY UNION

As a footballer, Gallaher became known for his fitness and his uncompromising physical play, as well as his skill as a dribbler. Playing as a front-ranker, he liked to impose himself on the game, thriving on starting a dribbling rush when on attack, disrupting an opponent's ball in the scrum, or being able to defend against a promising move from the opposing team by sacking the player with the ball. As long as the ball was in play, he was unbending. To spectators, although being a hooker in the midst of many a mêlée, he was easily identifiable by the fact that he wore his shin-pads outside his stockings. His reason for doing so was: 'I found that in the case of a kick in proximity to the buckle, the latter was apt to be rather a nuisance when next to the bare skin.' This may have had something to do with the childhood operation he had undergone on his left leg. Many players wore shin-guards, but it was hard to find another who wore them as Gallaher did.

Auckland representative sides were selected a week before they were due to play. Notice usually came by way of a newspaper article, which would also inform the players where they were to train on the Tuesday and Thursday evenings. There was often a cautionary note in the publication of the names — players were warned that 'absentees from the training shed will forfeit their claims to a place'. Generally, training took place of an evening in the central city in a large woolshed at Buckland's sale yards, on the corner of Albert and Wyndham streets. On the opposite corner, the newly erected Shakespeare Hotel (one of the last corner hotels now remaining in central Auckland) did a roaring trade when sales were on at a site formally known as the Haymarket.

Come match-day, the roads outside the ground at Epsom were filled with pedestrians who had walked from all parts of town. On wet days, there was no avoiding the mud that the passage of hundreds of pairs of feet created as they milled around the ground. There were the horses and carts which had transported wealthier patrons to the game to dodge, as well as the horse-drawn trams that slid along the rails to Tramways Corner. Spectators welcomed the provincial players as they arrived from the city on brightly decorated horse-drawn, four-wheeled carriages. The Auckland side travelled on a carriage pulled by imposing Clydesdales supplied by the Northern Roller Mills. Admission for matches was often sixpence for entry to the ground, and slightly more for a seat in the stand. Ladies were able to enter the grounds without charge.

The referee gave both teams three mandatory warnings that the match was soon to start. A bell was rung at 2.55pm for the 'punt about' to end. Five minutes later another peal indicated that the game was shortly to commence, and the final tolling was at 3.15 with all players to be ready to play. Some club matches were forfeited due to teams not being prepared to start when asked to by the referee.

At the conclusion of games, teams would head back into the city to bathhouses where they could clean themselves off with hot water and be reunited with their clothes. On club days, they would invariably head to the team's favourite public house to further discuss the play. When teams from outside Auckland visited, the custom — as it was around the country — was for the teams to attend a dinner and theatrical show together in the evening.

While the area for the Auckland city competition was geographically small, the Auckland union and its sub-unions occupied a huge area: from Hokianga in the north down to the southern Waikato and Tauranga. Inter-union matches, as they were known, were common, with much interest in Auckland's games against Waikato and the burly players from Thames Goldfields, as well as the provincial clashes with the likes of Taranaki, Wellington, Canterbury and Otago.

Gallaher had his first taste of 'rep' football when chosen for the Auckland 'B' team which played the Northern Wairoa sub-union at Potter's Paddock in August 1895. (Several weeks earlier he had played in a trial match between the prospective 'A' and 'B' sides before the 'A' side headed away on a southern tour.) The Auckland 'B' side raced out to a handy lead of 20–7, but by the time the referee whistled for the end of the match the visitors had closed the gap to only five points. Newspaper reports of the game had Gallaher as one of the picks of the forwards. The following week Auckland 'B' met Waikato on the same field in front of a crowd one newspaper described as 'moderate'. The home side won by a crushing 39–0. Match reports of this game also made mention of Gallaher's play, and general interest in the abilities of the front-ranker grew.

The following season Gallaher was named in the Auckland 'A' team. The 22-year-old made his senior Auckland debut a year after his 'B' outing, on 8 August 1896. Not only was it his first full rep game, it was also to be his first taste of international football. The Queensland side (who had initially planned to tour the year before) arrived for a six-game tour. Their first match was against Auckland, less than 24 hours after they had set their sea legs down on the city's quays after 10 days' sailing.

It was a fine, cool, windy Auckland afternoon, following a wet, wintry morning. Both teams were given a rousing send-off as they left the city by horse-drawn brake at 2pm. They arrived at Potter's Paddock with only 15 minutes to spare before the three o'clock kick-off, leaving just enough time for some to stretch their legs and for others to draw their last puffs from their pipes before having to take the field. Gallaher walked out into the middle of Potter's for his first senior rep game in front of a crowd estimated at 5,000. To the constant delight of the crowd, the game was played at quite a pace. Auckland won by 15–6, but their performance was riddled with mistakes and many felt the margin could have been larger.

Gallaher's first game for Auckland, a 15–6 victory over Queensland, 8 August 1896. Back row: J McLean, D Gallaher, J Swindley, F Surman, A Wilson, J Laing. Middle row: Frank Ohlson, S Brown, DL Clayton, AE Braund (capt.), R Masefield, I Mills, E O'Hare (trainer). Front: C Brady, Fred Murray. Absent: Elliott and Absolum. AUCKLAND RUGBY UNION

Gallaher then played in the remaining three provincial home matches that season, against Wellington, Taranaki and Otago. All were defeats for the blue-and-whites, with Auckland failing to register even a single point in the three outings!

The following season, all focus was on the upcoming All Black tour of New South Wales and Queensland. At the end of May 1897, a NZRFU selection panel chose 20 men for the 11-match tour. Captaining the team was Otago's Jimmy Duncan, a player who was equally at home at wing-forward or five-eighth. Gallaher's name was not among the tourists, to the disappointment of some keen observers of Auckland football, and no doubt to him, too. He, thus, also missed selection for the first-ever North *v* South match (won by the Northerners 16–3) which was played in Wellington on 26 June, the day the national side left for Australia.

Six weeks later the team arrived back in New Zealand having lost just one game, to New South Wales, one of three 'tests' they played against that side.

The All Blacks had one game remaining before disbanding: against Auckland. It was a chance for Gallaher to prove that he should not have been omitted from the side, despite the success of the tourists. While the national side had been away, he had been outstanding as a member of Ponsonby's Auckland club-championship winning side, which had won eight of its nine matches that season.

The Auckland union had asked for its All Blacks to be available to play for the province, but when this was turned down, newspapers gave them little chance against the side that had scored over 100 points in their last three Australian games. Those expectations were matched as the All Blacks moved out to a 7–3 lead in the second half. But then, as Auckland gained more and more possession, the run of the play went their way. Gallaher was prominent in a number of passing and dribbling rushes, as well as disrupting the All Black hookers at scrum-time. With three minutes to play, Auckland advanced again, sending the ball along the backline to the winger Absolum, who scored in the corner. The crowd went wild. Those in the grandstand stamped their feet with thunderous delight. One report noted that some of the spectators 'were quite carried away by the triumph of the moment, and substantial citizens might be seen cutting capers in front of the stand, with their hats reared high in the air at the end of their walking sticks'. The scenes of joy were repeated when the final whistle sounded, giving Auckland a win by 11–10.

There was a sour postscript to the All Blacks' defeat, however. At the after-match dinner, three All Blacks — William 'Cocky' Roberts, William Harris and Joe Calnan — caroused into the night. Their behaviour, and apparently some of the language they used, was not acceptable to the team manager, Isaac Hyams. He reported them to the NZRFU, who suspended them for two years. There were protestations, but the suspensions stood. None of the trio wore the black jersey again.

A week later, the triumphant Auckland side was off on a three-match tour of the lower North Island. In the space of six days they covered a considerable distance; they played Taranaki in New Plymouth, then went south to meet Wellington, before returning north again for a match against Wanganui. All three matches were victories.

That wasn't to be the end of Gallaher's travel for the season. As Auckland club champions, the Ponsonby side were to meet the Northern Wairoa sub-union champions, Aratapu, at the then-bustling town which lies on the shores of the Northern Wairoa river, south of Dargaville. The Ponsonby boys left Auckland on a Friday afternoon, travelling north by train from Auckland to Helensville. They then boarded an overnight steamer that chugged across the broad expanse of the Kaipara Harbour to the riverside town. On the Saturday afternoon they squared off against their hosts. A fierce contest was narrowly won by Ponsonby, and afterwards both teams enjoyed a most sociable evening. It was a weary mob that arrived back in Auckland on the Monday morning.

Once back in Auckland, Gallaher could hang up his boots for the off-season. He had established himself in the Auckland side, and as one of the best-performed in club football. The following season of 1898 should have been one to cement his standing, but it was not to be.

Although he did begin the club season, and turned out for Ponsonby when the representative programme was over, injury kept him out of the four Auckland home games that year.

PONSONBY DISTRICT FOOTBALL TEAM.

Gallaher as captain of the Ponsonby senior team, 1900. Back row: Blomfield, R Carder, Watson, Dunlop, J Carder, Dunning, R Rule. Middle row: Cossar, J Rule, Carlaw, Gallaher, Doran, Calloway. Front: Lendrum, Upton. SIR GEORGE GREY SPECIAL COLLECTIONS, AUCKLAND LIBRARIES, AWNS-19000706-10

Saturday was for football; Sunday was for church and family. David, Molly and the boys had reunited with Joseph and Nell and moved to Church Street (now Cowan Street) and attended All Saints Church which stood on the corner of Ponsonby Road and Church Street. The large wooden building, with an ornate wooden altar, was one of a number of churches of varying denominations dotting Ponsonby

Road. The size of the All Saints congregation had grown considerably in the late 1800s. Its Sunday school catered for over 600, and the body of the church had been extended to accommodate 500 service-goers.

There was a change of occupation for Gallaher, as he left the Northern Roller Milling Company and began working as a labourer with the Auckland Freezing Company. The meat company had a large, foreboding brick building standing alone on what was Auckland's Railway Wharf, a short distance along the city's quay from the milling company headquarters. Since 1882, the ability to refrigerate meat and game (and thus export it) had transformed the New Zealand economy. In Auckland, freshly slaughtered carcasses were brought from the 'Wester-field' abattoir, south of the city, and unloaded into large cool-rooms. Fifty thousand carcasses could be stored cold at the plant, while 1,600 could be frozen per day. A 70-tonne ammonia machine pumped cool air into the chillers, and 8 tonnes of ice could be produced daily from water tapped from the city supply, then boiled and filtered. This was in great demand during the summer months by local businesses attempting to keep their perishables cold. Ships berthed a short distance from the building, and frozen meat would be transported quickly from the factory chillers to the ship's hold.

While Gallaher's workdays were physically demanding — from the constant handling of the heavy animal carcasses to the cold temperatures in which he had to work — it was of benefit to his football career. Possessed of large hands and taut, round biceps, the work kept him fit and strong, particularly in the forearms and upper body.

Another way Gallaher kept fit was by walking briskly from his Ponsonby home to work in the city, a distance of roughly two miles. In suitable weather he joined a steady flow of workers in the morning walking down College Street on one of the area's first tarsealed footpaths. At the bottom of the hill, the Auckland Gas Company was developing a large parcel of land, and, a short distance from there, work was under way to reclaim a large part of the shoreline and turn it into a recreational area. As he continued on his way, Gallaher's walk was far from picturesque, as he made his way along streets that were dominated by the noise and smells emanating from a multitude of factories, sawmills and other industries. Arriving at the city's quay allowed him a view of the eastern hills, and of the ever-changing ships and boats that rested in their berths at the wharves, either emptying or filling themselves with passengers, cargoes of crates, and sacks or livestock. Beyond, as one looked north across the harbour, was the small suburb of Devonport, the duo of hills in Mt Victoria and North Head, and the dark shadow that dominated Waitemata Harbour — Rangitoto Island.

A view inside Gallaher's workplace, the Auckland Farmers' Freezing Company.
SIR GEORGE GREY SPECIAL COLLECTIONS, AUCKLAND LIBRARIES, AWNS-19080305-3-1

When the weather was poor, and the streets pooled with water or ran with mud, Gallaher could hail a horse-drawn tram in Ponsonby Road and ride it along the western rim of the city's undulating landscape, then down into Queen Street.

In the evenings, the progress for a number of those walking back to Ponsonby wasn't as swift. Three pubs — The Drake and The Rob Roy in Freemans Bay, and The Suffolk, halfway up the steep College Street hill — provided an opportunity for the weary to stop and partake of a refreshing ale or enjoy a game of billiards.

Besides work, church and football, Gallaher had also joined the United Ancient Order of Druids (UAOD). Today the word 'druid' conjures images of men with flowing beards and robes who possess special spells and potions. However, the UAOD was a friendly society, a lodge for (predominantly) working men or businessmen. Masonic Lodges still dot towns and cities around New Zealand, but long-forgotten are the Independent Order of Oddfellows (although their hall still stands in Ponsonby's Renall Street), the Ancient Order of Foresters, and the Manchester Unity Independent Order of Oddfellows.

These associations had regular meetings with ceremonial commencements, and promoted a spirit of fellowship among their members. This was best illustrated by the fact that members paid into a lodge fund. The purpose of this was that, should a member be faced with unexpected expenses or beset by financial problems, he could make a formal request to receive support via the fund. For a city with a small population like Auckland's in the early 1900s, there was a surprisingly large number of these societies in operation. Gallaher attended his lodge's night on alternate Mondays, tidying himself after a day at work, putting on his best suit, waxing his moustache, then making his way to the Druids Hall that stood in North Street (now

Galatos Street), in the neighbouring suburb of Newton. As well as the members' meetings, regular social events were held. There were Plain and Fancy Dress balls and supper evenings featuring 'Progressive Euchre 8–10pm, Ping-Pong 10.15–11.15pm'.

Over the next couple of years, as Gallaher's younger brothers matured, the various family members started to head off in their own directions: to other parts of the city and country, and even the goldfields of Australia. Gallaher, however, had become a Ponsonby man. Any departure of his from the suburb would only be intended as temporary.

To Africa

'An emergency has arisen: the occasion now exists
for us to prove our devotion to the Empire.'

What we commonly refer to today as the Boer War was actually the Second South African War. The first was in 1880–81, between British soldiers and Boer farmers of the Transvaal. (Boers were settlers of predominantly Dutch and German descent.) In the 1830s they had undertaken what was known as 'The Great Trek', which saw them leave the Cape Colony in the south — which was governed by the British — and make their way thousands of kilometres north to where they established the Transvaal and Orange Free State.

In 1886, gold was found in the Transvaal and a gold rush began, with many British from the Cape and Natal racing north to stake claims. While they were involved in the development of some of the mining industry, these *'Uitlanders'* were not welcomed by the Boers and their president, Paul Kruger. Tensions escalated in 1895 as *Uitlanders* agitated for citizenship of Transvaal (otherwise known as the South African Republic) and other rights, which they were denied. In the spring of 1899, as the Boers mobilized a well-armed army supported by the likes of Germany, hundreds of *Uitlanders* fled the Transvaal, passing British troops which were encamped on the Transvaal border. Kruger issued an ultimatum to Britain to remove the assembling troops and not to send any more to the Republic.

War had not yet officially broken out, but New Zealand's Premier Seddon, who was also Minister of Defence, was quick to offer troops to help England's cause. (Queensland had already done so.) He wasted no time in addressing Parliament on 28 September 1899, moving a resolution that:

> *... respectful address be presented to His Excellency, the Governor, requesting him to offer to the Imperial Government for the service in the Transvaal, a contingent of mounted rifles and that in the event of the offer being accepted, the Government be empowered after selection by the Commander of the Forces to provide, equip and despatch the force.*

Seddon, a larger-than-life character (weighing roughly 20 stone) who thrived on playing to a crowd, be it in the formal confines of Parliament or out in public, further addressed the House:

> *Mr Speaker — on no previous occasion have I risen in this House with a greater sense of responsibility that is cast upon me than I rise to make the proposal now submitted. An emergency has arisen: the occasion now exists for us to prove our devotion to the Empire and*

honourable members are called up today to pass a resolution offering
a contingent for service in the Transvaal.

Unanimous support for the resolution was not to be had, with six of the 59 members voting against it and 13 members abstaining or not able to cast their votes as they weren't present in the House. However, when the House rose, the national anthem was sung with great gusto and Seddon led three very hearty and patriotic cheers for Queen Victoria.

A week later the offer of a contingent was accepted by the Imperial Government and preparation began for the First Contingent of Mounted Rifles to sail to Africa as soon as possible. To serve, men had to fulfil a number of criteria: to be born within the colony; to be between the ages of 23 and 40, and unmarried; to be between 5 feet 8 inches and 5 feet 11 inches in height; to be 36 inches across the chest; to have served two years in volunteer corps. At the time, New Zealand's military totalled about 8,500. There were 300 artillery men, and the rest were volunteers. Some were veterans of New Zealand's Land Wars, while others had served for English regiments in the Crimea. Soldiers signed up for a year of service, but that could be extended by joining later arriving contingents.

With Kruger's ultimatum ignored by Britain, on 11 October 1899, with the support of the Orange Free State, Transvaal declared that a state of war existed between it and Britain. Ten days later the First New Zealand Mounted Rifles sailed for Africa on the SS *Waiwera*.

Initially, some contingent members supplied their own rifles, saddles and horses, and much fundraising was undertaken to help the patriotic sons of Maoriland pay for their gear and mounts. Saddleries gifted riding equipment. Horses were donated and purchased by the government from private owners. However, as the war progressed, the British Government funded the purchase of all of these items.

Four more contingents left the shores of New Zealand for Africa over the next year, and, as they served out their time of service, new recruits were sought by the government to replace the returning men. By the end of December 1900, 80 men from the greater Auckland area had already handed in their names at the Auckland brigade office as volunteers for the Sixth Contingent. Among them was Gallaher.

Those enlisting were subjected to a preliminary medical test. On New Year's Eve 1900, Gallaher underwent his at the Auckland Drill Hall (which stood in Rutland Street, on what is now the Auckland University of Technology site). His height was listed as 5 feet 11½ inches. His (qualifying) chest measurement was 39½ inches. The examining doctor wrote that he 'looks his age', which was written as 25 years old. Gallaher was by then 27. From here on, Gallaher would be known on official documents as a couple of years younger than he actually was.

Two weeks later, having easily passed the riding and rifle-range tests, he swore his attestation form: 'I, David Gallaher, do sincerely promise and swear that I will be faithful and bear true allegiance to Her Majesty Queen Victoria, and that I will faithfully serve in the Volunteer Force of New Zealand both within and without the colony until I shall be lawfully discharged.'

With the regimental number 3229, Gallaher became a member of the Sixth Contingent's 16th Company. The Sixth Contingent was made up of Companies 16–20: Auckland (16th), Wellington Province (17th), Wellington City (18th), Canterbury (19th) and Otago (20th).

Gallaher joined fellow members of the 16th for three weeks of training at the Auckland Domain, where dozens of tents with straw floors had been set up on the lawn which lies in front of the Auckland War Memorial Museum. Gallaher shared his accommodation with seven other men from Auckland and surrounding districts.

BACK ROW.—G. J. Dowson, Kaiwaka; W. S. Philips, Raglan; W. Ellis, Auckland; S. A. Dailey, Devonport; F. Gladding, Auckland.
FRONT ROW—A. L. Garner, Thames; P. Fahey, Bombay; D. Gallagher, Ponsonby.

Gallaher (front, right) and Sixth Contingent tent mates in the Auckland Domain, January 1901. SIR GEORGE GREY SPECIAL COLLECTIONS, AUCKLAND LIBRARIES, AWNS-19010125-7-2

On arrival, soldiers were issued a blanket, a tin plate, a tin mug, and a knife, fork and spoon. The camp was a busy one, with soldiers undertaking drills — mounted and on foot — learning bugle calls, tending to horses, and hosting a steady stream of visitors and curious observers who would gather daily to watch the men train.

While Gallaher was in camp, Queen Victoria died. Aged 81, she had been monarch for 63 years. Her passing was mourned throughout the Empire.

A ship called the *Cornwall* carried the Sixth Contingent to Africa, having earlier transported Australian troops to the war. The coal-fired steamer was a bulky vessel not blessed with speed or manoeuvrability. There was nothing luxurious about her. In fact, it could be said that there was nothing even comfortable about her. At the commencement of her role as a transporter, conditions aboard had been criticized when a Queensland Lieutenant-Colonel stated that the ship was not in a fit condition to be carrying soldiers and horses. To his mind, the hospital was in an unsuitable part of the ship and, more worryingly, was 'overrun' with vermin. He also found fault with the horse stalls and was concerned that horses would die *en route* to Africa.

In Wellington, on 26 January, following a speech by Finance Minister Sir Joseph Ward which was notable for its lack of brevity, the southern contingents boarded the *Cornwall*, which then moved out into the harbour for the night. (One of the soldiers on board was Joseph Linklater, a West Coaster, who had enlisted along with his brother. He kept a diary of his time in the Sixth Contingent which was later published as *On Active Service in South Africa with the 'Silent Sixth'*.)

The *Cornwall* sailed the next morning, and three days later arrived in Auckland. At dawn it berthed at Queen's Wharf, and during the morning the waiting Auckland Division drove their horses up long, wooden races to the stalls on the ship and organized their personal belongings on board. Each soldier was given two pairs of boots, a field service cap, a night cap, a greatcoat, a felt hat, two jackets, a khaki jersey, leggings, two pairs of riding breeches, shoes and drill trousers, braces, three cholera belts, two pairs of drawers, two undershirts, three pairs of socks, three grey military shirts, two blankets, two towels, a waterproof sheet, shoe brushes, and a kit-bag hold-all for eating and grooming implements. The newcomers were also allocated a new knife, fork, spoon, tin mug and enamel plate, and assigned a dining table with 13 others. The complete contingent now totalled 21 officers, 551 men, and a similar number of horses.

The Sixth Contingent marching into Queen Street on their way to the boat to sail to Africa, 31 January 1901. SIR GEORGE GREY SPECIAL COLLECTIONS, AUCKLAND LIBRARIES, AWNS-19010208-5-1

With on-board arrangements attended to, the contingent marched up Queen Street to the Drill Shed, where the Auckland members were farewelled by a large crowd, although the occasion was deliberately muted to show respect for the recently deceased monarch. Premier Seddon cabled a message, which was read to the soldiers:

Convey to the officers and men of the departing contingent my hearty and sincere good wishes for their welfare. I feel sure they will acquit themselves in a manner worthy of those of our contingents who are now in South Africa and bring home laurels to our colony. Give them my best wishes and wish them God speed.

The national anthem was sung and three cheers rang out. The men were then granted two hours' leave. At 5pm, they reassembled and marched determinedly back down Queen Street to the *Cornwall*.

The *Observer* noted that Gallaher had been given a send-off by:

> *... members and enthusiasts of the Ponsonby District Football Club assembled at the Ponsonby Club Hotel. ... Mr S.D. Hanna was in the chair, and proposed the health of the guest in a very happy manner. Several other well-known members spoke as to 'Dave's' good qualities, and the chairman then presented him with a well-filled purse of sovereigns. Corporal Gallaher replied very feelingly and thanked all his old comrades for the kind way they had treated him. At the camp in the Domain 'Dave' was very popular amongst his comrades.*

At the quay, with several hundred well-wishers behind them, the soldiers boarded the *Cornwall* and scrambled to vantage points across the top of the ship to wave their goodbyes, lining the deck and the top of the horse stalls, and climbing the masts.

Leaving its berth, the *Cornwall* pulled away slowly and sailed through Auckland's inner harbour, flanked by two ferry steamers packed with the soldiers' friends and family, who shouted and waved to their loved ones while brass bands added to the cacophony. Once the *Cornwall* left the relative calm of the Waitemata Harbour and then the Hauraki Gulf — steaming into the ocean proper — the heavier seas quickly upset the stomachs of dozens of men, who were ribbed by their mates for the time they spent leaning over the side of the ship 'feeding the fishes'.

The men slept in cramped quarters below decks, with the horses above them on the upper and main decks. To try to get some space, hammocks were often abandoned for the floor, although if the ship rolled the men lying there slid from one side of the room to the other, ending up in a heap! As a result of being below hundreds of horses — whose stall floors, although regularly cleaned and occasionally refreshed with straw, were constantly covered in urine and faeces — the air, according to one soldier, 'was none too pure. It was a common sight to see a great number of our men sleeping on deck on a fine night in preference to the hot hold below.' It was not only the heat and the smell that drove the men up from below; in rolling seas, the noise made by the horses' hooves on the floor of their stalls, as they kept moving to hold their balance, was incessant.

The Auckland men were berthed amidships, flanked by Wellington forward and Canterbury and Otago aft. Impromptu concerts would break out in the evening, and soldiers would hear an invitation to another part of the ship such as 'a concert in Wellington'. There were other spontaneous entertainments, such as that described by an Auckland soldier, Len Hook, in a letter home:

> *There was a little excitement this evening, a fight with fists, between one of the sailors and a cook, the latter must of [sic] weighed about 15 stone, the former was very small. They were stripped to the waist but they were half drunk, so that they didn't know what they were doing. It was over a billy of beer. Both lost blood as they fell on some iron and cut themselves, it drew crowds of troopers from all parts of the boat. They ended up by shaking hands.*

Soldiers' days began at 5.45am and comprised tending to the horses, fitness drills, and lectures. Lights went out at 9.40pm. Smoking was not allowed, except on rare occasions when officers agreed to it for an evening concert. This was a frustration to many, as the American Tobacco Company had presented the contingent with 5,000 cigarettes prior to sailing.

On 3 February, the boat was stopped for 10 minutes to observe the burial of Queen Victoria. All passengers were silent, giving the boat a ghostly air as it rolled and creaked.

An entertainment committee put together programmes such as musical concerts, minstrel shows, and even variety evenings which featured a comedian named Ernie Wall who had worked as a professional entertainer prior to enlisting. Sporting contests were another distraction from the daily routines, boxing being especially popular. Perhaps the most hotly contested event was the tug-of-war competition. Each of the five companies entered a team in the knock-out format which saw the Auckland team (of which Gallaher was a member) beat the boys of the 19th after a pull which lasted quarter of an hour! They then triumphed in the final over the 17th, who started with a lot of excitement and vigour but faded as the contest drew out to 13 minutes of stressing and straining.

Sunday Mass parades required all soldiers to be dressed in proper uniform. The men would also assemble in small groups to learn the contingent's haka. It was recorded in Linklater's diary as:

Tutahi hingatahi, tutahi hingatahi, purutia te mana ote Kingi. Ake-ake kia toa, ake-ake kia kaha. He, he, ha.

He gave the translation as:

Together we stand, together we fall and thus uphold the authority of our King. For ever and for ever be brave. For ever and for ever be strong.

Two brief stops were made on the voyage, at Sydney and Western Australia's Albany. Both were barely much more than a chance for the men to stretch their legs, shop for small items, and sightsee within a short distance of port. Not all could go ashore at once, as the horses needed to be tended to, so the men were broken up into large groups and had staggered times of leaving and returning to the *Cornwall*. The departures from these ports gave the contingent the opportunity to perform their haka to the large groups who gathered at the quays to see them off.

As the *Cornwall* made its way laboriously across the Indian Ocean, the first casualties of the deployment were horses. It was common to see them suffering from swollen legs due to the lack of exercise, which was remedied by the soldiers soaking their mount's legs with vinegar several times a week. In rough seas, if not securely chained on both sides of their heads, horses would be thrown around in their stalls, injuring themselves to the point where the only option was to put them down. A lame horse had no place in the columns which would be expected to cover thousands of miles in Africa. Nor was there time to wait for an injured horse to recover from its injuries. Carcasses would be winched up on deck and then, with the use of a makeshift derrick, lifted up and out over the side of the ship. Then the rope was cut and the weighty body of the dead horse would plummet into the sea. 'Planting a horse' it was called. Soldiers saluted the dead beasts by paraphrasing the popular song, 'The Soldier's Grave': 'With a splash and a plunge, and all was o'er/ And the poor dead horse was seen no more.'

The roughest night of the voyage occurred after a month's sailing. The ship ran into a violent storm, and Gallaher and the other soldiers had to rush to the stalls of their horses, ignoring all that was being flung about below decks. As the ship's captain did his utmost to steer his vessel through the surging swell, the men stood with their frightened horses, straining with every ounce of their own weight to make sure their mounts did not fall or injure themselves, with varying degrees of success. The Auckland horses fared worst as they were most exposed to the roaring storm, and 87 of them fell at some point. Men scrambled to get them back on their feet, while trying to hold their own, as the ship rose and fell in the huge seas. When the brief storm abated, no losses were counted. Repairs were required to a number of stalls, and injuries were sustained by men who had been stood on or crushed against stalls. Teeth were lost, fingers and collarbones broken, and blood ran free from noses. It all added to the workload of the Surgeon-Captain and his medical staff, who were also occupied with testing men against enteric fever (better known today as typhoid). The chief symptom of the deadly disease was a painful swelling and ulceration of the intestines.

Good hygiene was important with so many men and animals in close quarters, but cleanliness was not easy to maintain. Len Hook wrote: 'Yesterday was washing day and you should have seen the decks with clothes you couldn't move for them, this day is specified for the purpose, as the fresh water is only turned on at certain hours other times.' On hot days, many resorted to salt-water showers to try to remove the cloying sweat and grime from their bodies.

On 7 March 1901, Gallaher and the Sixth Contingent had their first view of the African coast, and excitement rose in the ranks as preparation was made to go ashore, including the issuing of equipment such as saddles and blankets. (Visitors to the Auckland War Memorial Museum can see on display the saddle used by Trooper James Madill, who was a member of the 16th Company alongside Gallaher.)

The greatly anticipated landing was to be delayed, however, due to an outbreak of 'plague' in Cape Town. Then the captain received instructions for the ship to make its way around the Cape of Good Hope to East London.

The Silent Sixth

*'I have had a couple of pretty close calls.
One day I thought I would have to say
good bye to old New Zealand.'*

As the *Cornwall* docked at East London on 14 March 1901, and the soldiers prepared to disembark with their mounts, Linklater made his first observations of Africa, writing that 'the gangs of Kaffirs — the first we had seen — seemed an amusing crowd. ... Malays and other fruit-dealers were carrying fruit to the boat all day, and got a ready sale for all they brought.'

There was no time for the soldiers to explore East London, though. Due to the delay in landing, orders had arrived for the contingent to proceed to the front with all speed. A count revealed that 15 horses had been lost during the six weeks at sea, and 21 men were still receiving treatment for illness or injury. Linklater wrote that: 'The greatest of good feeling was shown among the boys throughout the voyage, and that good feeling grew stronger as we got to know each other better.'

OFFICERS AND NON-COMS. OF THE AUCKLAND SECTION SIXTH NEW ZEALAND CONTINGENT.

Gallaher (top row, second from right) and fellow Auckland officers. SIR GEORGE GREY SPECIAL COLLECTIONS, AUCKLAND LIBRARIES, AWNS-19010208-8-1

Gallaher and the rest of the Auckland contingent loaded their horses into wagons on a train. It was always an exercise to get as many horses into a wagon as possible, the thinking being that it was of benefit to the horses if they were closely packed, as they wouldn't have room to move about or kick and knock each other. The sight of the spacious wagon would appeal to the first few horses, but as the numbers inside increased, makeshift whips, bare-hand slaps and stern voices were needed to force the horses aboard. Once the doors to the last wagon were closed, the Aucklanders departed. The other companies followed in four other trains. The soldiers were seated in small compartments of eight men that afforded little opportunity to stretch out, let alone sleep. Their destination was Pretoria, over 650 miles (1,050 kilometres) away.

Rifles and ammunition were distributed, and, with the men finding the action of the rifles unfamiliar, instruction was given on their use.

The better part of a week was spent sitting in trains, with stops to water, feed and lightly exercise the horses, but a number of the horses fared worse in the cramped wagons than they had at sea. The Kiwi boys, many of whom were from farming backgrounds, were fascinated by the landscapes they passed. The sight of very lush paddocks and healthy, large herds of sheep and cattle made many feel right at home. But as they moved, the landscape changed, becoming drier and less hospitable. At a number of stops they met 'Tommies' (English soldiers), who gave Linklater the impression that 'we are going to have a fine picnic and that the war was about over'. Further up the line, Australian Bushmen talked of 'Joey' (a nickname for Boer soldiers) being in the area.

Arriving in Pretoria, Linklater noted that it was a 'pretty town. ... The streets were crowded with mule and bullock transports, while the curious Eastern dress of part of the population made us realize we had truly arrived in a strange land.'

Here the Sixth Contingent was broken up into four squadrons under the command of General Plumer. These squadrons became known as 'Plumer's Column', and they were told that their task was to systematically rid the Northern Transvaal of Boer guerrillas and sympathizers. This was much easier said than done, as it was a huge area that the British had yet to enter.

Observing more of the detail of daily life in southern Africa, some soldiers had a curious degree of superiority when it came to judging the way the local black population was treated by the whites. Corporal Frank Twisleton, of the Second Contingent, wrote a book about his African experience, *With the New Zealanders at the Front*, and some of his comments — by no means unique — are very much of an age vastly different to that in which we now live:

> *The niggers are all in favour of the English. The Dutch treat the blacks worse than dogs; kick them out of their houses except when actually at work, and call them by the horrible name bastard. They are 'religious' but no black is ever allowed in a Dutch church. Their religion is a gloomy one; they are always drawling out hymns and praying. Most of their faces are too heavy and ugly to ever expand into a good honest grin.*

The interesting new land also introduced the fatigued, restless soldiers to strains of disease to which they hadn't previously been exposed. Measles broke out and quickly spread, meaning one camp had to be abandoned and a number of men quarantined. While they were treated, their healthy mates prepared to move off to join Plumer's Column, packing their horses for a final, uncomfortable inspection.

Besides a soldier's personal gear, and wearing bandoliers that could hold between 80 and 200 rounds of ammunition, they also had to carry water bottles, haversacks and equipment for their horses, such as horse rubbers, a curry comb, a body brush, a sponge, a head rope, a nose bag, forage nets, a picket peg, heel and pickets ropes, and a tin of Dubbin.

Linklater's view was:

> *A great mistake was made in issuing to us a great number of cumbersome articles that were of no earthly use to us, and which we took good care either to lose or get rid of on the first opportunity. The horses were more laden than they need have been, and we had*

great difficulty, on account of our heaped-up saddle, in mounting and
dismounting. … There was much bustle and confusion for a start,
through the boys having so much gear to strap on their saddles.

A column would move in formation, being led first by scouts, who
were chosen principally for their expert horsemanship but also for
having a keen eye, alertness and sustained concentration. It was a role
Gallaher found himself in, riding out in front, alone but part of a large
group, looking for any threat to his mates.

Roughly 100 metres behind the scouts trailed the advance guard.
Supporting the advance, 'flankers' rode wide on either side. Next were
the column's big guns — so placed that they could be readily used if
necessary. They had a protective escort which was followed by the
main body of mounted soldiers. At the rear were wagons of food and
baggage. The value of these to the enemy was reflected in their escorts
and the sizeable rearguard that protected the column from a surprise
attack from behind. Gallaher's contingent prided themselves on being
able to operate with a measure of stealth, nicknaming themselves 'The
Silent Sixth'.

Daily rations for soldiers were the following:

1 lb (approx 500 g) fresh or preserved meat
1¼ lb bread or 1 lb biscuit, flour or meal
⅔ oz coffee or ⅓ oz tea
3 oz sugar
½ oz salt
1/36 oz pepper
½ lb potatoes or other fresh vegetables
¼ lb jam

½ gill (quarter of a pint) of spirits (at the discretion of the Divisional Generals)

lime juice (when ordered by medical officers)

Feeding the horses was just as important as feeding the men. Allocations for forage were made depending on the size of the horse. Those over 15 hands high received 12 pounds of oats and 12 pounds of hay per day. Smaller horses were allocated 2 pounds less per day. A constant supply of feed could be maintained when men and horses were in camp, but it was an impossible expectation when contingents were in the field.

The Sixth covered thousands of monotonous miles in the saddle, and for days it would be only wattle trees providing tiny dots of colour, other than the brown of the earth.

Nights on the veldt were very cold, with the temperature dropping to freezing. When camp was set up, one of the first tasks was to find a supply of firewood before night fell. The barren veldt did not always give up much more than tinder, and on occasion men were known to tear down fences they found, simply for the fuel that the poles supporting the wire provided. Once fires were set, and a meal made from the unexciting rations, the men would settle in around the warmth and light of the fires, packing their pipes and telling colourful stories into the night.

Sleep was not easy or a constant, with the cold bringing on a restlessness of mind and body as soldiers wished away the hours and minutes until they could feel the dawn sun on their bodies. Moving columns often had a number of men who were asleep on their mounts after uncomfortable nights spent fighting the chill, which was a fine example of just how fatigued they were. Time in the saddle was not comfortable, and the pace of the moving columns was something Twisleton was highly critical of:

> *The military trot march is cruel to both horse and man. It is called a trot, but it is nothing of the sort; it is a double-shuffle — something a little faster than a walk. It is almost impossible to sit easily and steadily on the saddle, and the cavalryman bumps up and down in a manner painful to see. It is enough to break the back of an elephant. The rider is as stiff as a poker, and every limb seems cast in a plaster of Paris mould; there is no elasticity about them. It may do for a parade ground, but for the field it is simply cruelty to animals.*

Those who did manage to get to sleep at night were lucky if they didn't have it interrupted. Linklater wrote in his diary one morning of mosquitoes that 'made a fierce attack last night, as the swollen faces we wear can testify'. More of a nuisance were ticks, because they could cause sickness in men and horses, and they couldn't simply be swatted away. Twisleton noted:

> *The ticks are of two sorts — one is round and of a reddish colour, with a pair of forceps and about a dozen legs all round it. He works his head right into the flesh, and if left alone will eventually bury himself. The other one is a blood-sucker … His body is merely a bladder. When he begins operations he's about the size of a grain of rice, and the colour of blue grey. Horses and cattle that are bad with them just look as though you had got a dish of blue peas, dipped them in something sticky, and thrown them all over the animal, only when they are full of blood they are larger than a pea. At every halt on the march, every man is generally spending his time picking off the ticks.*

85

Mosquitoes and ticks were not an unknown to many of the soldiers, particularly those from rural areas, but one sight they hadn't encountered before had jaws dropping at its first appearance. 'It was on this march that we first saw the African locust,' wrote Twistleton:

> ... one of the greatest pests on earth; where such countless millions are bred is a mystery. When we first sighted them they were on the wing and formed a thick murky cloud, wavering about in a peculiar manner. When they begin to alight they just resemble a heavy shower of snow, and if there is any breeze a horse will scarcely face them. Almost every inch of the ground is covered with them, and they never leave any vegetation where they have camped.

Those clearing the Transvaal under Plumer participated in what is known as Lord Kitchener's 'scorched earth' policy, which was seen as a solution to the roaming Boer guerrillas. The Sixth Contingent had to move many Boer families from their farms, slaughter their stock, and raze their homes by setting fire to them, so that they could not be occupied or provide a sanctuary to the Boer guerrillas. 'The shifting of refugees was one of the saddest duties we had to perform out there,' wrote Linklater. 'Though they were our enemies, it was sad to witness the grief of those unfortunate people when leaving behind their homes and farms.' Large numbers of those being moved were transported to what were loosely called 'refugee camps'. Post-war examination has shown that the term 'concentration camps' would be more appropriate.

At the end of March 1901, Gallaher might have cast his thoughts home to the football season that was about to commence, with annual meetings, training and practice matches. Plus, New South Wales were undertaking a seven-match tour, culminating in a match with Auckland. Back in New Zealand, the *Observer* was noting his absence: 'Ponsonby will miss "Davie" Gallaher this season, but the team has some numerous young players who are bound to come on.'

Sixth Contingent soldiers carrying out Kitchener's 'scorched earth' policy, 1901. Sir George Grey Special Collections, Auckland Libraries, AWNS-19020605-16-2

There were football games played by the New Zealand soldiers in Africa. In one instance, some members of the Sixth Contingent played an Australian team in front of their respective rowdy comrades. The New Zealanders won 14–0.

Towards the end of May, Gallaher and his comrades found themselves trading 'hot fire' with a small group of Boers. A group of four soldiers had been sent to inspect a farm several miles from where the main column was camped. (When clearing a property, men would spread out in a circle around the house then slowly advance towards it using as much cover as was available.) As this party drew near to the farm, an unidentified man on horseback rode off into the distance. The quartet assumed it was one of their own. As they drew closer to the farm's main house, six Boer soldiers opened fire on them. As the men of the Sixth attempted to retreat from the hail of bullets, one of their horses was shot, and his rider, Private Hurrey, scrambled about looking for protection from the attack which now was focused on him. Attempting to return fire, he was shot. A bullet travelled through his left knee and into his stomach. According to a newspaper report of the incident, the other three New Zealanders 'took up a position behind a slight rising ground, and kept up a constant fire until Sergeant Gallaher, with Lance-Corporal Hunt and the others who were the advance party … came up and drove back the enemy.'

Private Hurrey died of his wounds later that night. His brother was in another column and rode some distance to see him. Sadly, he arrived only in time for the burial.

As the treks became longer, the daily ration for men was simply a pound of mealie flour. Hunger set in, and soldiers would forage what they could, when they could. It was not uncommon for men to drink milk straight from the teats of wild goats. At other times they completely stripped orchards of fruit when they came across them.

New Zealand soldiers' diaries and letters mention stopping for a 'skoff', meaning having something to eat. It could be from the African experience that Kiwis developed the slang word 'scoff'. As noted etymologist Max Cryer advised the author, the derivation of the word could be traced to 'scaff' which is from a Scottish dialect, and that became the English 'scoff' in the mid-1880s.

But there is also a connection with South Africa — but not from Afrikaans. Cape Dutch were people in the Western Cape of South Africa, starting in the 17th century descendants of Dutch and Flemish, and they spoke a dialect of their own. From Dutch they gained the word 'schoft' meaning a 'quarter of a day'. Among the Cape Dutch this became 'schoff' — and the quarter of a day significance was perceived as 'a meal'. Hence the development of 'schoff' and its derivative 'scoff' — to eat. The word did not move into the Afrikaans language, but was picked up by men fighting the Boer wars in the late 1880s. It is possible of course that both origins have validity — the Scottish and the Dutch. Quite often a word 'develops' from more than one influence and this could well be an example.

As time passed in the field, the men's condition deteriorated, as did their clothing. Some ended treks looking threadbare, as though they had been in the wild for years rather than months. Uniforms in such condition provided little protection from the worst of the elements. Linklater experienced a thunderstorm which:

… came up with great fury and violence. The lightning was vivid, the thunder deafening, while the rain poured down in torrents. As we had not expected the storm, we had no cover rigged, so quickly got very wet. The cold was intense and we suffered severely. Our New Zealand overcoats, which had by this time worn very thin, were very fair to keep out the cold, but were useless to prevent us getting a wetting.

Lightning was known to have caused severe shocks to soldiers struck by it out in the open, as well as killing livestock.

The horses didn't always fare any better from their months on the move. Hundreds died and were left where they fell. Those that didn't expire suffered sores from the rub of the saddles, or painful hoof conditions as they dropped shoes, or had cuts and abrasions, from thorny vegetation, that didn't heal.

During a period of rest after 10 months' trekking, a series of sports days were organized. Prize-money was raised from the troops. Gallaher featured in a cricket match for Colvin's Corps v Viall's Corps, where he reportedly scored 110 out of a total of 178, 'only giving one chance'. Viall's Corps was dismissed for 138.

Two letters in the Alexander Turnbull Library in Wellington (here unedited) survive from Gallaher's time in Africa. He wrote them on notepaper — in the wide, curling style that was his handwriting — to his sister, Molly. The first of them was written at the Charlestown Hospital, on 18 October 1901. Being hospitalized might have meant that Gallaher's spirits were at a low ebb, and he writes of a sense of loneliness and of his own mortality. Both letters show the genuine affection he had for his sister Molly. They are also good examples of just how heartening it was for soldiers at the front to receive any news from home.

Darling old Sis,

I suppose you weary waiting for a letter from me as it is so long now since I have had a chance to write a letter at all, that I have quite forgotten how to write even. I have received three of your letters lately or Sunday chats as you call them and also one from Nell and Joe. My word I tell you I was glad to get some news of the old place as I had not seen or heard of any for the past two months. Thanks very much for the cuttings from the Star *as every item of news is eagerly welcomed I can assure you. You tell me that you are still at the L.A.*

[Lunatic Asylum] you must find the place getting monotonous long ere this I hope to hear you have left it or if I ever come back to see you happily settled down. You say that Hugh has just returned from a fortnight's holiday down at Waihi. Surely the F.W. [Freezing Works] never granted him that or if so they must be getting generous all at once. I suppose that you have been at most of the Football Matches this year. By the time you get this you will be ready to spend your Xmas holidays and have a good time at the Duff and Goose. Well, Molly old girl, I hope that you have the jolliest time possible for anyone to have is all the harm I can wish you for. I think it is about up to you now after all you have done for us Sis Dear. I think that the last place that I wrote to you from was Utrecht if I am not mistaken, well since then we have been all over S Africa pretty well I believe, on the trek the whole time and it looks as if we will be trekking till the end of the Chapter. We have a fair share of the fighting all the time and I am still alive and kicking although I have had a couple of pretty close calls, one day I thought I would have to say good bye to old New Zealand but I had my usual luck and so came out all right though it had me thinking I can tell you Molly old girl. I could not help wondering what you would say when you heard the news. Well, we trekked north from Utrecht till we reached a place called Wonderfontein where we received news that we were to proceed as quickly as possible down to Cape Colony as the Joey's were playing up down there. We entrained at Wonderfontein and it took us five days to get to Bloemfontein, where we disembarked and started out on the trek again for the Modder River, and round Magersfontein where we spent two weeks hunting the Joey's out of a range of Kopye's. We got 70 of them. We left the Moddu and trekked down into Cape Colony where we had sundry fights and have been on the go all the time, the last go we had we lost three of our men, two of

the Auckland section and one of the Southern men. We were coming into Bloemfontein for a fortnights rest on Oct 1st but we got orders to go straight down to Natal as Botha is hard at work down there again so we entrained from Bloemfontein to Volksrust and are operating around Dundee and Ladysmith. I did not go out with them this time, as I had to go to hospital with malarial fever. I had a pretty bad time for over a week but I am getting right now and will be out on the veldt again in a couple of weeks. My word it is a change sleeping out on the veldt with your saddle and pillow and the stars for a roof for seven months to get into a good tent with a bed and sheets under you and a nurse to look after you, but I am sick of it already and hope to be out with my troop again soon. Molly, I got a photo of [brothers] Harry, Charlie and Dug when I was at Modder River, but having no way of carrying it about me I have posted it on to you. I hope that it has got there all right, as I would not like to lose it. I see that you have got my photo allright, you seemed to be rather doubtful about it one letter you wrote to me. So tell me the truth in the hurry and excitement of coming away I very nearly forgot all about them. How is dear old Nell getting along I suppose she is up to her eyes in work just at present getting ready for the holidays. I had such a nice letter from her just at the time when I got yours I was just beginning to think I was forgotten when I got them all in a heap. You understand old girl that this letter will be Molly, Nell and co as I do not get much time to write, but all the same expect you and Nell to write whenever you can. Give my love to Hugh and tell him he might find time to write, wish him a Merry Xmas and Happy New Year from me and now dear old girl I will have to wind up this rambling epistle and so I will wish yourself, Nell, Joe and family a bright and Merry Xmas and Happy New Year and best of love to you all. I remain your loving brother Dave.

Then he added at the top of the letter:

Molly dear, I wish you could send me a pound of Derby tobacco and I will pay you what it costs to send as I have not had a good smoke since I came over. Don't forget the price of it or I will never forgive you. Dave.

No doubt among the cuttings from the *Star* were match reports of Auckland's 25–9 win over New South Wales.

The New Year did not start in the best fashion for the Sixth Contingent, as Gallaher's second letter — sent from Hurricane Hill, Wakkerstroom, on 8 January 1902 — explained:

Dear Old Sis,

The old year has come and gone and I can tell you that I was getting very despondent at not receiving any news from you people for so long, when I got your letter also one from Hugh and a parcel of tobacco which I can tell you was very acceptable as it was the only good smoke I have had since I have been in this country so convey my thanks to Hugh for his thoughtful present. I can not understand you saying that you have not had any news from me for over six months as I have written both you and Joe a good many times in that space of time so something must have gone wrong with the postal arrangements to have caused such a delay. I hope that when next I hear from you that you will have received all the missing correspondence. I suppose that you have had a good time during the holidays though they will have become a thing of the past long ere this reaches you but all the same dear old girl I hope that all have had a real good time both at Xmas and at New Year. I hope to enjoy your share of Xmas comforts when they arrive which will be about the end of February I think, but they will be none the less welcome for being a bit late. We spent Xmas day partly in marching, started about 3pm. Had a biscuit or two and a bit of fried mutton for dinner and had to go on outpost that night. Next day was on observation post all day with Joey's dodging about, had sundry shots at one another, came into camp at dusk and received army ration of pudding and a drop of tea, turned in and dreamt it was Xmas. Trekked out again next day and had two very good fights before New Year, got in near Volksrust New Years Day to pick up a convoy with rations and was dead glad to get your two letters, no papers though, can't understand it haven't received one for months and months. Two days before Xmas were expecting to go into the line for Xmas and had visions of one good feed and a sleep at least, but that night received orders to be ready to march at midnight, no smoking no lights so we knew what that meant. Went like blazes all night with no transport and just as day was breaking we got right on to Mr Joey. The first volley was fired at daybreak and they held a pretty strong position about 1200 strong under Opperman and Botha but by 12 o'clock we had driven them off and occupied the position and they were going like the wings of h— you know, and our horses were too done up to follow them I got a bulls eye that day when they were doing a retreat but two of them came back and got him away between them and I did not have the heart to fire at them while they were doing so though you must think I am getting terribly hard hearted, it makes you so out here when you see how they treat some of our boys. We made another night march the night after New Year and on the morning of the 3rd of Jan sighted the enemy and had a good chase after them and a patrol of NZers went out after them, captured a wagon and some ammunition also some cattle and pushed on after the Joeys. Mr Blinkhorn, the officer of my troop, was told off to hold a ridge to prevent them cutting us off from the main body and 40 more of the A Sq pushed on over the next ridge with a hundred men as supports when they were cut off by 500 Boers surrounded and 5 of them wounded, our Serg Major killed and 38 taken prisoner. The Joeys stripped them of all their clothing boots and money, took their horses rifles and bandoleers and let them go and I tell you they presented a sorry sight. We held the ridge till night and then retired on the main body, as we were fully 12 miles away from them. The next day we started after them again with the main body and at dinner time we struck them, the Queenslanders who were advance guard suffered pretty heavily until the rest of us came up and we were engaged till after dark. We had a total of 22 killed and 36 injured and a few taken prisoners it was a pretty mournful sight to see the Red Cross bearers cruising around the field fetching in the dead and wounded who were laying all over the place. Six of us were on outpost that night and were all night within 10 yards of a Joey who was laying there shot through the head and did not see him till day broke, he was still alive and had a drink of tea though he died an hour afterwards. A lot of them were not found till next morning when they were attended by the ambulance men. We have to come in here to refit a bit and send in the wounded so have got a chance to drop you a line but will have to pull up now as I have a lot of work to do as have been promoted to Sergt Major. So with the best of love to yourself, Joe, Nell and family also Hugh and with hope that you are all in the best of health and remembrance to all encoring friends from your loving brother Dave.

The most telling passage in that letter is Gallaher describing 'getting a bulls eye' but then not having the heart to keep firing at those who went to rescue the wounded soldier. This, along with his musing of 'you must think I am getting terribly hard hearted, it makes you so out here when you see how they treat some of our boys' is a sentiment that wouldn't have been discussed between the men. It also gives some insight into his loyalty to his comrades and his ability to engage in fighting and carrying out tasks such as the razing of homesteads because he was under instruction to do so. He had sworn an oath of allegiance and he was bound by that. In football terms, he played to the whistle.

As for the battle with Opperman's forces, Linklater estimated them to be closer to 800 strong (while one history of the war has the figure as low as 200) but concurred that: 'We were all very downhearted over this day's work, as it was the greatest disaster that had ever befallen the Sixth.' Sergeant-Major Smith of A Squadron was the officer fatality. He was famous within the contingent for having vowed 'never to surrender to a Dutchman' and was gunned down after a valiant retaliation.

Daylight revealed a depressing scene. Dead and wounded from both sides lay scattered across the sandy battlefield. Haunting moans could be heard from those whose pain made them call out for relief. Rifles and bandoliers lay unclaimed on the ground. The hulks of dead horses were numerous and, as the sun and temperature slowly rose, flies were attracted to their open wounds. Other horses that were injured made futile attempts to get to their feet, the whites of their eyes a sign of their distress. Shots again rang out as many were put out of their misery by their handlers. Doctors and orderlies wandered the scene, evaluating and evacuating injured survivors while their compatriots dug crude graves for the fallen.

Clashes with the Boers were not, however, the greatest cause of casualties for the Sixth. Dysentery was a constant problem, and over the first two months of 1902 the contingent suffered a dozen casualties from enteric fever. The Sixth had lost three men killed in action, one had died of his wounds, two were accidentally killed (drowned and shot), and 13 had died of disease. The seriously wounded totalled at least 28.

The contingent then slowly made their way back to the coast, sporadically encountering Boers, but they were at the end of their campaign. As they waited to depart South Africa, they were addressed by General Plumer:

> *I shall not say much, except to tell you that your work has been as good as that of your former Contingents. You did not arrive in time to take part in the big fights. ... You arrived in time to take part in the march to Pietersburg, the last town held by the Boers, and thus take part in the last act of the first stage of the war. Since then we have been doing good work, gradually clearing the districts and reducing the number of Boers in the field, the only way to bring such a war to a conclusion. This is not such exciting work as big battles, but it gives officers and men better chances of distinguishing themselves than in big fights, and those chances that have fallen to your share you have made the most of. ... I think you can go home with proud feelings that you have preserved the good name which the former Contingents have had.*

On 10 April 1902, the Sixth Contingent sailed for home from Durban on the *Cornwall*, leaving behind 12 men and several officers. Among them was Gallaher, who had decided to extend his service, despite the homesickness that was apparent in his letters to Molly. He joined up with the Tenth Contingent, which arrived in Durban just as his mates of the Silent Sixth were setting foot back in New Zealand. His absence was noted by the *Observer* on 17 May 1902, when it reported that '"Dave" Gallaher's name does not appear in the list of the returned Sixth Contingenters, so he must have signed on for a further term in South Africa'.

Gallaher's extended service was a complete contrast to his first year. By now, the war was truly on the wane. The Tenth were sent north to Newcastle and awaited orders to move into the field. They did not come. Peace was declared at the end of May 1902. The Tenth did not see any active service, but suffered 11 casualties: 10 men died of disease, and one was fatally wounded in an accident.

Gallaher finally left Africa on 17 July 1902, some 16 months after arriving at East London.

The First Test

'Tena Koe Kangaroo!'

The Tenth Contingent arrived back in Auckland on 23 August 1902, and Gallaher settled back into the company of family and friends in Ponsonby and the routine of work at the Freezing Company. He returned from Africa having lost a noticeable amount of weight as a result of a poor diet and illness. Football was out of the question for him during the remainder of the 1902 season.

At the beginning of September, for his war service Gallaher received the Imperial South African War medal with clasps for Transvaal, Orange Free State, and Cape Colony. He was able to wear them to a formal welcome home on 8 September 1902, hosted by the Ponsonby Football Club for the seven members of the club who had served during the war: Gallaher, Dunlop, H Williams, Smith, Carder, Marshall, and Hugh Williams. Club chairman Tom Masefield celebrated the safe return of the group, but tribute was also paid to Stanley Rees Scott who had not been so fortunate. Scott had grown up in Ponsonby and served with the Utrecht Mounted Police, which was a colonial unit during the war, and had died in Durban. A fund to build a memorial drinking fountain to the fallen soldier was commenced, chaired by Alex Snedden. Two months later, a large crowd gathered respectfully at Three Lamps for the unveiling by Native Minister, The Hon James Carroll, of the tall, white marble sculpture. Attendees then adjourned to the Ponsonby Club Hotel. The first overseas war involving New Zealand troops was over. The delight at the arrival home of the fortunate was tempered by the more permanent tributes, to those who had not, that began to dot the nation.

Gallaher's Ponsonby, c.1905. Looking south to Ponsonby Road. Trooper Scott memorial left, top of College Hill. Ponsonby Club Hotel right, corner of Jervois Road. Sir George Grey Special Collections, Auckland Libraries, 35-R242

There was an exciting development at the Ponsonby Football Club. It had a new training shed and gymnasium, which was described by one newspaper writer who had attended its official 'house-warming' — along with an estimated 300 others — as 'the finest in the colony'. The parcel of land in Dignan Street (now Blake Street) and the construction had cost a little over £400. Money was raised by members through a concert, subscriptions, donations, and a grant from the Auckland union. It was completed in June 1901, barely three months after the tender for its construction was accepted. The shed became known as 'The Tan'. That name came from the fact that the floor of the shed was covered in soft, leftover materials from tanneries, such as bark that had been used in mixtures for soaking hides.

The new facility replaced the Ponsonby Hall as the main venue for club events. Socials were held regularly throughout winter. The programmes were made up of a succession of soloists singing with accompaniment. On less formal occasions, variety acts would perform, and it was not uncommon for Gallaher to give a solo singing performance. One of the early club socials was an evening to welcome a footballer by the name of George Stephenson. He had been an Otago representative in the 1890s, but became the first New Zealand convert to Northern Union when he signed to play for Yorkshire Football Club. As the guest of honour, he told the assembled club members that 'after touring England and visiting Yorkshire and Lancashire, the home of Rugby football, I consider that our New Zealand boys could hold their own in back play all over the world'.

There was another notable talking point for the people of Ponsonby when on 17 November 1902 the first electric tram began service, replacing the horse-drawn versions. Cheaper, bigger, more comfortable and somewhat faster, the new attraction's first day saw an estimated

25,000 people lining the streets to observe it as it passed along its route, and competition was fierce to be among the first to travel on it.

In terms of location, the headquarters of Auckland football was still in the same place, but it was now known by another name. Potter's Paddock had become Alexandra Park, in honour of the new monarch King Edward's wife.

Governor Lord Ranfurly had offered to gift a trophy bearing his name to the New Zealand union. Initially, a cup was proposed and NZRFU committee members made a variety of suggestions as to just what the Ranfurly Cup would be awarded for. One delegate proposed that it be played for by representative teams of the Queensland, New South Wales and New Zealand unions. An amendment was made that it be played for by the champion teams of both islands. This was further altered, until it was decided that the Cup be awarded to the team the NZRFU deemed 'in their opinion to be the Champion team' and then played for on a challenge basis, 'provided that the challenging union is prepared to play the holders on their own ground'.

The NZRFU's Management Committee agreed to give Auckland possession of the gift, based on its unbeaten record in the previous season. However, it would be a further 18 months until Auckland accepted and played its first shield game, because, due to the vagaries of scheduling, all of Auckland's 1903 representative matches were 'away' games. (Every four years the Auckland team toured the North and South Islands, meeting the major provinces on their home grounds.)

Selection of players for national honours was done by nomination. Unions put forward the names of the players they thought were the best in their respective positions. These names then went to a panel of selectors, who tended to be from Auckland, Wellington, Canterbury and Otago. On occasion there was disgruntlement from outside these regions that their players were being ignored by the selectors. The reality was that it was nigh on impossible for unpaid selectors to be taking time from their various jobs to travel by boat, coach or train to every province to observe players in action.

More than 80 players' names had been forwarded to the NZRFU selectors — among them Gallaher's as a hooker — from which to choose their 22-man squad for a 10-match tour of Australia. Gallaher had made his way back onto the football field in club play at the start of the 1903 season, and according to the *Observer* he had 'lost none of his dash. A couple of matches should see this player right back to his best form.' Remarkably, having not represented his province for two seasons, and being aged 29, Gallaher was selected to make the trip, along with six of his Auckland teammates.

The Ponsonby Football Club had been in existence for nearly 30 years, and had dominated Auckland football for periods during that time, but Gallaher was its first All Black. (To this day, in the club's rooms at Western Springs, his photograph leads off a long line of men from Ponsonby chosen to wear the black jersey.) He was the ninety-seventh player to be capped for his country, and would have been the club's second All Black had winger Bob Whiteside, who was chosen for the 1884 trip to New South Wales, not asked for his expenses to be covered. The request was not received at all well by union officials, and Whiteside was subsequently discarded from the touring party.

Prior to departure, a send-off for Gallaher and the other players from Auckland was hosted by the Ponsonby club. Gallaher was presented with head- and ankle-guards.

Captaining the 1903 side was Otago's Jimmy Duncan, who had

been a member of the 1897 side that had visited Australia. Six years later, some football writers were describing the man with a penchant for Speight's ale as a has-been. It was a moniker he then sarcastically referred to for much of the tour when dealing with the press men. Duncan had been a gifted player and was one of the key figures in the development of the game in New Zealand. He is credited with developing the dual five-eighth positions and could play as a wing-forward or a back. In Dunedin, as captain of Otago, he was revered for his tactical thinking, and he spent countless hours coaching lads from Otago Boys High School. While his contribution to the game was revered, the (by then) 33-year-old had a streak of vanity that did not endear him to all. He had gone bald in his early twenties, and subsequently insisted on wearing a woollen cap, and sometimes fingerless gloves, when playing. He also considered himself very popular with the ladies.

Among the forwards for the tour, mention must be made of a real character in the form of the big Canterbury lock Bernie Fanning. A blacksmith by trade, and slightly hard of hearing, his party trick was striking matches off the tough, rough palms of his hands.

The New Zealand team played Wellington Province prior to its departure, but the result was not the one hoped for by a team about to depart for an international tour. They lost 5–14 in conditions that were quite atrocious. All game, strong wind swept heavy rain across the field. Fewer than a thousand spectators saw Gallaher register his first points for New Zealand. He scored their only try, from one of his typical dribbling rushes, as the muddy ball was kept on the toe rather than in the hand. The try was converted by a promising young fullback from Wellington called William 'Billy' Wallace.

After the match, and warm baths that couldn't come soon enough, the teams appeared at a dinner put on by the New Zealand and Wellington unions. Seddon and his deputy, Sir Joseph Ward, were among the guests. The latter, in proposing a toast to the team, said that the afternoon's match 'could not be taken as any criterion of the abilities of the team'. Following the function, the players made their way to the quayside to board the steamer *Moeraki* and were once again at the mercy of the elements. This time, their vessel had to battle its way into one of Cook Strait's notorious southerlies, which did little to help some digest their large dinners.

A 'war-cry' had been written for the team to perform in Australia by a Mr C Parata, a brother-in-law of winger Albie Asher:

Tena Koe Kangaroo!	*How do you do Kangaroo!*
Tupotu Koe Kangaroo!	*You look out Kangaroo!*
Mo Tireni tenei haere nei	*New Zealand is invading you!*
Au, au, aue, a!	*Woe, woe, woe to you!*

A week after leaving Wellington, a crowd of 32,000 was at the Sydney Cricket Ground (SCG) to watch the All Blacks' first match against New South Wales. There was great excitement among the players to be playing at a vast venue that was far and beyond any in New Zealand. In the previous decade a number of stands such as the Ladies Stand and the Members Pavilion had been built at the ground, which had been the home to the New South Wales Cricket Association for 30 years. Another feature was the grassy rise known as 'The Hill', popular with those who were happy to stand rather than pay for more expensive seating, while the playing field was ringed by a cycle track which had lighting above it. It had hosted its first cricket test between Australia and England in 1882, and Gallaher, the competent club cricketer, enjoyed inspecting the facilities and talking to workers at the ground about the variety of sports the ground could accommodate.

Prior to the match, the All Blacks had their team photograph taken (see below). They were resplendent in black socks, knickerbockers, and the lace-up jersey with the silver fern on the left breast. Covering the chest and shoulders, in a triangular shape, was a canvas 'yoke', and chamois leather bordered the neck. The combination of the material around the upper body meant that, while the lacing had to be loosened to get the jersey on and off, it was not prone to tearing as other jerseys were.

The All Blacks *v* New South Wales, 18 July 1903. Back row: Ru Cooke, Gallaher, Archie McMinn, AL Armstrong, Bernie Fanning. Middle row: Dick McGregor, Henry Kiernan, FJ Given, Jimmy Duncan, Morrie Wood, AJ Long, George Tyler. Front row: Duncan McGregor, Albie Asher, Billy Wallace. AUCKLAND RUGBY UNION

The weather was perfect, and play from both forward packs was lively. Occasional scuffles broke out which required some dampening down from referee, Tom Pauling, an ex-pat who had played for the All Blacks on their 1897 tour to Australia. The All Blacks backs settled quickly. A fluent backline movement put winger Asher in for a try after four minutes, and Duncan McGregor followed suit midway through the half. Wallace added to the total with a penalty, and McGregor scored a second try in the second half after Morrie Wood had made an incisive run.

The friction between the two sets of forwards continued throughout the match, until, with only a few minutes to play, a fracas broke out between Ru Cooke and one of the New South Welshmen. Cooke retaliated to a punch from his opponent, but unfortunately his action was all that was seen of the skirmish by referee Pauling and the side-row forward was sent from the field.

There was a lighter moment in the 12–0 win. In the middle of one play, a New South Welshman grabbed the woollen hat off the head of Jimmy Duncan, resulting in a huge roar from spectators on 'The Hill', and taunts were directed at Duncan until his bald pate was covered once more.

The next tour game was against a Combined Western Districts team at Bathurst, which required a day-long train journey to get there. The Districts side was easily accounted for 47–7. Greater competition occurred prior to the match when some other 'locals' were the focus of the All Blacks. The players participated in a hare run and marsupial hunt with Gallaher displaying the shooting skills his teammates expected of a Boer War veteran.

For the third match of the tour, the team returned to the SCG for another meeting with New South Wales. Sydney had suffered heavy, steady rain for some hours prior to the match, and the surface quickly flooded. Some joked that it was Sydney's latest feature — a lovely lake. The inclement weather — and possibly the result of the first match —

discouraged many from turning out to watch, with the crowd roughly only a quarter of that which had turned out for the first game.

So wet was the ground, Billy Wallace recounted to journalist Morrie Mackenzie, that 'when the ball landed from a kick, it floated. I was lucky enough to kick a goal from a patch of mud.' They were the only points in the match. In Wallace's view, conditions weren't extreme enough to have the match postponed. To him, life-threatening lightning would have been the only justified reason to call the match off. While the ground may have been soft, collisions between players and boots were anything but. Gallaher suffered a bad cut to his forehead as the result of such a clash, and play was stopped while he had it bandaged before he then played on.

As was seen in Bathurst, the tour was not just about the sporting engagements, which drew good-sized crowds and resulted in win after win. The party was welcomed and entertained wherever they went. They enjoyed harbour and river cruises by day and smoke concerts by night. This was all welcome relief from the boredom of some of the lengthy train journeys they had to endure as they worked their way from Sydney to Brisbane.

The eighth match of the tour was a second meeting with Queensland. The All Blacks wore white arm-bands, having received news of the passing of Duncan McGregor's father. It was a notable encounter in the career of Gallaher, as for the first time in the black jersey he was chosen to play at wing-forward. The hosts were trounced 28–0 by the All Blacks, who played wonderful 15-man football. To a man, reporters acknowledged that Gallaher had been the best player on the field, thriving on the open spaces that were created by the dribbling rushes he led, and enjoying competition with the halfback around the scrum. He gave no hint that he was relatively new to the position. After only one outing he was on his way to making it his own.

The trip from Brisbane to Sydney was broken up by a match against a Combined Northern Districts side in the northern New South Wales town of Maitland. Spectators were treated to something of a festival match as the All Blacks ran in 15 tries. Gallaher bagged one of them, and the score could have been much greater than 53–0 if Wallace had not had an off-day, goaling only four times.

The next encounter was a hugely historic one. It was the first test match played by New Zealand, after 19 years of what could be called New Zealand teams. Over 30 matches had been played by those sides since 1884, but never an international, which reflects New Zealand's isolation. International football in the British Isles had begun in 1871 when neighbours England and Scotland played the first-ever test match. Australia had played its first and only test match at the same ground against Great Britain four years earlier, winning 13–3. So, the best players from Australia (namely New South Wales and Queensland) were lining up against the best from New Zealand for the first time.

The match took place at the Sydney Cricket Ground on 15 August 1903. The XV who became New Zealand's first test rugby players were: backs — Wallace (Wellington), Asher (Auckland), Dick McGregor (Auckland), Duncan McGregor (Canterbury), Wood (Canterbury), Duncan (Otago) and Henry 'Mickey' Kiernan (Auckland); forwards — Gallaher, George Nicholson (Auckland), Archie McMinn (Wairarapa), Cooke (Canterbury), Bernie Fanning (Canterbury), AJ 'Paddy' Long (Auckland), Daniel Udy (Wairarapa) and George Tyler (Auckland).

When the match began, the weather had vastly improved from earlier visits and so a crowd of over 30,000 was in attendance. The condition of the ground was conducive to running football, and both sides were of a mind to attack with ball in hand.

Wallace kicked the first points in a test match for the All Blacks, and added a goal from a mark before Asher scored the first try, displaying his tremendous pace and the great, flying swerve that had seen him nicknamed 'The Indian Rubber Man'. Two more tries were added, by front-ranker Tyler and three-quarter Dick McGregor. There was a minor dispute over the latter's try, as some of the Australian players thought he had put a foot into touch. However, there was no such ruling from the touch-judge.

Although the 22–3 scoreline might make it seem as though the match was something of a romp for the New Zealanders, it was anything but. All facets of the game were keenly contested, the difference being the All Blacks making the most of their opportunities.

A picture from the match, taken by a photographer for the *Sydney Mail*, shows Gallaher in action. Shin-pads clearly visible over his socks, he has the ball tucked into the crook of his right arm and is about to hare up the sideline. His pose is one of wariness as to just how close he is to the white line, looking to prop off his right leg to move infield. His left arm is raised like that of a tightrope walker, seeking that safe equilibrium. Duncan — wearing his trademark woollen hat and fingerless gloves — is appealing to the referee, and players from both sides seem to be waiting for the referee to stop the game. But there goes Gallaher, playing to the whistle.

The final match of the tour saw the side defeat New South Wales Country. Gallaher scored a try in the 32–0 win, which meant the All Blacks had been undefeated during their month in Australia. Their play had been enterprising and entertaining, averaging six tries per game. Interestingly, for two decades after the tour, rugby writers and many former players spoke of the 1903 side as the finest All Black team to take the field. They were given a great send-off in Sydney, but sailed back to New Zealand minus two players. Billy Wallace had broken his jaw in the final game and was advised not to travel for a few days, and the Otago winger John Stalker stayed on with him.

When they arrived back in New Zealand, Gallaher and most of the other victorious tourists lined up at Alexandra Park for the, by now, annual North v South match. The South won convincingly 12–5, with the highlight being a try by Morrie Wood where he ran through most of the North Island team to score untouched. (A rugby gypsy, the next season Wood moved north to play for Ponsonby and Auckland. He was the national long-jump champion in 1904, but a knee injury ended his career, by which time he had worn the colours of five provinces.)

Back in New Zealand, though, it wasn't the end of the travelling for Gallaher for that season. Auckland's provincial itinerary was its four-yearly tour of the South Island, so, less than two weeks after arriving home, Gallaher's bags were packed again and off he went with the team by boat to New Plymouth. It wasn't a good start to the trip. The Aucklanders lost their first three games to Taranaki, Wellington and Southland, albeit narrowly. The joy for Taranaki fans was immense as it was the first time their side had won a match in New Plymouth against Auckland. Four days later, Wellington fans were cock-a-hoop, too, as they beat Auckland for the first time in seven years. The final four matches — against Otago, Canterbury, South Canterbury and Hawke's Bay — saw vastly improved performances and a quartet of comfortable victories, although Gallaher missed the final game as he had to make his way back to Auckland for work. He had played 15 first-class games in 10 weeks, and only one of those matches was in Auckland. A tiring season had come to an end.

It was during this year that Gallaher began boarding at the home of the Francis family at 19 Church Street, Ponsonby. Gallaher didn't have the financial means to own a property, and time spent away from work playing football with no substantial recompense meant that keeping up bank and even rental payments would have been impossible. The best solution was to be a lodger. This way he could come and go as he — and the various rugby unions — pleased.

Arthur 'Bolla' Francis was a member of the Ponsonby club, playing as a forward. Tall and powerfully built, he was an imposing figure on and off the field. (He would make his Auckland debut the following season and later play for the All Blacks.) Bolla's mother, Nora, was a widow, her husband having passed away a dozen years earlier after notable service as a master at Auckland Grammar School. She had moved to Church Street and a lean, two-storey house in the early 1890s. She was mother to eight grown children, including a daughter, Ellen, who was 19 at the time. Known to most as Nellie, she was an attractive young woman, possessed of sparkling eyes and a shy smile.

As well as there being a rugby connection between Bolla and Gallaher, the Francis family were also regular members of the All Saints congregation, and Nellie was a member of the choir. David would later sing in it, too.

Now aged 30, a number of eligible young ladies had caught Dave Gallaher's eye, and he had exchanged photographs or courted several. He was even fobbed off by at least one who wasn't interested in the footballing storeman. When he came back from his All Black and Auckland trips, he had no parents to visit and to whom he could recount his adventures. His siblings were scattered around the country

and beyond. There was at the Francis house, however, the presence
of the quiet, delightful Nellie.

A previously unseen studio portrait of Gallaher, taken c.1897 and gifted to a
young lady he was enamoured with. He has written: *With best love from Dave*.
MATT ELLIOTT COLLECTION

Welcome, Great Britain

---

*'The vim and dash he put into his
play were really refreshing.'*

At the beginning of April each year, clubs around the country held their annual meetings. In 1904, Ponsonby club members assembled in the training hall for their Friday-night meeting, and among the business discussed was the satisfying reduction of the debt for the new hall by £200. The club delegates to represent them at the ARFU were selected, and consisted of Charlie Stitchbury (who stood down as club treasurer after some years in the post), Gallaher and DW Dunlop.

The following month, after nearly two years of discussion, the NZRFU was finally beginning to advance its preparation for sending a team to tour 'Home' (Great Britain and Ireland) the following year.

On 6 August 1904, Gallaher took to the field when the first-ever Ranfurly Shield match was played. Auckland, hosting Wellington at

Alexandra Park, was beaten 6–3 by the challengers. There was talk that Auckland — unbeaten at home for six years — had underestimated the Wellington side, evidenced by the fact that Auckland union officials didn't even have the shield at the ground to cover the possibility of a post-match presentation. It was a match in which the hosts boasted one of its finest forward packs of any era, which might have led to some off-field complacency. Playing at wing-forward for Wellington was Billy Hardham, who had won the Victoria Cross while serving as a farrier with the Fourth Contingent during the Boer War. The dry ground suited the visitors' fleet-footed backs such as speedster Duncan McGregor, and the outrageous natural ability of fullback (and captain) Billy Wallace. All the points came from tries: two for Wellington (one of them by McGregor) to a single touchdown from Auckland. Thus, Gallaher was involved in another first — he was a member of the first team to lose the Ranfurly Shield!

The men from the capital were cheered from the field by the reasonably sized Auckland crowd, who had a reputation for applauding and acknowledging stirring play, be it by their boys or not. While the crowd's appreciation sat well with the Wellington side, the actions of the host union did not. According to Billy Wallace, 'I well remember that the Auckland Rugby Union were unable to present the Ranfurly Shield to us as it was locked in a bank vault in the city, and we had to leave Auckland by ship for New Plymouth on the Sunday.'

The disappointment of losing the new provincial trophy could not be dwelt on. Six Aucklanders (Gallaher, R McGregor, Wood, Nicholson, Charlie Seeling and Tyler) had to make their way to Wellington — in the company of the victorious Wellingtonians — to prepare for the test match against the touring Great Britain side. After sailing to New Plymouth, they caught a train to Wellington where they were welcomed by a small but excited crowd.

The 1904 visit by the Great Britain team (who wouldn't become known as the 'Lions' until they toured South Africa in 1924) was an addendum to its 13-match Australian tour. It had been a decade and a half since the previous Great Britain team had visited. Another had gone to Australia in 1899, but arrangements, mostly financial, could not be settled on for them to cross the Tasman. In this instance, the NZRFU covered the team's expenses as well as paying half the net profits to the New South Wales union. Captaining the side was Scottish doctor and heavyweight-boxing champion, David 'Darkie' Bedell-Sivright. There are two explanations for his nickname. One says it was a nod to his style of captaincy, which relied on cynical and, on occasion, unsportsmanlike tactics. The other, that he had dark rings around his eyes.

Another member of the forward pack was former captain Blair Swannell. He had toured Australia in 1899 before serving in the Boer War. It has been speculated that his experience in Africa might have influenced his on-field play, which was described by a contemporary as 'controlled violence'. Swannell developed a poor reputation throughout an ill-disciplined and bad-tempered Australian tour.

In the match against Northern Districts in Newcastle, north of Sydney, Denys Dobson, the Newton Abbot and England forward, gained an unwanted place in rugby history when he was sent off during the match. His crime was using foul language when arguing with the referee. He had asked of a refereeing decision 'What the devil was that for?' and when his obstinacy wasn't tolerated by the referee, used language that was a lot more colourful. This led to an on-field argument before Bedell-Sivright took his team to the sideline for 20 minutes. The captain viewed Dobson's ordering off, and the refereeing of the match as a whole, as a slur against what he saw as the good character of his team. (As an aside, a dozen years later while in Africa, Dobson was run down by a rampaging rhinoceros, suffering fatal injuries. Word of the incident made its way back to England, and, when Dobson's former games master read a newspaper item recording his death, he is reported to have muttered: 'He always did have a weak fend.') Despite this controversy and criticism of Bedell-Sivright's boys' use of clenched fists during games, the side went through its 13 Australian matches unbeaten.

A positive feature of the touring party was the consistently adventurous play by the Welsh internationals in the backline: Rhys Gabe, Willie Llewellyn, William Jowett and Teddy Morgan. Inside them was an up-and-coming Welsh five-eighth by the name of Percy Bush. They were players of natural flair who together formed exciting on-field combinations — and the side scored five times as many points as it conceded.

After the five-day sea voyage from Sydney, the team arrived in Wellington where they were welcomed with a parliamentary reception hosted by Premier Seddon, who voiced his delight at being able to host a team from the countries so dear to the hearts of many New Zealanders. He congratulated them on their results in Australia, and assured them that during the next leg of their journey they would be challenged on the field and entertained off it.

The visitors travelled south to play matches against a combined Canterbury-South Canterbury-West Coast (on a Lancaster Park that had to be cleared of snow prior to the game, leading to a dispute between the New Zealand and Canterbury unions over who was to shoulder the cost of such) and Otago-Southland at Dunedin's Caledonian Ground. Both games were won by the visitors, continuing the unbeaten record of the tour, but this successful start to the tour was tempered by the fact that Bedell-Sivright badly injured his leg in the first match. He would not play again on tour. In preparation for the one-off international against New Zealand, the touring party returned to Wellington on one of the steamers, full of All Black supporters from the South Island crossing Cook Strait for the match.

There was enormous excitement before the match. This was the first test to be played in New Zealand. When reserved tickets for grandstand seats went on sale in Wellington three weeks before the game, more than 700 were purchased on the first morning. The anticipated demand for seats and the potential for scalping were acknowledged in a printed warning on the back of the ticket:

> *The ticket is issued upon the express condition that it cannot be re-sold at a higher price than five shillings. The New Zealand Union reserve the right to cancel this ticket if they have reason to believe that this condition has been violated.*

Accommodation was at a premium as people streamed into the capital in the days before the match. Special trains from as far away as Napier transported the football-mad to the capital. Shops and offices were closed on the day of the game.

The All Black side had a significant number of changes to that which had taken the field against Australia a year earlier, almost to the day. Gallaher had been named to play as a front-ranker in the side captained by Billy Stead, but changes were made due to the late withdrawal of original selections Ru Cooke and Harry Porteous; Gallaher moved to wing-forward as he had done during the previous year's Australian tour. Wallace, the McGregors, Tyler, Nicholson, Wood, Fanning and Gallaher were the survivors, while the newcomers were Eric Harper (Canterbury), Stead (Southland), Patrick Harvey (Canterbury), Billy Glenn (Taranaki), Tom Cross (Wellington), Seeling (Auckland), and 'Paddy' McMinn (Manawatu), who was the older brother of Archie who had played in the Australia test.

The New Zealanders had a week together at Days Bay on the eastern edge of Wellington harbour. There they prepared for their encounter with the unbeaten visitors, under the watchful eye of athlete Dorrie Leslie and the recently retired, now 'coach', Jimmy Duncan. He told one reporter that he'd never seen a better team, and predictions were that the All Blacks would win by a double-figure score.

On the day of the match, the team crossed the harbour by ferry and made their way to Newtown. Billy Wallace later recalled that Wellington was eerily quiet until they neared Athletic Park where an estimated crowd of 20,000 was bristling with audible excitement. Premier Seddon and members of his Cabinet were seated in the low, covered stand that ran the length of the eastern side of the ground. Behind the dead-ball line at both ends of the ground, tiered temporary seating was full. On the western side, hundreds stood chin-to-shoulder on the hill.

For the first half an hour of the match, play was tight. In spite of having had a week together, the New Zealand team looked quite disjointed and nervous in the early minutes of the match. They did, however, benefit from playing with the sun and a northerly wind at their backs. The visitors (led by stand-in captain Teddy Morgan) were required to do the majority of the defending. Wallace had five opportunities to kick goals, but all were missed, each to the increasing disappointment of the crowd. Then he finally put one between the posts, scoring the first points for the All Blacks in a home test, for a 3–0 lead. There was extraordinary jubilation on the sidelines as the ball sailed through the uprights. Hats went up in the air as the first number went up on the ground's scoreboard.

Both sets of forwards were going at the leather and each other, whether the ball was there or not. Clashes at the scrum were numerous. In one instance, Swannell was punched in the face by an All Black forward and responded by giving 'a display of temper' in using both feet against his attacker. In another incident, one All Black was thumped while he was on the ground and he retaliated with a kick to a rather sensitive area of the British player's body. On a lighter note, those close to the sideline hooted with laughter when front-ranker George Tyler enveloped the British halfback Vile in a high tackle just as the whistle went for a prior infringement. An irritated Vile made as though he was going to lash out at Tyler. He was patronizingly patted on the head by the ever-smiling Tyler, who said, 'Don't lad, don't. I'm bigger than you!'

Shortly before the break, offside was called against the hosts by the man considered the best referee in the country, Canterbury's 'Dutchy' Evans. A none-too-easy goal was kicked by Great Britain's Harding for 3–3 at halftime. While not behind, the All Blacks were well aware that they should have been much further ahead.

Come the second half, and facing the low sun and steady wind, the All Blacks kept the ball in hand. Much of their possession came from the British tactic of kicking their way out of their own half. That they secured the ball to do so was much to the credit of their halfback Vile, who was being given a torrid time at the scrum and in broken play by Gallaher.

Eventually, the New Zealand backline gelled, and crisp passing movements combined with the outright speed of winger Duncan McGregor saw him score two fine tries. When he placed the ball for the first, Jimmy Duncan was ecstatic on the sidelines, waving his left arm in celebration while using his right to hang on to his straw hat. According to one newspaper report, those sitting near him tried to 'take off the said straw hat and expose Duncan's bald pate to the admiring gaze of the assembled spectators'. Their attempts caused hilarity but were not successful.

At the end of the match — won 9–3 — McGregor was carried from the field on the shoulders of jubilant spectators. In the evening, the teams attended a smoke concert put on by the Governor General.

Football fans around the country were desperate to find out progress and ultimately the result of the match. The score would be telephoned through to branches of the Post Office or regional newspapers. Local papers would then print 'Extras' at halftime and fulltime, posting them outside their offices and around their towns where crowds gathered expectantly to read of the result. Special sporting editions with full reports of the match appeared on the streets later in the evening.

Gallaher was the All Black singled out for praise by the *New Zealand Free Lance* reporter, who wrote that:

Nothing cleaner, fairer, crisper, or more determined than his play has ever been seen on a football field in Wellington, and I have no hesitation in pronouncing him to be the finest wing-forward of his or any other day. Dave's methods were fair, and above board, and the vim and dash he put into his play were really refreshing.

A Wellington correspondent for the *Observer* wrote up the play for Auckland readers with similar sentiments:

> *One man who stood out above all his comrades was Dave Gallaher, as wing-forward. I had heard so much of the quickness and alertness of Vile, the Britishers' half, that I was prepared to see Gallaher out-manoeuvred by him but not once during the game did the Aucklander weary, and so persistent was he in his effective work that many in Wellington just now class him as the finest wing-forward that ever played the game. Much could be written about him, but suffice it to say that he was but once adjudged off-side during the game, and he repeatedly smothered Vile.*

The late rugby writer Sir TP McLean described the game as one that 'stirred the nation. It represented the birth of rugby as *the* great national game.'

The Great Britain side left for New Plymouth to play Taranaki-Wanganui-Manawatu (a match which was drawn 0–0), and Gallaher and his Auckland teammates also headed north. Once back in Auckland, he prepared his letter of expenses for the trip and submitted it to the ARFU, who, on behalf of the national union, would reimburse him costs in getting to the capital for the test match. Little did he know that the successful trip to Wellington would have serious ramifications for him in the months ahead.

After a week back at work, Gallaher and the five other Auckland All Blacks lined up at Alexandra Park against the side they had beaten seven days previously. The crowd was estimated to be 20,000 to 25,000, the largest seen at a football game in the province. Hundreds had come to Auckland from around the upper North Island to see the tourists in action, unperturbed by the heavy rain and squalls in the days prior. Temporary stands were erected around the ground, but only after some dispute between the ARFU and the NZRFU over who was financially responsible for their erection. Spectators were also seen carrying into the ground their own ladders and boxes to stand on to get a better view. A couple of traders selling stools ran out of stock in quick time.

THE TEAMS TAKING THE FIELD.

Great Britain *v* Auckland, Alexandra Park, 20 August 1904. Three cheers from the visitors. Gallaher stands far right. SIR GEORGE GREY SPECIAL COLLECTIONS, AUCKLAND LIBRARIES, AWNS-19040825-4-2

Following a haka by students from St Stephen's and St John's colleges, play got under way. The British team, having won the toss, played with the wind and started stronger than the blue-and-whites, but failed to register any points. One of their kicks at goal did hit an upright to the relief of the nervous home crowd.

The Auckland team then clicked into gear, and Gallaher had one of those games where he seemed omnipresent. He was into everything with great gusto, and his harassment of the Great Britain inside backs was unrelenting. Charlie Seeling had a more spectacular tackling style — that of getting airborne before he hit the unfortunate carrying the ball — but Gallaher's efforts were no less devastating. Several times in the match, play stopped dead as he drove players sideways and off their feet or simply threw them to the ground. He wasn't alone in nullifying the Great Britain pack. Lock Bill Cunningham bullocked his way around the field and was rewarded with a try. George Tyler was all elbows and knees in the loose, and George Nicholson was his usual reliable self at the lineout. With forward dominance achieved, the Auckland backs found themselves back in their own 25 only twice in the second half.

The Auckland team's defeat of the Great Britain side was even more resounding than that of the national team. The visitors failed to score, while Auckland put 13 points on the board. Of Auckland's four tries, one was by Gallaher, and it was spoken of for some years afterwards. Historian RA Stone, who attended most of Auckland's games in those early years, recalled in his book, *Rugby Players Who Have Made New Zealand Famous*, that just inside halfway:

> … *a great cross kick was taken on the bounce by Dave, who set off for the corner, drawing O'Brien, the British full-back, and then suddenly turning infield he caught O'Brien on the wrong foot, and finished a glorious effort by scoring by the post. Murray goaled; and how we boys did cheer.*

After the match, the players travelled back into town in their playing gear. They then went to a bathhouse to wash and clean up before attending dinner at the Royal Hotel. The Great Britain side were to play an unofficial match two days later against a Maori side in Rotorua, so instead of joining the Auckland team at a theatrical show, they headed to the train station and left the city. (Life didn't get any better for them in Rotorua: they lost 6–8.)

In an extensive write-up of the Auckland game, the *Observer* assessed every local player, and of Gallaher wrote that he:

> *... did great damage in breaking in amongst the British backs and did not give Vile much peace. He is now playing in better form than he has shown in his long football career, and this is saying a lot. Perhaps the British captain will change his ideas about wing-forward play after seeing Gallaher in the N.Z. and Auckland games.*

Bedell-Sivright did nothing of the sort. He departed New Zealand with his mood matching his moniker. He grumbled about Gallaher's role at wing-forward, a position not dissimilar to his of 'rover', and was not shy of predicting that the colonials would get their comeuppance when they eventually toured Great Britain. On a personal level he was frustrated that he had been unable to take the field in the important matches, and, as captain of the side, annoyed that they had lost their unbeaten record. He blamed the losses on fatigue from the length of the tour and the distractions of a variety of entertainments, rather than the superiority of teams they had encountered in New Zealand. (A newspaper article pointed out that Bedell-Sivright only mentioned the team being 'stale' when they had lost, not before.) Once home, he would not report favourably to his home union on the state of the game in New Zealand — despite the hospitality shown his players, including the presentation of tiki to all by the NZRFU.

With the international guests having departed, footballing attention turned back to the domestic competition. Gallaher lined up for the blue-and-whites to play Taranaki at Alexandra Park in the second-to-last game of the season, but suffered an injury in the second half of the 0–3 loss. The *Observer* newspaper commented that 'it is hard luck for Gallaher that after playing so well this season he should have to retire with a wrenched knee'. He then missed the final game against Otago.

Various team photos in which Gallaher appeared during 1904 show him without his trademark moustache. There is a story that he shaved it off as the result of a bet, the details of which are long forgotten.

In October 1904, a month after the provincial rugby season finished and still feeling the effects of his knee injury, Gallaher fell foul of the NZRFU. A dispute arose between him and the Wellington-based Management Committee over the expense account he had submitted to the ARFU.

At the time, the word 'professionalism' hung heavy over amateur rugby, as it did until nearly a century later. Players could not be seen to be making any money from playing the game. The game's managers in Wellington certainly were not impressed by any suggestion that a player might have been claiming or being advanced by their union more than was allowable, and, in effect, acting in a fraudulent manner. Claimed-for expenses underwent the strictest scrutiny, and it was common for players to be asked to explain their costs in greater detail. Following the 1903 tour to Australia, Jimmy Duncan and Fred Girven had both been suspended briefly over their expenses claims. Billy Stead's claim for expenses relating to the trip to Wellington — twice the amount of Gallaher's — was also under scrutiny after he claimed money from the NZRFU that the Southland union would not pay.

NZRFU Management Committee minutes record the development of the dispute:

Wednesday 5th October, 1904:
It was also decided to ask for details of the amounts of £1-14-0 and £3-0-0 shown as 'travelling expenses' in Mr Gallaghers [sic] statement in connection with the New Zealand matches.

Friday 11th November, 1904:
It was decided to telegraph to the Auckland Union for replies re. Gallaghers [sic] a/c and Grand Stand matter.

At the same meeting, George Fache, on behalf of the Selection Committee, submitted his list of the 50 players from which the team to tour 'Home' would then be finally selected. Such was the role of the wing-forward that Gallaher's name was included among the 'backs' rather than the 'forwards'. Although he was on the list, the dispute between Gallaher and those governing the local game had not been resolved. In fact, for Gallaher, the situation worsened:

Friday 9th December, 1904:
It was resolved that D. Gallagher [sic] (Auckland) be suspended until a satisfactory statement of his expenses rendered by him in connection with the Auckland Representatives in the New Zealand British match is forthcoming.

There is no suggestion that Gallaher's request for reimbursement was in any way fraudulent. His stubbornness in settling the matter with the NZRFU was probably a result of him firmly believing that he was claiming back what it had cost him to travel to the match and no more. The union's accounts at the time totalled more than £2,000, and so, while it did have one eye on the cost of the upcoming tour to the northern hemisphere, one or two pounds would hardly be the difference between the trip going ahead or not. Suspensions were the most common punishment for transgressions on and off the field. So, with preparations being made for a team to travel the following year and newspapers and players talking excitedly about who would be on the boat 'Home', Gallaher found himself on the outer with the very men who would decide the composition of the most important event in New Zealand's short sporting history.

The Touring Party

The choice of Gallaher as captain was a curious one.

While Gallaher and the union's Management Committee were still at loggerheads, the Selection Committee made known their chosen 24 to tour Great Britain. They were: Ernie Booth, Steve Casey, William Johnston and Donald Stuart (Otago); Billy Stead (Southland); Billy Wallace, Duncan McGregor, Fred Roberts, Eric Watkins and Tom Cross (Wellington); Eric Harper, Bob Deans and Patrick Harvey (Canterbury); Jimmy Hunter, Harry Mynott, William Glenn and Jim O'Sullivan (Taranaki); D Whisker (Manawatu); John Corbett (West Coast); Hector Thomson (Wanganui); William [Hay-] McKenzie, George Tyler, Charlie Seeling and George Nicholson (Auckland).

After further discussion, several key decisions were made. One was that George Dixon would manage the side. Born in Huddersfield, Dixon had come to New Zealand as a 20-year-old in 1879. He played football himself, then served as the ARFU secretary from 1887 to 1900. Moving to Wellington, he was Auckland's delegate to the national body. He was a keen judge of character and an able businessman, managing both the New Zealand *Observer* and the *New Zealand Times* newspapers, founding the *New Zealand Free Lance*, and later becoming the first Life Member of the NZRFU.

Two extra players — a forward and a back — were to be added to the squad, and there would be no public announcement of the selections until players' form was scrutinized once the local season had begun. They would also have to undergo medical examination and be passed as fit to travel.

Monthly NZRFU Management Committee meetings continued to have as an item on their agendas the Gallaher suspension:

Friday 27th January, 1905:
The Treasurer of the Auckland Rugby Union wrote of (under date 3 January) that Gallagher [sic] was forwarding statement of his account 'next week'. The secretary reported that the statement had not been received.

23rd February, 1905:
Letter from Treasurer, Auckland Union, was read giving details of the amount claimed by Gallagher [sic] as expense of Auckland and Taranaki players returning home after New Zealand match. It was decided to 'insist' on refund of the £4-14-0, the suspension to remain in operation until amount paid.

Despite Gallaher being *persona non grata* with the national union, he still took his place as the Ponsonby delegate, in the company of a number of Ponsonby men who held high office, at the ARFU's annual meeting. Gallaher's main contribution to the meeting was consideration for the wider game. He was particularly concerned about ways to keep junior footballers playing and, thus, then moving into the senior ranks. One way of doing this, he proposed, would be to send the junior representative team on a tour. 'If our juniors had something more to look forward to they would take a keener interest in the game,' said Gallaher. His proposal was later acted upon.

The issue with NZRFU finally reached a resolution with Gallaher reluctantly sending a mail order of the disputed monies:

28th April, 1905:
From Treasurer, Auckland Rugby Union, asking for copy of statement supplied by Gallagher [sic] re. expenses — supplied by Treasurer.

10th May, 1905:
D. Gallagher [sic] wrote enclosing M.O. £4-14-0 being amount due for which he was disqualified, sent under protest. Mr Fache gave a personal explanation of private correspondence between himself and Gallagher [sic] on this subject. After consideration by Cme. the Secretary was instructed to reply that no satisfactory explanation having been received of the expenditure of the amount in question. Committee can do nothing more.
Disqualification to be removed. Auckland Union to be notified.

With the shroud of suspension lifted, Gallaher was free to represent the North Island for the second time in the encounter with the South Island, at Athletic Park on 3 June 1905. The sides were two of the best to ever assemble for the inter-island encounters. However, it was a resounding win for the North, 26–0. They scored six tries, with Wallace converting four of them. Gallaher was in the same form as that shown against the Great Britain team the previous year.

Following that match, further selection changes were made to the proposed touring side. Stuart was omitted after failing a medical test. [Hay-]McKenzie, Harvey, Watkins, Cross and Whisker's names were crossed out, too. Harvey's was an unusual case in that he was the only lip-reading teacher in the country and, despite an appeal to the government, was not granted leave for the tour. Included at their expense were Frank Glasgow (Taranaki), Alex McDonald (Otago), Fred Newton (Canterbury), George Gillett, William Mackrell, George Smith and Gallaher (Auckland).

Critics of Gallaher have liked to claim, with some derision, that Gallaher's inclusion came about only because his form in the North *v* South game was magnified beyond reason by Auckland newspapers, such as the *New Zealand Herald*, which described his play in the 26–0 rout of the Southerners as the finest on the field.

That is a short-sighted view. Gallaher had been an All Black for the past two seasons and a consistent performer as such. His name appeared in the early selection lists, but the NZRFU could hardly be seen to be endorsing a player for such an important tour while he was, under its own strict rules, disqualified from playing. Players didn't make their way into the national side on the back of one game … unless they were George Smith.

To say Smith was an all-rounder is something of an understatement. So extraordinary were his achievements that some refused to believe them. Smith played rugby for Auckland's City club and represented the province in 1896, 1897 and 1901. He was chosen for the North Island and New Zealand sides of 1897, and had last represented New Zealand in 1901. But what had he been doing between stints on the football field?

According to the Auckland Amateur Athletic and Cycle Club's golden jubilee publication of 1928, he had won the New Zealand title for the 100 yards between 1897/98 and 1899/1900, and again in 1901/02 and 1903/04. He also won the 220 yards event in 1899/1900, and the 120 yards hurdles in the years of his straight sprint successes. But he wasn't just an athlete blessed with explosive pace over the shortest distances. He was also an athlete of great stamina, as proven by the fact that he held the local title for the 440 yards hurdles in the same years as the 100 yards. (The 1900/01 title was won by Eric Harper.) Smith won four titles when the national championships were held at the Basin Reserve in Wellington in 1900, running seven races, including a couple of heats, in the one afternoon. All were on an undulating surface that was less than suitable for the speedsters. He won the Australasian hurdling title in 1901 and 1904, then travelled to England to compete in the English Amateur Athletic Association (AAA) events in 1902. He won the 120 yards hurdles at Stamford Bridge on 5 July 1902.

Before departing for England, in a March event at the Auckland Domain, Smith equalled the 'world' record of 15.4 seconds for the 120 yards which was held by American Alvin Kraenzlein, who had won the English champs over that distance for the past two seasons. That afternoon at the Auckland Domain, Smith may in fact have broken the world record. He was timed by five watches. One stopped at 15.0 and four at 15.2. The New Zealand Amateur Athletic Association (NZAAA) generously asked their Australian counterparts to ratify the record as 15.4.

Renowned athletics commentator and statistician Peter Heidenstrom noted, in a history of New Zealand track and field, that Smith's 15 national titles was a total not bettered for decades until one John Walker took national and international middle-distance running by storm in the 1970s.

When not occupied with those pursuits, Smith could be found with a cue in hand at a billiard or snooker table. Another biographical detail relating to Smith that has been repeated for over a century is that he spent time as a jockey, and rode a horse called Impulse to win the 1894 New Zealand Cup at Riccarton. Many have doubted this. Rugby historians have questioned this, based on the fact that the jockey of the day weighed a mere 7 stone 9 pounds. With this in mind, many have said that Smith couldn't have been the jockey, as he was 20 years old and, by the time he started playing representative football three years later, he would have had to put on nearly 4 stone in weight.

Researching this little mystery, the author believes that while Smith wasn't on the winning mount in 1894, it isn't far from the truth. In 1894, Impulse did win said Cup, and on her back was a jockey named Smith. It appears that this was a boy called 'Tip' Smith, not George. However, *three years earlier* — which would make him only 17 — George did ride Impulse to win the Auckland Racing Club's Easter meeting Autumn Handicap. Smith also apparently rode horses such as Patchwork, Quadrant, Morion and another, Wakawatea, which was trained for a time by his brother, Fred. He gave riding away when he had an accident riding a steeplechaser. Just what the injury was is unknown. At the age of 33, he was the oldest of the tourists.

There were more controversial selections. Wellington football followers were upset that one of their forwards, the infamous Joe Calnan, wasn't included. Aucklanders felt aggrieved when [Hay-] McKenzie was the only member of the North Island backline to miss selection. There was also widespread annoyance at the lack of an extra halfback, particularly when it was announced that Otago's Jimmy Duncan would be travelling as the coach. The reaction to this from the northern newspaper scribes was not one purely of consideration for the make-up of the team and the economics of such a trip. There was some back story to their opposition.

When the 1903 side returned from Australia, the supposed 'has-been' of a player and captain, Duncan, and apparently a couple of the Otago players, had made a number of disparaging remarks about some of the Auckland players and their overall abilities. They compared them with Otago players whom they thought were better. Duncan's chief target was halfback and wearer of white boots, 'Mickey' Kiernan, who had played in eight of the 11 tour matches. Duncan's gripe was that he didn't consider Kiernan a very good defensive player. (Bear in mind that the side conceded only 13 points in 10 games in Australia!) The Australian press had highlighted Kiernan's play in a number of reports; he'd scored three tries on tour, whereas Duncan had been somewhat lambasted. One Sydney writer had commented:

Old-man Duncan is about the clumsiest runner and ugliest 'passer' of a ball imaginable. But his 50-year-old agility, stamina and unselfishness — in a footballer — are marvellous. Running like a labourer with heavy, muddied boots, handling the ball more awkwardly than a schoolboy, how he gets there and accomplishes as much as he does is something to ponder on.

The Auckland papers were furious at the lack of respect for teammates, and their provincial men, on an unbeaten tour. In the *Observer*, one of the most bilious attacks on a footballer ever was printed:

> *Poor disappointed old man, Jimmy Duncan. Is this what you, the much-boomed footballer and would-be sport have descended to? Don't you think you would have acted a more manly part after your return to your native heath by having less to say against the boys who have played the game right up to the hilt? Don't you think that you have been rather contemptible and guilty of casting a reflection on your fellow committeemen? Aren't you satisfied that there was at least one better man in the N.Z. team than Jimmy Duncan? Don't you know that for the past twelve months you have been boomed through the N.Z. Press and engineered into the team by puff paragraphs? Don't you realize that you have proved yourself a complete failure and should never have been included in the team? Have you forgotten that you are the man who never scored a point during the tour, although you have been called a 'pointer'? Are you not a bitter disappointed, egotistical football failure, and won't you miss that trip to England with the N.Z. team? Burn your jersey, Duncan and turn the game up. You have had your day.*

Football watchers joked that if Duncan could play football as well as he could talk, Otago would be invincible.

When it became known that he was to 'coach' the team to Britain, Auckland papers fomented an outcry which spread throughout the country. To the opponents, the decision was unfathomable. The view was that taking Duncan 'Home' was at the expense of an extra player or two who might be sorely needed on a tour of over 30 matches.

Certainly, Duncan had 'coached' the team against Great Britain and the NZRFU had presented him with a gift as acknowledgment of his service. Many followers of the game were also against such an appointment. To their minds, players knew what had to be done on the field and looked after themselves. The issue of Duncan's role became a national debate when the Auckland Rugby Union formally opposed the appointment.

Duncan was also speaking publicly about the play of the backline, and that he strongly disapproved of Mynott's cross-cutting and running in. For him, the way to beat the opposing backs was on the outside, through quick passing. He was, he said, determined to change the way Mynott and Hunter played and wanted to get them 'running out'.

When the Management Committee met on 25 July 1905, it decided to appoint Gallaher as captain, the thirteenth man to be so honoured. Billy Stead was given the nod as vice-captain. They would then make up the tour selection committee, along with George Dixon, Duncan, and Billy Wallace.

The choice of Gallaher as captain was a curious one. He had captained his club side, Ponsonby, but he did not captain his province. The previous year Billy Stead had led the team. Just why Gallaher came into the reckoning as the leader of the team for the tour — when some even questioned his place in it, and there was his recent suspension from the game — may be explained in the following way: Premier Seddon.

In the small, close-knit community of Wellington, George Dixon was well known to the Premier. The capital city was a small business and political community. Seddon had personally chosen officers for the Boer campaign and contingents, among them his own son. He had visited South Africa during the war. Seddon saw the importance of the tour, not just to the colony, but also to his own standing in the upcoming general election. His personal interest in the success of the tour might have led him to suggest to the NZRFU that Gallaher was the man to lead the tourists.

NEW ZEALAND REPRESENTATIVE TEAM, 1905.
Back Row—G. Gillett, S. Casey, D. McGregor, A. McDonald, F. Roberts. Second Row—E. T. Harper, J. O'Sullivan, C. Seeling, R. G. Deans, W. Johnstone, G. H. W. Nicholson, J. Corbett, W. Cunningham, F. Newton, J. Duncan (Coach). Third Row—H. L. Abott, W. G. Wallace, G. W. Tyler, D. Gallaher (Capt.), G. H. Dixon (Manager), J. W. Stead (Vice-Capt.), W. Mackrell, F. Glasgow, W. S. Glenn. Front Row—J. Hunter, H. J. Mynott, G. W. Smith, E. E. Booth, H. D. Thomson.

The 1905 'Originals'. AUCKLAND RUGBY UNION

For Seddon, this tour was like a military operation. The finest footballing bodies were being sent to the other side of the world to conquer the Home nations. The leader should be a man of discipline, maturity and courage, who knew the importance of preparation and was not easily fazed. He would have to be capable of carrying out innumerable off-field duties, such as representing the team at civic receptions. Gallaher could move easily in the company of both the working man and the businessman. He was not flighty in his behaviour. An intelligent man, with a measure of shyness, he was a keen observer of people, behaviour and events. To some he may have seemed aloof. He didn't suffer fools, and made considered decisions and took some convincing to move from them. Add to this his physical presence, his unchallenged place on the field, and a keen sense of humour. In Seddon's eyes, Gallaher was the man to lead the team.

Seddon's commitment to the tour did not initially extend to a financial one. So when the NZRFU failed to raise enough money via a bond issue to the provincial unions, it decided that the players should embark upon a short seven-match tour of New Zealand and Australia, captained by Jimmy Hunter and managed by union Treasurer, Neil Galbraith.

Gallaher was to travel, but withdrew, lining up instead for Auckland (alongside Tyler and Mackrell) against the All Blacks in their first game of their pre-tour tour. This was the second of his two appearances against the national side. Although matches by the All Blacks against New Zealand provincial sides were much more common in those days, it still marked him out as one of the few in the history of the game to have played for and against the All Blacks on more than one occasion.

The game at Alexandra Park was billed as a clash between the All Blacks' pacey backs and Auckland's imposing forwards, and that was how it played out. To the delight of the nearly 10,000 spectators, the weather on that first day of July was warm and dry, conducive to running rugby. Hunter, McGregor and Smith had plenty of opportunities to show their pace and abilities in beating their men either on the outside with sheer, exciting pace or with breathtaking swerves and jinks. All three scored tries. Despite Wallace having an off-day with his kicking, the All Blacks still won 9–3. The press praised the backs, but dismissed the forwards as 'lacking the dash or vim expected of a colonial combination'.

Before they left for Australia, several senior players also voiced their objection to Duncan's appointment to the NZRFU. (Gallaher was not among them.) The response to the disquiet was that the decision had been made and it would not be reversed.

The tour to Australia (two big wins and a draw in the final match against New South Wales) had shown that, despite their dominance, the All Black locking stocks needed shoring up. It must be remembered that at the time there was only one lock in a 2-3-2 scrum. Enter Bill Cunningham. He had made a name for himself as a footballer in Waihi club football, and, as the Thames-Goldfields area was part of the Auckland union, was selected for the blue-and-whites in 1899. Two years later he played for the All Blacks against New South Wales, and moved to Auckland to play for the City club before returning to Waihi. He was a solid man, physically and in personality and temperament. As some large men are, he was also remarkably agile, but his reputation as a forward was based on the fact that he worked as a woodsman. His large shoulders and broad chest were typical of those who, in the pre-mechanized age, brought trees crashing to the forest floor with long, rhythmic strokes of long saws. He was fit, strong and a real character, too. Never short of a joke or a prank, when it came to entertainment evenings his star turn was to dress as a lady, with hilarious results.

Having missed the tour to Australia, then a drawn match against Otago-Southland and a big win over Canterbury, Gallaher's time as leader did not start well. On 29 July, the New Zealand team — playing in jerseys that were lettered rather than numbered — lost its 'farewell' match against Wellington (as its 1903 predecessors had done), 0–3. Billy Wallace recalled that the weather for the match (the seventh that Smith, Johnston and Glasgow had played that month) was:

> ... *a terrible winter's day with a cruel southerly wind, and we all tried to dodge the game. I was lucky enough to get out of it. No sooner had the match started than the ball began to go down, and everyone reckoned someone had stuck a pin in it. We had only one ball for a match in those days, so a kid had to be sent over to the Melrose Football Club to get another. While he was away all the players came up and sat yarning with the crowd.*

(Wallace missed the game because he had broken his collarbone in a match between Otago and Wellington, following a throw from All Black teammate Ernie Booth. He feared the injury would see him replaced for the upcoming tour, but a doctor confidently assured the NZRFU he would be alright to travel and the injury would be healed by the time the team arrived in England.)

A souvenir booklet of the tour was produced for sale at the Wellington match. Curiously, while Gallaher does appear in the team and individual photographs, and is listed as a member of the team at the beginning of the book, in the player provincial records his name is the only one missing from the squad!

Following the defeat, a farewell dinner for the team was held at the Wellington Town Hall, attended by Premier Seddon and other officials. Speeches were made, toasts raised, and a gentleman by the name of 'Goff' Warren sang a pun-laden tribute to the team called, simply, 'The New Zealand Football Team':

In days of old the Maori put up a sturdy fight;
This land has great traditions, let's strive to keep them bright.
We're not much good at cricket, but at the Rugby game,
We've won a bunch of laurels, and mean to keep the same.
So that is why we here have met, upon this festive evening,
To bid farewell unto our boys who tomorrow will be leaving,
To cross the briny ocean, and on many a hard-fought field,
Prove they are worthy Britain's sons, and ever scorn to yield.

(Chorus)
Here's success unto the fern leaf,
The emblem of our band;
May we welcome them as victors
From the good old Motherland!

A tower of strength is Gillett, their last line of defence,
For Wales they have a Harper, and Deans, who is immense.
For Scotland, William Wallace, a name of great renown;
Wee MacGregor lived in Glasgow, but will play against his town;
And when the Mackrell Hunter returns unto his Glenn,
And thinks his own dear 'Mona' loves with the strength of ten.
In-Stead of loving welcome, the village Smith he'll see,
And shout, 'Let her go, Gallaher!' to the couple 'neath the tree.

The Army's represented, for they have got a Booth,
And General Freddy Roberts, an Oriental youth,
And when the ball's out in the scrum, and he shouts: 'Oh, Mynott
fair!'
In Casey cannot get it, George Tyler will be there.

And when the word is 'forward', they've got a Trojan pack,
With Corbett, O'Sullivan, Nicholson, and likewise Kaikorai Mac.
With these are 'Baby' Newton and Johnstone — players neat.
Last, but not least, comes the Seeling, and the building is complete.

But, as no building's perfect until it has a 'lock',
We've added burly Cunningham, who's sturdy as rock.
Since Freddy is a bachelor, no better half is there,
But there's an Abbott in the team if he should want to pair.
Every big family needs a 'coach', so there's old warhorse Jim —
He doesn't get his hair cut now, and there's not much left to trim.
If any player plays it up, or tries his funny tricks on,
He'll be brought up with a round turn by genial Manager Dixon.

The general public showed little interest in the event. The team that had lost to Wellington was given little chance of success when away. Newspaper writers described the side as 'rotten'.

Aboard the *Rimutaka*

Disunity had surfaced.

On the morning of 30 July 1905, under grey skies and constant drizzle, the team boarded the steamship *Rimutaka* for its passage to England. The ship had carried passengers between England and New Zealand for over a decade. Among a number of farewell gifts, each player had been given a copy of the 'On the Ball' sheet music, signed by EW Secker.

Manager Dixon's personal diaries record his excitement at departing and his initial perception of the team as one where 'appearances point to party being a happy family', they 'seem very nice sociable lot of fellows' and ' "Uncle" Jimmy Duncan [is] making himself useful and appears to be well liked by everybody'. He also wrote of the task before them that they 'must pull through successfully if humanly possible'.

Not all the players were well known to each other, but it didn't take long for them to settle into becoming a team. A card-playing 'school' was quickly established by the gamblers in the side, to help pass the time. When the stakes started to rise considerably, Dixon had to put an end to it. In getting to know the players he noted in his diary that 'Deans and Newton seem disinclined to exertion'. Cunningham was team funny man, with able support in the humour department from Tyler and Thomson, who would stage mock wrestling bouts. Cricket matches — All Blacks *v* Passengers — took place on deck where large nets were set up. In fact, just about every activity was grounds for a competition — quoits, pillow fighting, potato races, sack racing, an obstacle race, chalking the deck, blind boxing, elbow wrestling and tug-of-war. One afternoon, Gallaher and Duncan began a competition to see who could catch one of the Cape pigeons that was flying at the stern of the ship. Soon, more of the team were joining the aerial angling, and lengths of light string and cotton were being sought. Several birds were caught then released. In the evenings, progressive euchre tournaments were hosted along with impromptu concerts, when the ship was stable enough for someone to take the piano stool.

Gallaher, Stead, Smith and Duncan began to prepare training arrangements, and Dixon observed that 'All seem thoroughly impressed with importance of undertaking.' It was announced that Gallaher and Cunningham would drill the forwards while Smith and Stead would run the backs training. This left the official 'coach' Jimmy Duncan somewhat on the outer.

After a week at sea, the team assembled in the smoke room to formally discuss for the first time on the trip what lay ahead. But the 'happy family' that Dixon had written of was not in evidence. Disunity had surfaced, and Gallaher's ears were burning. There was talk of a coup, of him being asked to relinquish the captaincy to satisfy some of the southern players who were aggrieved at the pre-tour debate that had raged over Duncan's appointment and the way in which they believed he was being sidelined from duties now that the team was on its way. Adding to this was another crucial point: the NZRFU had appointed Gallaher captain. On the 1897 and 1903 tours to Australia, when the touring parties had assembled, the players had held a meeting and chosen the captain, vice-captain and selection committee themselves. Some thought that if the players were capable of coaching themselves, why were they not capable of selecting the man they thought best-suited as their leader, as they had done in the past?

Knowing how destructive low morale could be in a military setting, Gallaher realized he had to put an end to the negativity as quickly and painlessly as possible. Two dozen factionalized men at sea would land in England a team contributing greatly to its own downfall. What followed was an act that defined his leadership. Gallaher rose and addressed the assembled. Without being directly accusatory, he addressed the team as a whole and spoke of his concerns about what he was hearing. For Gallaher, the team came first. If the team thought him so unsuitable, he would resign in the best interests of the team and the campaign that lay ahead. The team was stunned into silence, with several wondering if Gallaher was trying to call the bluff of the agitators. Seconds passed. Then Stead rose and offered to also resign if Gallaher did. Now the southern dissenters risked losing one of their own from a key leadership role. Dixon was next to address the side.

On a personal level Dixon, understandably, would have been a Gallaher supporter, given his association with Auckland rugby, despite chairing many of the meetings that had discussed and enforced Gallaher's recent suspension. However, Dixon was also Chairman of the NZRFU. In his strong Yorkshire accent he made it quite clear to the team that the decision to make Gallaher captain was one made, not by the players, but by the union itself. As manager of the team, he had to uphold such decisions while away. Frank Glasgow, the Taranaki forward and a bank clerk by profession, then proposed a motion that the group 'heartily endorse the appointments made by the Managing Committee'. A vote was had. Those in favour were 17, against were 12 — a narrow majority. Although not an overwhelming result — and one that could almost be broken into northern and southern lines — it was democratic. That was the end of the matter. It remains a remarkable incident in All Black history.

Other matters were discussed, and then at the meeting's end Dixon again spoke to the team, urging them to be 'loyal to each other and to the team ... in no case should they on tour or after their return to New Zealand discuss each other with outsiders'. What goes on, on tour, stays on tour. He also asked that any information for the press should go through him. All players agreed, and thoughts turned towards their preparation for the first game.

The drama of the morning meeting was matched by the elements in the evening, as a fierce storm, typical of the Southern Ocean, blew up. Large waves broke windows and water flooded some of the players' cabins. An area of wooden planking was lifted and splintered, and some of the railing was twisted and bent by the force of the breaking waves. Fortunately, no one suffered injuries as the ship was pounded by the ocean's sudden fury. It was the start of a week of cold weather and rough seas. Snow fell on the decks and the icy tips of the seething waves sent constant spray against the portholes. With the weather so bleak, a number of players took a sudden interest in shovelling coal into the steamer's boilers. It was hard work, but it was a dry, warm place to do some exercise.

The team had been allowed a week's respite before the organized practice regime began, and an improvement in the weather meant such could begin. Not everybody was accepting of compulsory exertion, however. Seeling belligerently announced that 'I didn't come on board this ship to work!'

'That's exactly what you did,' replied Dixon.

Of great concern to Gallaher when he studied the 14-week tour itinerary was the fact that the test against Wales was game number 28. He had seen the skill of the so-called 'tired' Welsh backs in the Great Britain side the previous year, and was wary of them playing in a side that had had months to prepare for their meeting. The challenge was to keep fit and healthy, not just for the December clash with Wales, but for all the matches on the itinerary. Their off-field preparation had to be as precise as their on-field play. His mantra, often said to his teammates as they prepared for matches, was: 'Give nothing away; take no chances.'

The daily fitness and training routine was dependent on the weather and the roll of the ship. A physical drill at 7.45am was followed by a bath and then breakfast at 8.30am. At 10am the team would reassemble on deck in their training gear, whereupon Smith would lead them on a run around the deck before taking the backs for a series of sprints. While they were occupied with that, Gallaher and Cunningham led the forwards in scrummaging for half an hour. One advantage the All Blacks would have over the teams they were to meet, that was apparent to Gallaher, was that in Great Britain a player's position in the scrum was dictated by when he arrived for its formation. If he was there first, he would be a front-ranker. The slower forwards tended to assume the positions of the side and back-row forwards. The New Zealanders were chosen for teams based on which forward position they played. Thus, when being drilled in scrum practice, much could be made of the individual positions in the scrum and the technical requirements, rather than just practising pushing.

Both groups then came back together, and Gallaher led the team in some other drills, before passing was practised and other exercise undertaken. Following this exertion they would bathe, have a rubdown, and reassemble for a hearty one o'clock lunch. Every second day there were organized fitness sessions at 3pm, and at 5pm there was a team discussion about rules and tactics.

As the steamer made her way east through the cold, grey seas, a constant watch for icebergs had to be kept. When there was a sighting in the middle of one night, Billy Stead was quick to make his way up on deck to view it. He described it for a column he contributed to the *Southland Times*:

> *On first discerning it, I was paralysed with the creeping, ghoulish feeling that one always associates with ghosts. So quiet, mystic; not a sound of any progress; one could hardly help imagining the results of colliding with such a monster. I should say it was about 200 feet high and about half a mile long.*

Two weeks after leaving Wellington, the *Rimutaka* rounded Cape Horn and several days later anchored off Montevideo. The team had a day ashore, marvelling at their first taste of the chaos and colour that was South America. One of Stead's more humorous observations was that 'the Spanish female up to about the age of thirty is, generally speaking, a beautiful, graceful woman but, over that, you would think she was sixty'.

A large number of Argentinian passengers boarded at Montevideo, and as the ship resumed its passage they were intrigued by the All Blacks training sessions and the rehearsing of their war cry, in the same way as there had been when Gallaher travelled to South Africa with the Sixth Contingent. 'Ka mate' was their haka, and the Maori (and English translation) were recorded at that time as:

Ka mate ka mate ka ora kaora,
Ka mate ka mate ka ora kaora
Te nei te ta nga ta pu huru huru
Na na e piki mai whaka white te ra
Hu pa nei, hu ka nei, hu pa nei kau pa nei white te ra

Together we live, together we die
This man we bring is the murderous one,
He slew as long as the sun shone.
So shame on him! Shame on him!
Shame on him as long as the sun shines.

Once out of the Southern Ocean, sailing conditions improved and heat replaced cold — which created its own problems. O'Sullivan suffered sunstroke and Gallaher suffered an illness for a few days. It was suspected to be related to the sickness that had hospitalized him in Africa. Fortunately, there were few serious accidents on the trip. Gillett fell on the deck and suffered a cut around the eye. Johnston, too, fell badly, grazing the skin on both shins, which became infected. McGregor suffered a bad strain of some sort, while Tyler twisted his back in a scrum session. Newton was clobbered in the chest during a boxing bout and had to refrain from practice for a number of days. Wallace, whose shoulder was still strapped, suffered from a painful toothache. A dentist passenger suggested that the offending incisor should be pulled. However, he had no instruments and the weather had been too rough to conduct such a procedure. Mackrell, too, was ill.

Although the warmer weather was greatly preferable to the cold, several players began to suffer from boils. This was indicative of both the physical demands of the team's training and the extent to which it was difficult maintaining an active sports team's personal hygiene on a ship. Small cuts and bruises became infected, and in the warmer climes bacteria quickly spread between players. The infections certainly weren't symptomatic of poor diet — most of the players were gaining weight on the journey.

The *Rimutaka* steamed on towards England.

A couple of days out from Plymouth, a fancy dress ball was held. The sporting contests that the players had been competing in came to their conclusion with a series of finals. Gallaher came third in the potato race behind the dead-heating Hunter and Harper. He also won chalking the deck. Such simple events had proved a good light diversion from the heavier demands of training, and were important in keeping the players in good spirits.

On 8 September, in the wee hours of the morning, the players made their way up on deck to see the Eddystone Lighthouse and, shortly before dawn, they were disembarking from the *Rimutaka* onto a tender to be taken to shore. After six weeks at sea, the team had arrived 'Home'.

'Home'

'Look at that terrible man, Gallaher; offside as usual!'

Having been at sea for a number of weeks, Gallaher and team had no idea just what sort of reception there would be when they arrived in England. Their departure had been somewhat muted, and they had, since Montevideo, been in the company of very social Spanish passengers with little interest in football. Thus, they were completely surprised by the large number of people who turned out to welcome them when they arrived at Newton Abbot, a small township in Devon. Their base for the beginning of the tour was the Globe Hotel, and here was taken one of the most famous photographs of the touring party in their playing strip.

A journalist by the name of JA (John) Buttery from the *Daily Mail* made himself known to the team. He would be the only reporter to see every game the team played, and he is credited with first using the term 'All Blacks'. The passage of time has shown that New Zealand footballers had been referred to as the 'blacks' in print prior to the tour, and Dixon used such a term in his tour diary. Mind you, Buttery was filing the greatest number of stories about the side — in one of the newspapers with the greatest circulation in Britain — so he certainly can be credited with popularizing the term.

In the week until the first game, the time was spent training and sightseeing. They also went to watch one of their future opponents, Devonport Albion, play Torquay, leaving the stands at the conclusion of the game even more convinced that their methods were going to prove far superior to those of many of the teams that were lined up to meet them.

The team had its pre-match rituals, which involved a 'rattling good meal' at midday, then the players went to their rooms for an hour to allow their lunch to digest, and in this time they were expected to begin to concentrate on the match ahead and their roles in it. (Some players became known for a noisy form of deep concentration that involved the eyes being closed and the mouth wide open!) They would also be rubbed down before and after each match by the 'breathers' (non-match-day players) and Jimmy Duncan, using a special 'training oil'. The concoction was 60 per cent eucalyptus oil, 30 per cent whisky, and 10 per cent hartshorn (which was made from horn or antler of the male red deer).

Their first match was against Devon at Exeter on 16 September 1905. A coterie of English Rugby Union (ERU) officials were among the crowd of 7,000 enjoying the sunny, warm afternoon. All had come to the ground expecting a close match. It quickly turned out to be nothing of the sort. Excitement at finally getting on the field to play fired the All Black forwards and backs. Smith raced in for four tries, while Wallace scored three and kicked eight conversions in registering half of the team's 55 points. Such was the pace of the game played by the All Blacks with ball in hand that the taking of conversions was a chance for several to sit down and catch their breath.

Gallaher with trademark shin-pads outside his stockings, having held the ball for Wallace to kick, *v* Devon, 16 September 1905, the first game of the 'Originals' tour. MATT ELLIOTT COLLECTION

The Devon side struggled to counter the play of Gallaher, were bewildered by the fact that their eight-man scrum was being out-muscled by only seven All Black forwards, and their backs were almost tripping over themselves trying to defend against their speedy opposites. In response, they could muster only a dropped goal.

A famous story has oft been told of a British newspaper editor who, upon receiving the result from a reporter, thought there had been an error in communicating the score and printed it as Devon 55, New Zealand 4.

After the post-match dinner, the All Blacks returned to Newton Abbot, arriving back shortly before midnight. At that late hour, one would expect the town to be ghostly quiet. It was the exact opposite. A carnival atmosphere enveloped the team, with a brass band playing and hundreds turning out to welcome back the new sporting stars. Such a response from members of the public was to be an ongoing feature of the tour, with endless invitations to visit businesses and councils, and young women making themselves known to players after matches or writing to team members in the hope of becoming the belle of an All Black.

When readers opened morning newspapers for full reports of the game, much ink was dedicated to Gallaher's wing-forward play. It is worth noting that the referee of that first match was Percy Coles, secretary of the ERU. He found little reason to penalize Gallaher during the game. However, local fans had not expected their side to be so completely demolished by the colonial upstarts. Humbled supporters and newspaper men looked for something or *someone* to blame other than the failings of their own team.

Hamish Stuart wrote for the *London Daily Chronicle*:

One really novel feature of the New Zealand system was far from pleasing. I refer to the wing-forward, who wears shin guards — an unusual thing in rugger. Let the omen be absent, but the wing-forward as we saw him on Saturday is such an irritating person, and plays such a decidedly unlawful game from our point of view, that his prudence in wearing shin guards may be commended ... if he had met with his

*deserts [he] would have been penalized into effectiveness. He may be
described as a scrumhalf who claims the privilege of a forward in the
scrum. His part is that of a passive and active obstructionist.*

The *Daily Telegraph* correspondent wrote:

*The most interesting and most watched person on the field naturally
was Gallaher, the 'wing-forward', and there can be no question
that he had much to do with putting the Devon team off their proper
game … [That] a player may passively obstruct or prevent an opponent
from getting at another player who is in the act of passing, without
rendering himself liable to a penalty, must, of course, be a matter for
the referee's judgment. It occurred to us on Saturday that Gallaher
sailed very near the wind on several occasions.*

The *London Sportsman* was more direct in writing that the All Blacks'
'winging forward is not a forward, but is a wolf in sheep's clothing'.

Gallaher's play stood out even more because in Great Britain he
rarely had an opposite. Playing in New Zealand, be it for club or
province, as a wing-forward he had an opponent in the same position.
Both men tended to cancel each other out. However, with no one lining
up against him, Gallaher suddenly had free rein and the interpretation
of the position became very different. Years later Wallace said of
Gallaher's play that:

*… the British players didn't have many clues about the type of football
we played … and our scrum work with the two-three-two front gave
us such a monopoly of the ball that Dave didn't have much to do in the
way of breaking up attacking play by the opposition.*

Debate over the legality of Gallaher's play would blaze away all tour.

The next two games — versus Cornwall and Bristol — were identical in the way the game was played and in the result on the scoreboard: 41–0 to the All Blacks.

Three matches into the tour, Gallaher gave the lengthiest interview of his career, sitting down with journalist Buttery, who described him as 'a fine man, over 6ft. in height and, consequently, of a bigger build than might be expected'. He began by asking Gallaher what his impression of the first few weeks of the tour was. Said Gallaher:

We are all delighted with our visit so far, and the reception we have had everywhere. We have met with the greatest kindness and hospitality on every side. We are, of course, delighted with our three victories, but we do not overestimate them. I fully realize that English clubs are only just commencing the season, and have not yet got 'going'. Devon and Cornwall showed evident signs of this, and lacked combination; but I thought Bristol a good side, especially in the front rank, and I think this is our best win to date.

What are the prospects for the team as the tour progresses?

Well, it is hard for me to say yet. We are looking forward very much to our game with Durham, as I hear they are always a good side; and I have also heard a very good report of the Leicester 'pack', and shall be more than interested to see whether we can hold them with our seven forwards, as we shall not play more than that number in the 'scrum' in any match.

On the subject of the different methods of play between the English
sides and the All Blacks:

*I have been asked many questions as to my opinion of the merits of
our 'packing' as compared with English methods. Every man in my
team has his allotted place — not that he cannot play elsewhere —
and on scrumming each man goes down in his own place. We do not
waste time in this way, having put in a great deal of practice; and
as the result has been that with seven men we have held opponents,
surely further comment is unnecessary. Your three-quarters hardly
run straight enough. There seems scarcely room enough on the ground
sometimes for four three-quarters. Some of the men we have met go
beautifully straight, but others, I fancy, are inclined to 'bore' towards
the wing too much, and, consequently, often waste the chance of the
wing-man, who is thrust right on to the touchline before he gets his
pass and cannot then do anything, even if he were the finest sprinter
in the world. I notice that our methods have met with some amount of
admiration. Imitation is said to be the sincerest form of flattery, and
in the match against Cornwall they pulled a man out of the scrum to
play as a wing-forward; while Bristol are going to try their hand with
three men in the third line.*

His response to a final question about his play as wing-forward was
described as 'diffident':

*The spectators are not unkind as a whole but some writers' criticisms
are hardly kind. I think my play is fair — I sincerely trust so — and
surely the fact that both Mr Percy Coles and Mr D.H. Bowen — two
of the referees of our matches, and fairly representative of English and*

Welsh ideas, have taken no exception so it ought to have some weight. I do not think that it is easier for me not to infringe the rules while behind a winning pack. If they are getting beaten it will not make any difference. I have studied this style of play very keenly, though I have played in every position on the field. Some exception, I notice, has been taken to my wearing shin-guards, one critic being very severe on the point. I'm afraid I caught his eye because mine were outside my stockings. As a matter of fact, the whole team wear shin-guards, but mostly inside their stockings; and I fancy many of your English players do also. I must do it, we all must do it. We have a very long tour to get through, and only those who have had a bad kick on the shin know what it means.

The comprehensive wins continued through the Midlands and up to the North East of England, leaving a trail of bemused opponents and star-struck spectators:

28 September: *v* Northampton at Northampton, 32–0

30 September: *v* Leicester at Leicester, 28–0

4 October: *v* Middlesex at Stamford Bridge, 34–0

Towards the end of the Middlesex game, Stead was kicked in the stomach. In pain, rather than leave the field and leave his team a player short, he went to fullback where he could see out the match with less physical contact. Gillett who was at fullback moved to wing-forward, Gallaher moved to halfback, and Roberts went from halfback to Stead's original position of five-eighth. Gallaher then sprained a knee. It wasn't a serious injury, but it was something he had suffered from over his career and this time it put him out of the next three matches. That included the 7 October encounter with Durham which he had told Buttery the side were looking forward to. As it turned out, the northern county champions did have a competitive set of forwards but had to start the game with only 13 players as two of their side had missed the train to the game! The first try was conceded on tour by the All Blacks, but they still won 16–3.

11 October: *v* Hartlepool Clubs at West Hartlepool, 63–0

14 October: *v* Northumberland at North Shields, 31–0

Six matches in, only three points had been conceded by the All Blacks against over 200 scored.

While Gallaher saw the differences in playing styles as the key ingredient in the team's early successes, Premier Seddon, who had been cabled by the *Daily Mail* for a response to the team's impressive start to their tour, buoyantly responded:

I am not surprised that the British public is amazed at the brilliancy of the New Zealand footballers. … The natural and healthy conditions of Colonial life produce the stalwart and athletic sons of whom New Zealand and the Empire may be justly proud.

Seddon's cable was followed by a longer, more florid letter to the *Daily Mail* from the High Commissioner in London, William Pember Reeves, who added:

First of all the climate is a great factor. It is brisk, breezy and bracing, with a combination of sea and mountain air. Our country is peopled with a race inheriting the sporting instincts of a British stock, with vaster opportunities and inducements to practise open-air games.

He highlighted better living conditions, working hours, sanitation and education and concluded with:

For these reasons, the men of New Zealand have thrown themselves passionately into the pursuit of the game of football. … In short, there is nothing mystical about our team's success. They play, as it were, with both ends — their heads and their feet.

On and on the black juggernaut rolled, moving down to the south of England, but still they found little resistance.

19 October: *v* Gloucester at Gloucester, 44–0
21 October: *v* Somerset at Taunton, 23–0

While in Somerset, some of the touring party visited the Cheddar caves in the Mendip Hills where two years earlier Britain's oldest skeleton had been found. While exploring the subterranean landscapes, Hunter, Glenn and Gallaher scratched their names on a cave wall. (They were still visible two decades later, when the 1924–25 All Blacks toured Britain.)

There were high hopes for Devonport Albion to make their match a close one, as they had been beaten only twice in the past two seasons. The club president, the Reverend Ponsonby, ceremonially began the match by kicking off for the All Blacks. There were occasional periods of resistance from the hosts, but then the All Blacks would swarm the length of the field for wonderfully taken tries, one of which was claimed by Gallaher in the 21–3 win.

Three days later Midland Counties fared marginally better on the scoreboard (21–5), but the play was some of the most evenly contested thus far. Gallaher had a great tussle with the opposing halfback, Braithwaite. Standing only 5 feet tall, he was small and sinewy like a jockey, but gave as good as he got in his contest with the imposing All Black captain. Their running battle was exciting in itself. At one point in the match, Gallaher received a nasty kick to his head. As he sat on his backside rubbing the spot on his head that was still stinging from the blow of a boot, the non-playing Billy Wallace joked, 'It's the first time I've seen any halfback make Dave think.' At the end of the match, Gallaher was asked for his thoughts on the game. With sweat running down his brow, he puffed that Midland was 'a fine side [with] an exceedingly good halfback'.

The outing against Surrey at Richmond on 1 November, won 11–0, was recalled by Billy Wallace as an occasion 'none of us are ever likely to forget … not because of any particularly brilliant piece of play, but because of the grilling we got from the referee'.

Gillett took Gallaher's place at wing-forward. Gallaher spoke highly of his friend's ability to move from fullback to play wing-forward, going so far as to say: 'He begins where I end.' Stylistically, they were quite different in one key area. Gillett was a man who always fed the ball out to his backline when he secured possession, whereas Gallaher's play tended to favour slightly older tactics. If he was near the ball, rather than picking it up and feeding the backs he would either keep the ball on the toe and work his way downfield with long dribbling rushes, or he would pass to his fellow forwards and they would use short, close passes to advance. Nonetheless, the other 14 players in the side had no trouble responding to the differing styles of play. Some years later, Billy Stead commented that 'I will always think of Dave Gallaher as the impetuous, bustling, aggressive wing-forward'.

When the two sides took to the Athletic Ground in London, the surface was very slippery due to wind and rain in the hours prior to kick-off. Heavy rain clouds settled low in the skies above the ground, weighed down with rain that was emptied on the assembled during the match. Those conditions made play disjointed enough, but the game became even less of a spectacle for the 8,000 thanks to the referee — a Mr Williams from the Rugby Committee — and his incessant interruptions. One spectator counted 33 penalties awarded in one 15-minute period. So farcical was the officiating that Buttery labelled the match 'The Whistling Fantasia' and delighted in sending up the referee's performance in his write-up of the game:

This gentleman … was evidently under the impression that everybody had come to hear him perform on the whistle, and as he was in charge of the stage, so to speak, he was enabled to indulge his fantasy to his heart's content. The finest artists are said to shut their eyes when whistling their hardest, and judged on that hypothesis, the referee must have had his eyes closed on and off for the greater part of the game. … As one of the rules of rugby is that you may not kick or handle the ball while the whistle is blowing, it is obvious that there was very little football. … As for the game, there was no game. It was an exposition of the power of music to tame even the New Zealand rugby footballer.

Local fans didn't have many more clues about the wing-forward play or even Gallaher himself. For, while his name was well known due to the amount of print local newspapers were devoting to his position, he could have walked down any high street in England in civilian clothes and few would have recognized him. A fine example of this occurred in that match against Surrey. As Gallaher sat in the stand with the other 'breathers' to watch the match, all game he heard Surrey supporters barracking against him with constant cries of 'Offside, Gallaher!' and remarks such as 'Look at that terrible man, Gallaher; offside as usual.' Unperturbed, Gallaher is said to have wryly remarked, 'By crikey, I didn't know I was so popular.'

Five more wins followed, scoring at an average of 30 points a game, and not a point conceded.

4 November: *v* Blackheath at Blackheath, 32–0

7 November: *v* Oxford University at Oxford, 47–0

9 November: *v* Cambridge University at Cambridge, 14–0

11 November: *v* Richmond at Richmond, 17–0

15 November: *v* Bedford XV at Bedford, 41–0

After 19 games, it was time for the first test match. Oddly, the team had to travel from the south of England up to Edinburgh to face Scotland. One might have thought playing England in London would make more sense in terms of geography and travel but that was the agreed-to itinerary.

The warm welcome that had been a feature of arriving in every new town was completely absent when the team arrived in Edinburgh on the evening of 16 November. There was only one representative of the Scottish Rugby Union (SRU) to meet them, and the SRU had already evinced little interest in the fixture. When initial arrangements for the tour were being undertaken, the SRU had refused to agree to give the NZRFU a guarantee of £200, offering instead the gate takings. This backfired on it in spectacular fashion when over 21,000 came to watch the game at Inverleith. The fact that the All Blacks were 'three bob a day' men, receiving a *per diem* of three shillings, had the Scots questioning the amateur status of the side. The pre-existing ill-will also meant that the Scottish players weren't awarded caps for the match, and no precautions, such as covering the ground with hay, were taken to prevent a very severe frost from settling on the ground.

Gallaher tackles an Oxford University player, 7 November 1905.
AUCKLAND RUGBY UNION

About noon on the day of the game, 18 November, the Secretary of the Scottish union sent a message to Dixon that he and the Scottish captain Bedell-Sivright — the cranky captain of Great Britain the previous year — were going to inspect the ground and in all probability the match would be called off. (They hadn't even finalized their team by this late stage.) Dixon told Gallaher of the news, and the two called for a cab to take them to the ground as quickly as possible. There, they found the surface of the field frozen. The referee for the match and the Scottish union official wanted to abandon the game, but Gallaher and Dixon would hear nothing of it. Adding to their argument for the match being played was that the sun was breaking through, suggesting a thaw was imminent.

By the time of kick-off, the sun had disappeared again, however, and the uniforms of a brass band and pipers were the only colour on a dreary afternoon.

The insistence of Gallaher and Dixon to play the game, and not succumb to the Scottish apathy, nearly worked against the All Blacks. The players would have been better with ice skates than football boots, as manoeuvrability on the glassy surface was nigh-on impossible. Adding to this, the ball supplied by the hosts had been too highly blown, and Gallaher instructed that it be soaked in water to try to make it heavier. Dixon recorded in his diary that the ball was of a:

> ... very long torpedo variety and being too lightly blown, consequently very light, the difficulty of playing good football (already great) was largely increased. I never saw a ball cut such extraordinary antics in my life and having regard to the slippery foothold it is wonderful that the players of both sides caught and fielded it as much as they did.

Gallaher led his team out on to the field, becoming only the fourth man to captain the All Blacks in a test match. (While the All Blacks were away, an Australian side was in New Zealand and played a test at the beginning of September, where another All Black side was captained by Wellington's John Spencer.) The All Blacks started the match well, but the Irish referee — Mr W Kennedy — disallowed two tries on account of forward passes, ruled by him from 20 metres behind the play. Scottish back Simpson dropped a goal for Scotland to lead by 4–0. The All Blacks replied with a try to Glasgow, which was followed by a try to Smith. They were ahead, 6–4. Shortly before halftime, the Scottish forwards rushed from almost halfway to score a try which saw them ahead by one point at the break, 7–6.

The score remained in Scotland's favour and time was running out. Stead later wrote: 'Shall I ever forget the look of my captain when (during a temporary lull in the game) he said, "Only six more minutes, Billy." ' Then with less than five minutes to play, after absorbing a series of Scottish attacks right on the All Blacks' goal-line, Smith made a great break (even more impressive on the slippery surface), went around the Scottish fullback, and scored for a 9–7 lead.

Play restarted with a fury, but it was the All Black forwards who made the best progress and a long dribbling rush resulted in a final try to Cunningham. He unsuccessfully attempted the conversion, as Wallace was groggy after a late charge had sent him crashing back-wards onto the hard ground, the back of his head hitting the surface with a sickening thud.

When the referee whistled for the end of the match, the relieved All Blacks were somewhat stunned by the silence, broken only by celebrations from a small group of Australian and New Zealand spectators, most of them medical students studying at Guy's Hospital. Gallaher left the field limping noticeably. Through the final minutes of the match he had been something of a passenger, having had his right leg hacked with a boot in a period of rough play that had also claimed two Scottish players.

The ill-will from the SRU continued when the All Blacks were not allowed to keep the ball as a souvenir of the game. There was no official after-match function, the players instead being guests of the Australasian Club.

In his summary of the game, Dixon noted that: 'It certainly was a hard keen game desperately fast all through and making due consideration of the conditions, a fine exhibition of football.' He added that 'Scotland laid out to play a spoiling game' and 'the Referee [who] went out unprovided with bars on his boots', struggled to keep up with the play and 'as was natural under the circumstances, made occasional mistakes'.

There was only one more game in Scotland — against the West of Scotland, four days after the test. The players had expected an even chillier reception following the test match, but were pleasantly surprised when the exact opposite occurred. This was due to the game being played at a soccer ground — that of Queen's Park — and the club's staff were warm, welcoming and there was nothing they would not do for the team … even after the home side had been disposed of 22–0.

The team sailed for Belfast and, 27 years after leaving the country of his birth, Gallaher was back on Irish soil. However, he was beginning to feel unwell as a result of his leg injury, which had become noticeably red and swollen.

By the time the team moved down to Dublin, Gallaher was very crook. His leg was painful to touch and he felt as though he was suffering from a very bad cold, being unable to get warm. So, while his teammates went off to St James's Gate to sample the delights of the Guinness brewery, Gallaher took to his bed at the Imperial Hotel. A local doctor — with the less-than-comforting name of Burke Savage — was called and, after inspecting Gallaher's swollen limb, diagnosed cellulitis. Gallaher was instructed to stay in bed with the leg elevated, and medication was prescribed. Most disappointingly, he was told he should not play for at least 10 days. He was to miss the test against the emerald greens.

Captaining Ireland was a man becoming very familiar in backlines opposing the All Blacks. Basil MacLear was playing his third match against them, having also turned out for Blackheath and for the Bedford XV. (He would line up for Munster, too, three days later, meaning he played as many games against the tourists as the invalid Mackrell played for them!)

Both sides played the match at Lansdowne Road in great spirit, buoyed by the festive atmosphere of the 12,000-strong crowd. The score was only 5–0 to the All Blacks at halftime, Deans having taken a good try and Wallace converting. In the second half Deans crossed the line again, and towards the end of the match McDonald drove over from a scrum on the Irish line. Wallace converted both tries and the match ended 15–0. Both sides dined together in the evening, and the craic, as they say, was mighty.

Dixon wrote of the match:

Ireland relied almost entirely upon their forwards for attack … fast, fearless and dashing … their headlong rushes down the field were of a character to stir the blood — little wonder that the excitable Irishmen around the field were worked up to a state of almost delirious joy.

The Irish forward play was something he hadn't witnessed 'since the 80s when a similar class of forward play was common in NZ'.

It would have been a great disappointment for Gallaher not to play in a match where the opposition were such willing participants using a style of play that he thrived on. He described waiting to hear the result of the match as 'one of the most anxious times I have ever lived through'. At halftime, the score was phoned through to him. Once he'd heard it, 'I could neither smoke nor read; in fact I could hardly keep still until I heard the result and knew my boys were safe.'

The team moved off to Limerick, still without Gallaher. Munster were beaten 33–0, but there was a downside to the win. George Smith injured his shoulder. (He would play only once more on tour.)

Reunited with their captain, the team ferried back across the Irish Sea to prepare for the test against England on 2 December.

Buttery asked Gallaher if he would be playing in the England game. 'I am a great deal better but it is not yet settled whether I shall play,' he said. 'If I don't, it will not be for want of trying. I am most anxious to take my place. I have had enough of lying in bed.'

The *Observer* newspaper noted that the crowd at Sydenham's Crystal Palace 'was probably the best dressed that ever gathered to watch a match' there, that the crowd was free of 'burly Northerners', and it wondered just how many in the crowd actually knew the rules of the game. It was considered that the reputation of the All Blacks preceded them. The muddy conditions around the sidelines saw a roaring trade in small wooden stools and boxes to stand on. Estimates of the crowd size vary between 40,000 and 80,000. This variance is because, although there were official gate takings, a large number made their way into the ground without paying or took whatever vantage point they could on the perimeter of the ground (such as tall trees) to watch.

Almost 100 years after the Crystal Palace match, several minutes of film footage taken that day was found in — of all places — a South Island garage. At less than four minutes in length, the film is mesmerizing. The 'photo faces' of the All Blacks and the English team come to life. As rugby commentator Tony Johnson told the author: 'It is like watching ghosts.'

As the film begins to roll, we see the bleak London December day. Long, bulky coats are the common feature of spectators' clothing. First the English team stand on one goal-line, some warming themselves against the cold and pre-match nerves. One, the skipper Cartwright, playfully lobs the noticeably round ball at the cameraman.

Then the New Zealand boys appear, led by Gallaher. There is nothing nervous or twitchy about his movements. He comes carrying the ball, head slightly bowed, having some last words with manager Dixon. His walk is that of a man confident in the team who follow him. As much as the crowd have come to see their home side play — many still making their way to their seats — they have come to see these 'Colonials' who have cast aside 23 teams *en route* to this clash. The rest of the team walk out behind Gallaher. A mix of heights and shapes, they nonetheless look imposing. Two bandsmen standing nearby step back slightly as they pass. Trailing them is the lean, side-row forward George Nicholson, taking the sideline flag for the match. He looks much taller than his 6 foot 3 inches, and trudges past the camera puffing on a cigarette. The All Blacks line up as the English did, and the camera moves along the line. Gallaher, holding the ball against his lower thigh, is flanked by Tyler and McGregor. It finishes on referee Evans, who stands slightly apart from the All Blacks but with a hint of a smile that shows his delight to be part of the auspicious day. The All Blacks then break ranks and Gallaher heads towards the dead-ball line where referee Evans is standing. As he goes, he turns and kicks the ball back to his teammates.

Why has Gallaher run in the opposite direction from his team and why does the referee want to talk to him in front of where the crowd line one of the pitch extremities? It was a practice — if not a requirement — for captains to check the touchlines for anything intruding on to the field of play. (Gallaher knew all too well where not doing so, or failing to agree with the opposing captain that the ball striking a spectator was dead ball, could count against a side. In June 1899, Newton and Ponsonby were embroiled in one of their usual close matches at Potter's Paddock. The ball was kicked hard by a Newton forward through the Ponsonby 25 and into goal. Most of the players, and spectators, expected the ball to roll dead, but it struck a wee lad who was standing in goal, inside the railing, for a better view of the match. A Newton wing, following up on the ball, dropped on it as it stopped and the referee had to award the try.)

As the film continues, the English team move up from the opposite end of the field, passing the ball with some aptitude before it becomes more like lobbing a beach ball. A day at the seaside this isn't! We briefly see the finale of the All Blacks' 'haka' before the English kick off. We can only imagine the roar from the crowd as the ball first leaves the toe and sails through the air to begin the game.

Play moves around the field and we get to see Gallaher in action. He prowls around where the dribbling rushes have broken down. At a scrum, he is stooped, watching the passage of the ball through the feet of his opponents, turning to appeal to the referee. When feeding a scrum, he then stays bent over, his protruding backside an obstacle an opponent must go around in order to put pressure on the All Black halfback. On other occasions, when play has broken down, he stands with his hands on his hips, surveying the scene, digesting the referee's decision, calculating his next action. When play moves to the open, his running style betrays the fact that he was still having trouble with his leg. He begins his chase with small steps to assure he doesn't slip on the muddied ground, despite wearing long studs on his boots, then lengthens his stride. But he never straightens and runs tall. He is always slightly bent from the waist in readiness for a collision or to go down on the ball.

The footage is remarkable, absorbing. When watching it one can forget it is only three and half minutes long, not 80.

The match resulted in a 15–0 win to the All Blacks. In a scrappy match, McGregor scored four tries and Newton one. (The former's feat was a New Zealand test-match record that stood until John Gallagher and Craig Green both scored four tries against Fiji in the 1987 World Cup.) Of Gallaher's play in the match, one newspaper report said he 'really should have rested from this fixture, but his keen desire overmastered his discretion. He showed wonderful grit in tackling, but lacked his usual aggressiveness.'

In the evening, a large dinner was put on by the ERU at the Trocadero restaurant in Piccadilly. Guests included Pember Reeves and Lord Ranfurly. Gallaher, feeling the effects of the match on his sore leg, made an entertaining speech in response to a toast to the team. They had in England, he said, 'met with clean sport and sportsmen, and, as cousins from across the sea and chips off the old block, had a reception which exceeded all expectations. We have come Home to wake up the Old Country, which, in its conservative spirit, had gone to sleep. We wanted to stir up John Bull a little but once we stop stirring he might take a lot of stopping!' Laughter and cries of 'hear, hear' rang out from tables around the restaurant.

George Dixon addressed Rowland Hill, mentioning the NZRFU's support for the rejection of the professional game and of a desire to see an English team make a visit to New Zealand in the not-too-distant future. From the back of the room came a cry of 'We will beat you!' which brought about much laughter. The English captain, Cartwright, was most good-humoured in acknowledging that his side had been well beaten, and he asked the reporters in the room to record the All Blacks win as '15 points, rather than five tries — it looks better'.

Pember Reeves spoke at length about the team's success and the role of colonies in the Empire. He concluded with a warning about the approaching matches in Wales: 'I have been told there is a wonderful fence, post and rail, ditch and bank, being prepared for the team at Cardiff. I am sure the New Zealand horse will go straight for it!'

Post-match reports overwhelmingly praised the performance of the All Blacks and commented that the poor state of the field affected the New Zealanders more than the English as it negated the speed of the three-quarters. Under the title 'A Colonial Triumph', the *Observer* newspaper also made much of the temperament of the players:

It was most strenuously contested from start to finish, and the gay way in which hard knocks were given and received proved the chivalry of the rival champions. Some men got temporarily knocked out, but no serious accident occurred, and the intervals, while the New Zealanders assisted in attending to an injured opponent, or a similar courtesy was exhibited on the other side, only served to display the admirable spirit in which the game was contested.

Between matches a small group of players visited the Royal Agricultural Show. A large pen of cattle took their eye, and as they were discussing the beasts an entourage made their way past, in the midst of which was King Edward. He stopped briefly and asked who the captain was as he would like to shake his hand and congratulate him on the team's effort thus far. The ever-mischievous George Tyler stepped forward, pronouncing that he was the captain. Then he and the king shook hands before the monarch was moved on by his staff.

Cheltenham (18–0) and Cheshire (34–0) were next swept aside before the team moved on to Leeds to play Yorkshire on 13 December. Yorkshire were still recovering from the breakaway of Northern Union clubs and their establishment a decade earlier, but nearly 25,000 descended on Headingly, the only venue in Leeds capable of accommodating such a crowd. Gallaher enjoyed discussing the cricketing history of the ground, but the players were kept from being caught up in too much conversation. Northern Union scouts were known to be at the ground, intent on making approaches to individual All Blacks about switching codes. Several players spoke of being offered £500 to sign up for a Northern Union club with a weekly stipend of £3 10s. With the match easily won by 40–0, it was probably the most memorable aspect of the visit for some.

The focus was now on the part of itinerary that had most concerned Gallaher from the outset of their journey: Wales.

Cardiff

---

*'I have always made it a point never to
express a view regarding the referee in
any match in which I have played.'*

The controversy over Gallaher's role as wing-forward, and the
legalities of the position in general, might have been the lasting
sentiment of the 1905 tour were it not for one incident in the fourth
test match of the tour against Wales.

The All Blacks went to Cardiff a tired team. They had played 27
games in 88 days. Although still unbeaten, there were injuries and
there was illness, predominantly the result of fatigue. Boils were the
most common, painful ailment.

On the other hand the Welsh team had developed a formidable
reputation. They had won the 1905 International Championship
played between the Home Unions. In doing so, they claimed the Triple
Crown by beating England, Ireland and Scotland. In fact, they had been

undefeated on Welsh soil since 1899. The unofficial title of 'Best in the World' was at stake. In preparation for their meeting with the All Blacks, the Welsh players and management had attended several tour matches. They had also partaken in a number of practices, focusing on executing special backline moves that they hoped would lead to victory.

When the All Blacks arrived in Cardiff, every person they spoke to told them that Cardiff Arms Park would be at, or beyond, its 42,000-person capacity, that special trains were bringing spectators from all over the country's valleys to the capital, and they were about to lose their unbeaten record.

The concern Gallaher had felt months earlier about the scheduling of the Welsh test, and the state of his team by the time that match came around, proved correct. After a practice run the day before the game, the selection committee struggled for *seven* hours to select 15 fit players to take the field. Billy Wallace recalled: 'We had only twelve or thirteen fit players for that game. Lots of chaps had boils, and I had a poisoned knee.' Crucially, Cunningham, Smith and Stead were unavailable through injury or illness. Stead later said he stepped aside for Mynott to take his place because he felt stale. It seems an unusual decision for the tour vice-captain to make. Other members of the side have said they thought he had boils, too, or dysentery. The latter may be correct. Stead ran the touchline during the match but had to leave the field, and was relieved of his flag by Nicholson as the match progressed. He wrote of having had trouble sleeping for some time. So, the team was named as follows: Gillett, Wallace, Deans, Hunter, McGregor, Mynott, Roberts, Gallaher, Seeling, McDonald, O'Sullivan, Newton, Glasgow, Casey, Tyler. The Welsh XV was: Winfield, Llewellyn, Gabe, Nicholls, Morgan, CC (Cliff) Pritchard,

Bush, Owen, Harding, Joseph, Hodges, Williams, CM (Charlie) Pritchard, Travers, Jones.

The All Blacks stayed in The Queen's Hotel, a short distance from the park. All morning the players had been able to hear the gathering Welsh masses in full, expectant voice. Welsh representative (and visitor to New Zealand in 1904) Rhys Gabe stopped in at the hotel to see the All Blacks. What he saw heartened him. He told his teammates that Gallaher's men looked 'keyed-up and ill at ease, with the thought of a possible defeat'. Being unbeaten had been an aim at the start of the tour, but as the weeks wore on, the record started to become a heavy burden. No one wanted to be in a side that lost a game. The confident, carefree players seen in Devon were now men weighed down by their own achievements and the expectations of the footballing public in New Zealand (who expected them to win) and in the British Isles (who were hoping to eventually see them lose).

As the players took the mandatory rest after lunch, the body could relax but their minds were awash with a multitude of choruses. Looking out their windows, they could see the human tide swelling, slowly moving through the streets towards the gates of Cardiff Arms Park. At half-past one the ground was at its capacity and the gates were shut. From then until the players took to the field an hour later, the excitement built. There was something in the air that began to say it was going to be the Red Dragons' day.

When both sides came out on to the field, the crowd erupted. Match time at last! The All Blacks grouped together for their haka, and the crowd fell respectfully silent. Following the enactment of the war cry, the delighted masses roared their appreciation, clapping and cheering. Then they suddenly fell silent again as the Welsh team clustered together in the middle of the field. The players in red began to sing their anthem. Their voices were joined by 40,000 more, and a thunderous, rousing rendition of 'Hen Wlad Fy Nhadau' ('Land of My Fathers') reverberated around the stadium and its neighbourhood. These were special moments in football history and unlike anything the All Blacks had experienced before.

Refereeing the match was a former Scottish international, 27-year-old John Dallas. From the opening whistle, Dallas saw nothing legal in Gallaher's play, particularly when it came to feeding the ball into the scrum. The ball would barely leave Gallaher's hands before the shrill of Dallas's whistle was heard and an advantage given to Wales. As time wore on, in absolute frustration but with a confidence in his own players, Gallaher instructed his front-rankers not to hook the ball. He would put it in and the Welsh team would win the scrum. It was better to try to defend from the area of the scrum than to constantly cede territory through penalties. Dixon observed:

Gallaher was frequently being penalized, and the spectators showed a degree of bitterness towards him and other members of the team that did not coincide with the warmth of their welcome and was in striking contrast to the generous spirit of many other crowds, and notably of the Irishmen.

The tumult on the sideline continued unabated as the Welsh side had the better of the first 30 minutes of the match and their supporters willed their boys to score. The New Zealand backs somehow contrived to muddle many of their moves and fluff easy passes. Their kicks were aimless and defence unorganized as the Welsh counter-attacked. Gallaher and the other forwards found themselves running forward and back, following the leather that flew over their heads to whence it had just come. But for all that, they held their line until a scrum was held just inside the All Black 25. As the scrum crabbed from side to side, Welsh halfback Owen made as if he was going to run down the blindside. The New Zealand backline defence was drawn towards his intended run. Then he stopped, turned the other way and sent the ball out to his backs. Quickly it went through Welsh hands — Cliff Pritchard then Bush then Gabe — as the All Black backs scrambled to defend the space left open by Owen's cunning misdirection. Welsh winger Morgan met Gabe's pass at full speed, and was past Gillett and over the line in an instant. The crowd's joy at seeing Morgan ground the ball tested the very foundations of the stands — the noise of stamping feet, clapping hands and cheers rolled around the park, as hats went skyward and hugs of delight were shared. Although the goal was missed, Wales were ahead 3–0. In the minds of the crowd, the undefeated Colonials were on their way to being toppled.

As they prepared to restart play, whatever quick words Gallaher said to his team snapped his men out of their malaise. They had a renewed vigour and the backs suddenly discovered their accuracy. It was the turn of Wales to defend. Every tackle that felled an All Black drew a roar from the crowd. Then, two minutes before halftime, with the All Blacks hammering away at the Welsh line, referee Dallas unexpectedly whistled for the interval.

During the break, as Gallaher stood with the other members of the team, Stead approached him. Gallaher was deep in thought. His own play was under terrible scrutiny from the inexperienced referee and the vocal crowd. His backs — with the exception of Roberts — were giving their worst display of the tour. The quality Welsh side were reaping the benefits of this and their own thorough preparation. Stead's view of the game from the sideline led him to offer a suggestion to his skipper:

'Why don't you play two wing-forwards and one five-eighth and let the Welsh have the ball?'

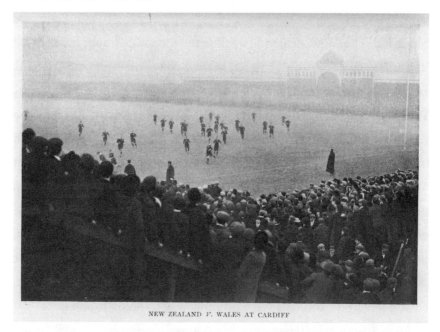

NEW ZEALAND V. WALES AT CARDIFF

The All Blacks on attack against Wales at Cardiff Arms Park, 16 December 1905, the only loss of the 'Originals' tour. MATT ELLIOTT COLLECTION

Gallaher looked at his diminutive vice-captain. He knew the little Southlander had an extraordinary feel for the technical aspects of the game and the ability to envisage aspects of play that few dared, or could, imagine. He pondered the risky proposal. 'In front of this crowd? Would you be game to?'

The game resumed with no positional changes.

The All Blacks were dominant throughout the second half and had their chances. Errors and tremendous defence — such as Welsh players holding Mynott up over the line — continued to render them scoreless. A score by McGregor was ruled out after Dallas and the line umpire adjudged the final pass as forward. The clock continued to tick, and the shadow of defeat began to rise up behind the team.

Then, out of nothing came another opportunity. After the ball had been hacked through by the Welsh forwards from a lineout, the covering Wallace scooped up the ball. On the left-hand side of the field, and just inside his own half, he saw more space than defenders ahead of him. Off he went, building a scything run, typical of the wonderful pace and vision he possessed. Several defenders were unable to even land a hand on him. He continued on to inside the Welsh 25. The tryline loomed. The crowd was yelling for their boys — for *anything* — to stop him. The equalizing score was the blink of an eye away, but there was still one red-jerseyed man who could save the day: Welsh fullback Winfield. He hadn't put a foot wrong all game. Then, at his shoulder, Wallace heard Deans calling for a pass. Drawing Winfield he sent the ball to the young Cantabrian who charged on. There were no red jerseys in front of him, just a white line. Changing direction slightly, he headed towards the posts mindful of the team needing a try and a goal to win the match. This change of angle was a blessing to a chasing, desperate Welsh defender, Morgan. Deans was now within reach. As the solid centre made his dive for the line, Morgan's arms wrapped around his legs and the players fell to ground. What happened over the next few seconds has been a matter of conjecture ever since.

The New Zealand players' view — best recounted by Wallace as he had been right up with the play — was that Deans grounded the ball over the line and then was pulled back into the field of play by the arriving Welsh players. The ball, he said, was moved similarly. Gillett, for one, had no doubt that Deans had scored. 'Deans went over the line by about nine inches and grounded the ball. A man from behind him pulled him back, and another who was on the line pushed him. I was close up to Deans at the time.' Nicholson had taken one of the sideline flags from Stead and watched the play unfold. 'It was a try, true enough,' he later said.

The Welsh opinion was that Deans was brought down about six inches short of the line. Gabe is said to have asked Deans after the game: 'Why did you try to wriggle onward?'

Referee Dallas was some way behind the play, and when he arrived (with the crowd in stunned silence according to some reports) he saw the position of the ball and whistled 'no try'. The silence was broken by the ecstatic crowd and the protestations of several of the All Blacks.

Did Deans score? Rugby historians have playfully argued over that question for a century. No examination here will change the score. The controversy was one between two rugby-mad nations, and it became a moment, not to divide two rivals who have rugby as their national game, but rather an important moment shared.

Play resumed, but there was no fairytale finish for the All Blacks. The final whistle sounded. Wales had won 3–0.

As the jubilant crowd celebrated, Gallaher went and shook the hand of Welsh captain, Nicholls, and was then stopped and interviewed by a Welsh reporter, perhaps hoping, in the heat of the defeat, to get some controversial words from the tour's most debated player. Not surprisingly, Gallaher didn't make an issue of it. He knew his side had not played well. Ultimately, they were responsible for their loss, not the referee. The reporter asked Gallaher what he thought of the match. 'It was a rattling good game played out to the bitter end with the result that the best team won.'

'Is there any point about the defeat which you regard as unsatisfactory?' he probed.

'No. As I said before, the better team won and I am content.'

'Did your team play up to its best form?'

'On that point I have nothing to say.'

'What of the refereeing? Have you an opinion favourable or otherwise to express?'

Apparently, this question brought a wry smile to Gallaher's face and he replied: 'I have always made it a point never to express a view regarding the referee in any match in which I have played so you must excuse me.'

Another press-man reported Gallaher's comments to him as: 'We have met our Waterloo. Wales beat us at our own game, and all I can say is that Welshmen ought to feel proud of their side. Winfield, at back, was excellent and I have not yet seen a centre to beat your "old crock" Nicholls.'

Such graciousness in defeat drew praise from the *Welsh Daily News* who wrote that 'Gallaher ... is, like the rest of the members of the team, a thundering good sportsman.'

Manager Dixon wrote in his diary post-match: 'That [there] was an absolutely fair try there is overwhelming evidence, including Gabe who tackled Deans as he was fading and pulled him back into play and Llewellyn the Welsh line umpire.' While he had no beef with the Welsh players, he was highly critical of referee Dallas.

The refereeing was not what would be called first class according to my standards. What would be thought of a referee in NZ who went out to control a first class game on a greasy surface in ordinary walking boots, no buttons on them and clad in heavy ordinary clothing including orthodox stiff high collar?

However, Dixon did concede that 'I am of the opinion that on the day the NZ team did not deserve to win but they actually made a draw of it I am assured. Draw fair reflection of play.' He also commented late that 'I have never known a player to be so violently and unjustly attacked as was Gallaher by the Welsh papers after the International match.'

The *Manchester Guardian*'s correspondent reported that Cardiff 'was throbbing with excitement'.

Plethoric with the emotions of their team's great victory, Welshmen everywhere are singing and dancing and cheering and generally enjoying themselves with good humoured extravagance of conduct. … Immediately after the match, I encountered a company of men, with leeks in their caps cheering and dancing.

As word spread that the win for Wales may have been controversial, the *Daily Mail* sent a return cable to the All Blacks' hotel asking who claimed to have scored. Deans sent a famous reply. 'Grounded ball 6 inches over line. Some of Welsh players admit try. Hunter and Glasgow can confirm was pulled back by Welshmen before Referee arrived. Deans.'

Perhaps the answer to the controversy lies in that very answer by the 21-year-old who had the ball at the crucial moment. Bob Deans was a man whose sincerity, maturity and unquestioning generosity were remarkable for someone his age. He was honest as the day is long. Never was his integrity questioned in any capacity by those who knew him personally or played alongside him. There is no reason to think that his character would change to the extent that he would lie in the aftermath of a match.

Back in New Zealand the result did not come through until Sunday morning. In Christchurch, the *Lyttelton Times* reported that 'for an hour after the announcement Cathedral Square was dotted with groups of talkers, nervous, dejected-looking critics who spoke calmly enough, but very sadly, of the national calamity'. Premier Seddon's son Tom recalled:

> *On the afternoon when New Zealand sustained this staggering blow my father took my brothers and me for a consoling drive in a cab to help us forget the sad fate that had befallen our heroes. The cab horses clonked along Jervois Quay until we came to the curving shore of Oriental Bay — and there we saw groups of men clustered at various points, all discussing the dismal Sunday afternoon news.*

As time passed and the full report of the match was published in New Zealand newspapers, so incensed was the rugby public by the 'stolen' result that even schoolchildren sang a jingle which began: 'Taffy was a Welshman, Taffy was a thief.'

There is a nice story about a small Welsh lad who was selling mourning cards in the aftermath of the All Blacks' loss. He approached a man who was standing smoking on the steps of a hotel. The boy, who had no idea he was approaching Gallaher, asked the man if he wanted to buy a card. Gallaher smiled and politely declined, saying, 'No, thanks, I was at the funeral myself.'

It was a controversy that remained alive. In 1924, Teddy Morgan signed a dinner programme for Billy Wallace, writing the words *Deans did score*. For decades New Zealand rugby fans, accompanying All Black tours to Wales or on their own travels, visited Cardiff Arms Park to make a pilgrimage to where the incident occurred, and ground staff obligingly escorted them to that 'spot'.

The unbeaten record was gone. Now the task was to make sure that that was the only loss. There was no respite for the side and little time for disappointment, as they had to play four more games in Wales — against Glamorgan County, Newport, Cardiff and Swansea. Those sides now had confidence that they could also topple the no-longer invincible All Blacks.

In the lead-up to the match against Glamorgan, countless hours were spent by Dixon in a dispute with the Welsh union over the lack of consultation regarding the appointment of the referee. So heated did the issue get that Dixon threatened that the All Blacks would not play the game. Gallaher, apparently at the urging of local councillors and businessmen, was the mediator responsible for the game going ahead.

Glamorgan were dispatched 9–0. They played a niggly game, highlighted by the fact that Gallaher suffered a badly bitten finger. He missed the next game, against Newport — an encounter played at a cracking pace for a 6–3 victory — as a result of the chomp on his digit. The match with Cardiff was played on Boxing Day. The team had celebrated Christmas Day by themselves in a large dining room, eating, drinking, and opening telegrams from family and friends back home. For many it was the first time they had experienced a winter Christmas — and this one was memorable, not for snow, but for fog.

The Arms Park was the venue once more, and again a merry crowd flowed into the park, expecting the All Blacks would be defeated by the black-and-white hoops of the champion Welsh club side.

It was another game played at great pace, with both sides spending periods on attack that stretched their opponents' defence, but the breaches were few. The noticeably weary All Blacks had to contend with Cardiff backs who had in their number the internationals

Winfield, Gabe and Nicholls. Gallaher suffered a cacophony of hoots and whistles every time he put the ball into the scrum, until he moved from wing-forward to hooker, when O'Sullivan fell awkwardly in a tackle and broke his collarbone. This not only left the All Blacks a man down, but also ceded possession to Cardiff for the put-in at every scrum.

The match was won 10–8, but could easily have been lost were it not for a howler of a mistake from the Cardiff captain and flyhalf, Percy Bush.

With the scores locked at 5–5, and only 15 minutes left to play, Seeling led the forwards in a dribbling rush, then toed the ball forward over the Cardiff goal-line. Bush was at the ball first, but, rather than just touch the ball down for a restart, he looked to hack the still rolling ball into touch. As his foot came down, the ball took a mocking turn on its point and rolled away. Bush had to watch as Seeling, with Nicholson close behind, dived on the ball for the try. Wallace converted. Cardiff scored a late try themselves, but the goal was not successful.

The All Blacks knew they had been fortunate to win. Gallaher told a reporter that 'It was a very hard game, and the result was in the balance to the end. I think Cardiff is a long way the best club side we have met.' Bush was inconsolable, with one newspaper reporting that his 'acute mental distress at his acknowledged blunder was obviously great. Tears welled in his eyes as he said, "I don't know how I did it; I don't know why I did it, but it will be a life-long memory for me".'

Swansea was the last Welsh challenge to be met and repelled, but again it was a narrow escape. Assembling a side to take the St Helen's Ground was still an issue, and Gallaher had to play at hooker. It was a sunny afternoon, but a strong wind was at Swansea's backs in the first half. At halftime the All Blacks were 0–3 down, but turned confident that the wind behind them would aid their flagging efforts. As the minutes ticked by only one scoring opportunity presented itself, and Duncan McGregor thought he had scored a good try but it was disallowed. According to Wallace, he:

> … *grounded the ball over the goaline but the line umpire raised his flag for stepping into touch. Our chaps protested and when the straw [that had been raked to the touch lines having covered the ground to protect against frost] was cleared away we found Duncan had missed stepping into touch by at least a couple of yards!*

Ten minutes from the final whistle, Wallace caught a clearing kick, ran forward towards the Swansea 25-yard line, and, taking into account the wind, let fly with a drop kick that broke Swansea hearts as the brown dot sailed between the posts.

The match ended shortly after, a scrambling 4–3 win. The rugged December of rugby was over.

France, North America, and the Return

The crowd called for Gallaher to speak.

It was a relief for the team to leave the fervent valleys of Wales and make their way to Paris for a match (not originally planned) against France, although some members of the party openly expressed the feeling that they would rather be sailing for home than across the English Channel to Calais. They were tired, some were unwell, and Gallaher himself was looking drawn and weary. George Dixon noted:

> *In the early stages of the tour, it was a treat to watch the boys enter the field of play — eagerly, with free, buoyant steps, every man evidently bubbling over with vitality, for all the world like a team of young racehorses. But towards the end they demeaned themselves, by comparison, like a team of working bullocks. The eagerness, the*

exuberant vitality, were all gone, and the impression created was
that the game ahead of them was regarded no longer as a pleasure,
but a task.

There was excitement to be had in being on the Continent and in one of its most fabled cities for New Year's Eve, though. With little thought for the match the next day, the team went out for the night, visiting such Parisian landmarks as the Folies Bergère and the Olympia Theatre. Poor old Jimmy Duncan got lost and wandered the streets for some time before he finally came across Gallaher and Dixon, who guided him back to their hotel.

In the morning, after a leisurely start to the day, the team was driven in motor cars the 15 miles to the match at the Parc des Princes ground. It was a journey the players found hair-raising, as the Parisian drivers raced each other on icy roads. Once at the park, there was a relaxed atmosphere to the occasion. An estimated 8,000 spectators, including a large number of Englishmen, had assembled to watch France's first-ever test match. (France had won a gold medal for rugby at the 1900 Olympics held as part of the World's Fair in Paris, although the other two teams were club sides from Germany and England.) The game took place on a gravelly surface which was ringed by a velodrome. The surface was probably in a worse state than that of Inverleith earlier in the tour: still hard with overnight frost and a light drizzle was falling, adding to the cold. The difference, however, was that the hosts were warm, amiable, and thoroughly appreciative of the visit by 'les Zélandais'.

There were some small difficulties with communication due to the fact none of the New Zealanders spoke fluent French, but this became sources of amusement rather than frustration. The French captain —

Henri Armand from the Stade Français club — was delighted that the team who had developed such a reputation across the English Channel was taking the time to meet his charges on the field. With a geniality reflective of this excitement, he insisted there be no coin toss and that Gallaher choose in which direction they wanted to play. Gallaher responded to this compliment by taking the less advantageous side, playing into the wind and light rain. Gallaher was always quick to respond to the challenge laid down by an opponent, but he enjoyed nothing more than seeing players assemble simply for the love of the game. Billy Wallace observed that Gallaher and Armand 'took an instant liking to each other, as one would expect of two such fine sportsmen'.

The All Blacks quickly discovered that, although the French had some of the largest forwards they had encountered on their tour, and could tackle with some ferocity, they were technically immature when it came to play. But that did not stop them achieving something which most of the teams in Great Britain had found impossible to do — score a try. This sent the crowd into waves of Gallic delight, much to the amusement of the All Blacks on the field and sitting in the stand. Running rugby was the nature of the game, as nobody wanted to be manhandled onto the rocky ground. By halftime the visitors were out to an 18–3 lead.

At the break, Gallaher instructed his team to take it easy for the early part of the half, which resulted in another try to France shortly after play recommenced. Again the crowd burst into celebration, shouting their praise and even mimicking the haka. With the score at 18–8, the All Blacks returned to playing a bit more seriously, and, thanks to slick midfield passing and well-rehearsed moves, ran in another six tries to win 38–8.

At the conclusion of the match Gallaher (sporting a cut to his face from falling hard on the gravelly surface, which had seen him have to leave the field temporarily) and Armand exchanged jerseys. A reporter asked Gallaher for his thoughts on the match. 'They are fine sportsmen, these French. I am surprised to see that they show such a comprehension of the game, which is greater than any evinced by very many of the British teams we have met,' he said. 'The work of their forwards was admirable, although the backs left a good deal to be desired.' He told another that he considered the French spectators to be the most sporting and unbiased of any he had played in front of.

At last the tour was over. They had played in as much of a celebratory mood as they could, given the conditions, and the French players had been enthusiastic companions. That evening the two teams dined together at the Champeaux restaurant. As the wine flowed, communication became easier and the sides mingled more freely. Toasts were made. Gallaher and Armand could often be seen in close conversation, Gallaher enjoying the expressive Frenchman's delight in talking football with the famous captain. The teams moved on to the nightlife of Montmartre, where, at a ball, the All Blacks were asked to perform their haka.

The next two days were spent sightseeing. Gallaher, the military man, was particularly interested in visiting Napoleon Bonaparte's tomb at L'Hôtel national des Invalides, a large series of buildings dedicated to French military leaders and history, as well as the recently opened military museum, Musée de l'Armée.

When their stay was over they went by train back to Boulogne, where they boarded a ship to England. They arrived wearily, but with thoughts of packing their bags one final time and at last heading home. That was until Dixon received a cablegram from the NZRFU, informing him that Premier Seddon's government would pay for the team to travel on to America for well-earned rest and relaxation … which would also involve a series of exhibition matches. The government hadn't supported the tour financially at the outset, but now that they were a success Seddon wanted the rugby missionaries to continue their work, under the guise of reward.

Dixon was unimpressed. In his words, the addendum to their tour was 'a confounded nuisance. Would much rather have gone aboard the steamer to enjoy a six-week rest and immunity from letters, callers, newspapers and worries generally.' The players' reactions were mixed. Some wanted to come home — and in fact Harper and Glenn left the party to return via the Suez Canal, while Seeling and Johnston made their way back via direct steamer. Others considered it a once-in-a-lifetime opportunity to visit America. The side now had the best part of three weeks' break before departing for America.

While Dixon set about organizing the logistics of the trip, some of the team headed off around the British Isles to visit relatives. Numerous invitations were received from clubs and societies wanting to host players at social functions or have players turn out for their football teams.

Two days before the All Blacks' departure for America, High Commissioner in London William Pember Reeves sent his impressions of the tour to Premier Seddon, praising the 'admirable personal conduct' of team members:

… the feeling that prevailed amongst them was one of remarkable cordiality and loyal co-operation. Something [that] was no doubt due

to the tact and firmness of their manager and to the sportsmanlike example of Mr Gallaher, the captain; but the main credit, of course, has been owing to the men themselves. It is with genuine pleasure that I am able to bear testimony to the manner in which they have upheld the good name of New Zealand in the Mother Country, not only as athletes but as sportsmen and gentlemen.

In his reply, Seddon boastfully wrote:

The success of the team is unparalleled in the history of athletics. Their only reverse, small as it was, is more attributable to the fortunes of war than to any superiority in the team that carried the laurels on that historical day. It was indeed a glorious victory, and one of which the Welsh are rightly proud. ... The triumph of the team is not only a credit to the colony, but to the Empire. ... Such exchanges are of great material advantage, as they keep distant parts of the Empire in touch with the centre, remove false impressions, promote commerce, and encourage interdependence and goodwill, and these principles are especially true when the visitors are men and gentlemen. They were all splendid men, well captained and well managed.

The *Daily Mail* summed up the crux of Seddon's reply in simple, economic terms: 'The New Zealand Agency may spend £1000 per annum advertising New Zealand but the "All Black" "ad" is worth "millions".'

A large crowd gathered at Waterloo Station to farewell Gallaher's men, among them Rowland Hill, Percy Coles, and assorted members of clubs and counties. A handful of the players were decidedly fatigued after a farewell dinner and dance hosted by the London New Zealand

Society, where Gallaher, as captain, had been presented with a bronze medal inscribed with the tour results on it. His fellow players received a photograph of the medal.

Reporting on the departure, one newspaperman made a point of noting that none of the team had been lost to the Northern Union game. A spontaneous singing of 'Auld Lang Syne' broke out from the well-wishers, and the All Blacks responded with their haka. As the team were preparing to board the train, a newspaperman asked Gallaher for a message. His parting words were: 'Boys who want to play football well must take pains, be good sportsmen, play the game as it should be played, and keep very fit. That is what all young New Zealand boys do who aspire to become great players in time. There's nothing like rugby for a boy.'

A large crowd waited for them to then arrive in Southampton before they made their way to the ship that would carry them across the Atlantic, the SS *New York*.

❧❧✦❧❧

Seven days after leaving England, the ship arrived in New York. Two days were spent absorbing the sights and sounds of the streets of New York, and marvelling at its Manhattan skyline. The team then played an exhibition match in Brooklyn against a New York team. The whole arrangement was makeshift. The field was usually used for baseball, the New York team had six of the All Blacks in their ranks (and eight Englishmen) while Dixon refereed. A crowd of only 500 watched the All Blacks run out winners by 46–13. This was the most points conceded by the team on tour — but they had all been scored by their own teammates!

From there the team travelled to Niagara then Chicago, Kansas City, the Grand Canyon, and finally San Francisco. Two games had been arranged on the west coast at the University of California Los Angeles and at Recreation Park, San Francisco, against players from Vancouver assembled as a British Columbia side. Both were comprehensive victories, 43–6 and 65–6.

Before the team finally boarded a ship for home, they had two days in Los Angeles. Excluding the New York exhibition match, the side had played 35 games, losing just the one. They had scored 243 tries and a total of 976 points. They conceded a mere 59 points, with 20 of those coming in the last three games. Gallaher and Wallace had played 26 games, Glasgow 27, Stead 29, and Fred Roberts 30.

Over a century after the tour, a number of point-scoring records remain from the visit by Gallaher's men to the British Isles and Ireland, such as Billy Wallace's 217 points and Jimmy Hunter's 40 tries.

Given that over a dozen tours of the British Isles have followed in the footsteps of the Originals, these are remarkable records. The dawning of the professional era saw such tours reduced to the point where the rugby calendar is now dominated by test matches. Rarely is the term 'midweek game' heard in relation to a touring rugby team. So, one can say with certainty that these records will never be beaten, further immortalizing the 27 players, guided by Gallaher, who set the precedent of style and attitude for All Black teams visiting the northern hemisphere.

While there had been little interest in the departure of Gallaher's side, their return was an entirely different matter. On 6 March 1906, word quickly spread around Auckland that the ship carrying the team, the *Sonoma*, was within sight, and hundreds streamed down to the quayside. At mid-afternoon, with the anchor set, a health officer and Premier Seddon (making sure he was one of the first to greet the team) and rugby union officials went out to the ship. The players — most of them having put on weight while they were away — were milling on the decks, being courted by circling ferry steamers that were full of excited well-wishers. When the health officer had given the players and other passengers the all-clear, another steamer drew alongside and the players filed onto it for the short trip to the quay.

By now an estimated 10,000 had surrounded the landing point, taking whatever vantage point they could to see their heroes. Their response to sighting the players was deafening. Archival film footage of the day shows the players alighting from the boat, shaking the hand of the delighted ship's captain. Most have cigarettes in their hands. Some carry trophies of the trip. The players look very relaxed, even a little relieved to be home at last. One by one they descend before they make their way to the carriage that would take them firstly to their hotel and then up Queen Street to their civic reception in Philson's Square (since built on, opposite the Auckland Art Gallery on the corner of Wellesley and Kitchener streets). The team, in their white-and-black-banded straw hats atop a brake, was piped up to the town square. Cheers and hoorays broke out along Auckland's streets as they passed. Alighting from the brake, they made their way through the excited crowd to a platform in the middle of the main square. The Mayor of Auckland, Mr Myers, and Seddon were among the official party. As the All Blacks made their way to the platform, cheers rang out for each. A newspaper scribe noted that the 'heartiest being not unnaturally for Gallaher, the popular captain'.

Myers welcomed the side, paid tribute to their success, and said it was Auckland's privilege to be the first to greet them. Seddon received a rousing cheer as he stood to address the assembled. It was a colourful speech by a noted orator, but one which probably caused some embarrassment to members of the team. (In fact, in a photograph of the reception included here, as Seddon talks, Gallaher sits uncomfortably, head bowed, chin on hand.) 'The team went with the intention of playing the national game. A team had gone before,' Seddon bellowed:

... and the Native team had left its mark, but when the 'All Blacks', superseding the brown and representing the all whites, went to the Old Country what a change their play worked! In the Welsh international match the men had gallantly fought an uphill game to the finish. They had not questioned the result, but in their hearts and in the opinion of most people, it was recognized that morally this was not a defeat, but try to try. ... Nothing in Wales had happened for years that had brought it into such prominence as the try against the New Zealanders.

He proposed three cheers and the response was 'such as perhaps had never before been heard in Auckland'.

George Dixon responded that the welcome was on a scale unimaginable to the team as they were returning. He spoke of how well received the team had been in the Mother Country, from the King down to those not greatly interested in football.

Then the crowd called for Gallaher to speak. The cheering was thunderous as he got up from his seat. He thanked the previous speakers for their kind words, and in a short reply said:

When the team set out we had hopes of winning every match, but, as Premier Seddon said, we were beaten by the Welsh leek. We did not

go behind our back to talk about the Welshmen, but candidly said that
on that day the better team had won. I have one recommendation to
make to the New Zealand Union, if it was to undertake such a tour
again, and that is to play the Welsh matches first.

He finished by paying tribute to Dixon and the NZRFU for appointing
him manager.

The Originals are welcomed home by Premier Seddon and the Auckland
public, 6 March 1906. Gallaher (centre), sporting a team white boater, has his
hand on his chin. AUCKLAND RUGBY UNION

A NZRFU-hosted dinner was held that evening for the team and 200
guests, including representatives of many other sports. It was a long
night for the weary players, with a steady stream of toasts and as
many as 20 speeches given. Gallaher stood and spoke once more,
waiting for continuous applause to subside. Among his thanks on

behalf of the team, he commented that 'the team had attempted to do away with all provincialism and had succeeded', words that had Seddon nodding his approval, but might still have made at least one of the southern members of the touring party shift slightly in his seat. However, that Saturday in August on the *Rimutaka*, when Gallaher had tendered his resignation, was a long way behind the team now. The players were presented with a medal and a photograph of their touring party. The next morning they began to disperse to their homes around the country.

Making their way back to the South Island, Deans and Duncan were interviewed by a reporter in Wellington. Deans was glad to be home. 'It did get pretty tiresome towards the end and the fellows were pretty sick of it before we finished up in England,' he said. 'It was the travelling and want of rest, and then the hard matches were left to the last.'

Then came a question about the Welsh match. Deans looked at the reporter. 'You mean my try? Well, it was as fair a try as has ever been scored.'

Duncan added: 'I can't see how the referee could not see it as we could see it from the far end.' The reporter then asked about the treatment of Gallaher by referee Dallas. 'The referee went out to penalize Gallaher — there is no doubt about that,' said Deans.

'But Dave never turned a hair, and as to his unfairness of putting the ball into the scrum, look at the Cardiff match,' added Duncan. 'Gallaher had to go in the scrum yet we got the ball pretty well all the time. The people who attended the matches were pretty good sports, but the Welsh have only one eye — an eye for their own men.'

Once back in Dunedin, Duncan did speak out against Gallaher's position: 'There is one part of our formation I hope to see obliterated before long. I refer to the wing-forward. The innovation should be abolished because it spoils the game, and is responsible for continual offside play.'

However, while there was great outcry over Gallaher's positional play and the role and legality of the wing-forward, it remained a feature of New Zealand teams for almost 30 more years, and the next All Black side to tour the Home nations (in 1924–25) was captained by Cliff Porter, who played in the same position. The wing-forward became obsolete when changes to the scrum laws regulated that front rows must contain three players, rather than the two New Zealand had persisted with.

The years 1903–06 were, arguably, the most extraordinary and important in New Zealand rugby history. The first All Black test was played against Australia; Great Britain were hosted for the first domestic test; and Gallaher's Originals cemented in place the reputation of the men in black, one that future sides would look to emulate. The black jersey (fortunately to this day still more of a uniform than a moving advertising hoarding) was well on its way to becoming one of the most recognizable and revered strips in world sport.

The Complete Rugby Footballer

*'The best work that has been
published on the Rugby game.'*

While Gallaher had been less engaging with newspapermen, apart from Buttery, as the tour had progressed — due in large part to his treatment in a variety of sporting columns — at its conclusion he contributed some of his thoughts to a 1906 *Daily Mail* publication compiled by Buttery called *Why the All Blacks Triumphed*, which chronicled the trip alongside comment from a number of the All Blacks' opponents. Gallaher's piece for the tour souvenir was titled 'The Secret of our Success', in which he argued for the legality of the wing-forward and compared playing styles between his team and those in Great Britain and Ireland.

Manager George Dixon's diary entries were the basis for another tour souvenir called *The Triumphant Tour of the New Zealand Foot-ballers*. It was a very affordable and popular release, selling locally for a shilling. (Original editions are now prized collector's items worth several hundred dollars.) Principally a game-by-game account of the tour, combined with newspaper reports of matches, there is very little in the way of behind-the-scenes content. No mention is made of Gallaher's offered resignation aboard the *Rimutaka*. In fact, the boat journey received only one paragraph of coverage, which concluded: 'Of the relationships of the members of the team, it can only be said that it was a very happy family and that Gallaher, in the capacity of skipper, proved himself thoroughly and justifiably popular.' Gallaher contributed 'The Captain's Retrospect' to this book.

As the tour of Great Britain had progressed, and the New Zealanders' on-field wizardry amazed crowds, stunned sporting scribes and puzzled administrators, Gallaher was approached by an English publisher, Henry Leach, who, with a history of publishing sports books, saw a market for a book on the skills and tactics of the All Blacks. Books on the evolving game's skills and tactics were not uncommon. Prominent players in England had turned their hand to instruction manuals on the fledgling sport.

In New Zealand, Tom Ellison had published *The Art of Rugby Football* as recently as 1902. Its release was a return to prominence of sorts for Ellison. Following his key role in the establishment of the NZRFU and his admission to the bar — he is believed to be the first Maori to achieve this — he attempted unsuccessfully to enter Parliament three times. On each occasion he failed to secure the nomination as the candidate for the Southern Maori seat. The reason for that may be found in an event no mention of which appears to have been made in profiles celebrating his achievements. In 1895 he was allegedly involved in the death of a 14-year-old girl whom he was sexually involved with. When she fell pregnant, Ellison — according to court reports — paid

£25 for a back-street abortion. The girl died. Ellison and two others were charged with conducting an illegal operation.

His book was a thin tome, but one which was technically adept and perfectly encapsulated facets of play that made up the New Zealand 'style' of football.

The 1905 tourists' play was seen as so revolutionary — and had created such enormous interest even in those who had no real knowledge of football — that Leach was certain such a book would sell well in the aftermath of the tour.

The offer was £100 for the work. Gallaher had reservations about the project, given the relatively short timeframe for delivery of the manuscript. He discussed it with Stead. The idea appealed to the vice-captain, so, after agreeing to terms with Leach, they went to his home to begin work. At the publisher's Herne Hill residence, both men were assigned a stenographer to record their words. This arrangement wasn't fruitless, but the content — more memoir than textbook — wasn't in the direction the players wanted it to be. Gallaher and Stead went for a wander around nearby Clapham Common. Stead later said that Gallaher, presumably frustrated by the disjointed nature of their pairing and the looming deadline, wanted to abandon the work. But Stead's mind was already at work, and he told Gallaher he'd write the text if Gallaher could assemble photographs and drawings to accompany his words. Gallaher, with help from good mate George Tyler, set about his task of sourcing photos and having diagrams of scrum formations and back play drawn. The story goes that a week later Stead had written 80,000 words long-hand and the payment from Leach was used to put on a party for the team.

Whether the deadline for the book was only seven days is another of the myths attached to this team. Certainly, the deadline would have been a short one, especially as the team was due to move on to North America. The writing most likely took place in the weeks between when the All Blacks returned to London from France on 4 January and when they departed for North America on 20 January. Stead spoke of spending much of the last week in England sightseeing, so even a mere two weeks is still a remarkable timeframe to produce such a book. Unfortunately, no copies of the contract or other details from the publisher's records remain. Speculation as to the brevity of the time allowed for the writing of the book merely adds to how remarkable the book is.

The book is usually referred to as *The Complete Rugby Footballer*, as though Stead and Gallaher were writing a book on how to become such. However, the full title of the book is *The Complete Rugby Footballer on the New Zealand System*. This is quite different and implies that, in fact, Stead and Gallaher are the complete footballers and this is their interpretation of the New Zealand way of playing football. Many — players and public alike — were keen to have the 'secrets' of their play revealed. The players acknowledged such in their Preface:

Only half of our system, or perhaps not so much that, could be discovered by the most careful student of it who merely saw it at work on the field of play. The remainder was secret to ourselves and we conceived it to be our advantage to keep it so until we had finished our engagements.

Looking at other instructional sporting texts of the day, Mr Leach may well have thought he was going to receive a much slimmer volume from the authors. Nineteen chapters, 35 photos, set-piece plays, and extensive appendices make up the 322 pages of the book. It begins with the development of rugby in New Zealand, and ends with a summary of the 1905 tour. In between, there are all-encompassing chapters on the idea of the game, possession of the ball, the wing-forward, scrum and lineout play, tactics, captaincy, dangers to the game, how the 1905 team prepared for their matches, and the laws of the game.

In 'Chapter XV: Good Rules', there are pieces of advice which retain their relevance and could be adhered to by amateurs and professionals in the modern game:

A little bad temper will neutralize a lot of very fine skill. A reputation for the former will overshadow a reputation for the other, and a player of magnificent ability may find his prospects ruined by his disposition. Play right up to the whistle. Remember that what may appear to you to be a breach of the rules may not appear so to the referee.

Never play to the gallery. You have quite enough to do to play your proper hard game, and any player (except perhaps a full back) who remembers comments made by people in the crowd has certainly not been as keen during the match as he should have been.

Never play 'dirty' or 'foul'. Do to others as you would like them to do to you. Nevertheless, when you tackle a man, tackle him hard, and see that you put him down. Accidents resulting from real hard tackling are very rare.

Stead's was the hand that wrote out the text, but there are sections that indicate quite obviously that Gallaher was standing over his shoulder much of the time. This is best illustrated in descriptions of club football, which have quite an Auckland slant, or the methods of play for forwards. In the 'Good Rules' chapter, one item and its content (some highlighted by the current author) stand out as that of the Boer War veteran rather than of a Southland man whose off-field occupation was bootmaker:

The situation is sometimes tantalising when a man injured on the other side insists on continuing to play, though at a great disadvantage and possibly in pain. What are you to do when he has the ball, and it is your duty to take it from him? Take it from him. You must without doubt treat him exactly as if you were unaware of his injury or indisposition, and tackle him just as forcibly. The simple rules of war must of necessity apply to all such cases. The man who remains on the field must be treated as a combatant. *If he is unfit to play he has no business to continue to do so, and must accept all the risks involved in his persistency. If a player were to make the slightest allowance for an injured opponent,* he might one day find himself shot at by a man who had flown the white flag. *Rugby football matches must be conducted on sound business principles, and sentiment can have no place in them.*

Curiously, in the opening chapter of the book, which charts the evolution of football and the key men responsible for the development of it in the United Kingdom and New Zealand, there is no mention whatsoever of Tom Ellison, one of the country's best-known and most influential players and administrators.

Gallaher was well aware of the Natives tour of 1888–89 and of their achievements. Being part-Maori, Stead was, too. He claimed to have had a schoolboy thrill in carrying the boots of the great Joe Warbrick when the Natives (with Ellison as part of the team) played Southland, in August 1888. However, the history section reads as though it was written by somebody other than Gallaher and Stead. If so, it would seem even more puzzling for there to be such an oversight. Also overlooked is Jimmy Duncan.

Such are the authors' insights into the basics of the game that the tome remains a timeless one. Technically, the book is marvellously astute. There are even suggestions for referees and law-makers, such as changing some penalties to free kicks, which were eventually adopted decades after the book was published.

However, there are instances where the sociological aspects of the game have changed enormously and some passages betray the period in which it was written. One such piece — 'The Influence of the Fair Sex' — refers to the role of 'ladies' in New Zealand football:

Everywhere ladies are admitted free to both ground and stands, and, while this is a nice compliment to pay to the sex, it is from the business point of view of the Union very much more than a compliment. … It may not always be realized how powerful is the influence of one's womenkind in a game like this. If the ladies are encouraged to take a keen interest in the game, to understand it thoroughly, and to follow the doings of the clubs and players with enthusiasm, their favourable attitude affects the game in several ways. When a man finds his form and the performances of his club matters of criticism, not only among his own club-fellows, but in his home circle among the ladies belonging to it — and among the ladies in whom he may be interested in other home circles — he obtains a stimulus which in some respects is perhaps more powerful than any other, though he may not admit it, and may not even be aware that such is the case. The situation of such a player is far happier and brighter than that of a man who in his own household finds complete ignorance concerning his chief hobby, in which he is so closely interested, and either silence concerning it or else irritating expressions of indifference or even contempt, with occasional lofty but quite mistaken sermons on the evils attending the waste of one's time. … Some people who have not thought the matter out, and who do not know the sex very well, might be inclined to say that if ladies wanted to see a match a paltry sixpence or shilling would not deter them from attendance; but the desire to get everything that is to be got for nothing is much stronger in the lady than in the man.

The subject of smoking was also addressed. The risks of the habit were then largely unknown. Had the All Blacks' jerseys borne a sponsorship logo in 1905, it undoubtedly would have been that of a tobacco company or brand of cigarettes. Gallaher and Stead wrote:

The majority of our men are fairly heavy smokers, and … were to be seen pulling away at their pipes with great vigour in the dressing-room just before going out on the field of play. Suppose that for the sake of argument smoking does very slightly impair one's powers of wind and digestion, we are sure that any advantage to be derived in this respect from abstention would be more than counter-balanced by a lowering of spirits and irritation at the abstention. Pipe smoking is the best.

Reaction to the release of the book in September 1906 was unanimously one of awe. Einstein had published his first theory of relativity that revolutionized the world of science and particularly physics the year before. Gallaher and Stead's work was the sporting equivalent, theorizing on the movement and actions of players on the football field. London reviews were reprinted in New Zealand newspapers, such as that from the *Sporting and Dramatic News* which described the book as 'in some respects, the most engrossing book which has ever been written on any sport'.

It is so full of things new and strange, of a spirit of study and enterprise, which one would not have thought existed in connection with a pastime played in any country, that one feels loath to put it down until the last chapter has been perused. This book deserved to be read by everybody.

A relatively informal photo of a smoking Gallaher (back row, third from left) and other members of the 1905 team in Great Britain. AUCKLAND RUGBY UNION

EDH Sewell reviewed the book for the *Evening Standard*. Among his lengthy comments, he didn't agree with Gallaher and Stead's remarks on the wing-forward and the definition of roles for forwards at the scrum, but did write that the book was 'the best work that has been published on the Rugby game', 'the book gives us very fully, and in excellent language, the Rugby game as it must be played to attain unto the standard of New Zealand, which is, at present, clearly the highest', and finally that 'every Rugby man must have the book which needs no further recommendation'.

Decades later, Welsh historian Gareth Williams wrote that the book 'brought a startlingly new technical dimension to rugby literature, raising it to a level of sophistication previously unheard of and rarely exceeded since'.

Veteran New Zealand rugby writer Lindsay Knight commented in his book *They Led the All Blacks* that the reason the book remains so important a century after its publication is that:

> ... *with its analysis of tactics and the game's mechanics, and its tips on training and preparation, it is the virtual blueprint for that pattern and precise planning which have become such features of All Black rugby. ... [T]here is little doubt that its distinctive clarity and logical thinking had their genesis in the strong minds of Gallaher and Stead and in their deep comprehension of rugby in its many facets.*

It remains one of the rarest and most prized sporting rugby titles. Copies, when they do appear for sale, which is rarely, have been known to sell for over a thousand dollars.

Some months after the release of Gallaher and Stead's book came another. Wellington postal clerk and club footballer AH Baskerville wrote his *Modern Rugby Football: New Zealand methods* because, according to his introductory piece:

> ... *the writer of this book conceived the idea of compiling a work describing the methods in vogue in New Zealand, and how the Maorilanders train for the game. The writer is not aware that there is a book at present on the market explaining the modern game in such a manner.*

Baskerville surely was aware of fellow Wellingtonian Ellison's book, and one can question his ignorance of the existence of the Gallaher and Stead work, given the amount of publicity about its impending publication and the promotion of local sales at Whitcombes booksellers. His text, drawings, photographs and insight pale against those of the All Black captain and vice-captain's work. While his overview is relatively engaging, the detail is not as comprehensive or compelling, and some advice on the outfits required to be worn by players have a century-old charm to them:

> *If the rules of your club allow it, wear black trunks. They do not, after a few tumbles on a muddy field, look as dirty as a white pair does. … Underneath the jersey and trunks it is advisable to wear a cotton combination bathing suit. This is serviceable in more ways than one. It absorbs the perspiration, which would cause irritation if the woollen material were next to the skin. It also gives a player a feeling of safety and unconcern if he should at some stage of the game become aware that the greater part of his trunks is in the hands of an opponent.*

He recommended 'long brisk walks' to prepare for the rugby season but warned against the practice of 'extremists [who] go to the seaside … and there take sun baths to harden the constitution'.

Baskerville's book was no competition for Gallaher and Stead's (at barely a third of its length) and is rarely mentioned or seen today, but another of his entrepreneurial enterprises was to have much greater and longer-lasting success.

Union and Disunion

---

*'The crowded congregation was an evidence
of the esteem in which the young couple
are held by their many friends.'*

Upon Gallaher's return from the seven-month tour, the Ponsonby
Hall was packed to capacity as the Waitemata Druids Lodge
welcomed home 'Brother' Gallaher, along with Tyler, Nicholson,
Gillett and Mackrell. All made speeches, and singer of renown Mr Abel
Rowe gave his rendition of 'The All Blacks' song as part of an evening
described by one newspaper as 'the largest Druidic gathering ever seen
in Auckland'. This was just one of the many invitations extended to
returning All Blacks to attend celebratory functions. They were the
toast of their towns and cities.

Several weeks later, Gallaher was an organizer of a football match
fundraising for the Auckland Cricket Association's Cricket Coach Fund.
The two sides were footballers who donned whites during summer

against those who didn't. George Smith and a number of Auckland players joined Gallaher in the Cricketers team, but they were beaten convincingly, 0–11. It was reported that the ball used for the match was the very one used in the test match against Wales.

Dave's old colleagues from the Sixth Contingent acknowledged his success in leading the All Blacks in a May 1906 edition of their magazine:

The All Blacks — A New Zealander isn't a New Zealander unless he has rejoiced at the striking successes of our footballers in the United Kingdom. Sixers have been particularly interested in the doings of Dave Gallaher, to whom we extend a hearty welcome home and whom we congratulate on having captained the best team of athletes that ever travelled. Dave, as the first exponent, of any note at least, of the wing forward position in the Old Country was the most observed and talked-of person in the whole team, and much has been said and written for and against him (or rather his play as a winger), but principally against him. You may have noticed that a good sportsman generally turned out a good soldier, and we know Dave to be both. If he was not a good sportsman he would probably have some worse things to say against certain referees he met at Home than he has.

Around this time Gallaher wrote to the Defence Force requesting additions to his previously awarded medals: 'I beg to apply for the South African Bars for years 1901 and 1902 to which I am entitled having served over 18 months with the Sixth and Tenth contingents — the same being continuous service for that period.' They were promptly dispatched to him.

On 10 June 1906, the New Zealand public was shocked at the news of Seddon's sudden death. The big man, whose health had been deteriorating for several years, was on his way back to New Zealand after visiting Australia. He suffered a massive heart attack on board a ship that was a couple of days out of Sydney. The vessel had to return to Australia for his body to be embalmed before heading out into the Tasman again, bringing home the Premier for a state funeral.

While Gallaher had been away, the Auckland Freezing Company had become part of the Auckland Farmers' Freezing Company, but the name change didn't mean the work became any more glamorous.

Auckland's quays and Gallaher's workplaces c.1907: The Freezing Co. building (left distance) and Northern Roller Mills (far right). SIR GEORGE GREY SPECIAL COLLECTIONS, AUCKLAND LIBRARIES, 1-W1048

Constantly changing surrounds on his walk to work were reflective of a city that was growing in terms of commerce and of the operations that an elected council was responsible for. Trams now made their way up and down College Hill. At the bottom of the hill Gallaher passed the Auckland Gas Company's huge iron gasometers, with their accompanying smell. A short distance further on, the city's Destructor (now the site of the well-known Victoria Park Market) was fully operational. Its large chimney billowed smoke from the furnace that consumed the city's waste, and that, too, had its own pungency. The large reclamation that had taken the best part of 20 years was now open for use as a public space called Victoria Park. For the final part of his walk, Gallaher traversed the paving alongside the dock where he and his All Black teammates had been greeted by thousands of cheering supporters.

When Mr Fred Murray (who had been an All Black in 1893 and 1897) stood down as sole selector for Auckland, Gallaher was appointed to the position. It was a way for him to retire from playing, yet maintain his close involvement with the game. Plus, Auckland had regained the Ranfurly Shield while he was away, beating Wellington 10–6.

The style of football played by Auckland changed dramatically when Gallaher took over as sole selector and coach. Dour wrestling matches between the forwards where neither side really gained an advantage became a thing of the past. Suddenly, Auckland was consistently winning margins of 25 or even 40 points thanks to a game based on pace and the sweeping backline play that had served the Originals so well. Local spectators were thrilled by the exhibitions and flocked to matches to sample the style of play that had so enthralled those at 'Home'.

Having retired from playing, Gallaher was now able to think about settling down. He must have felt that he had spent most of his life on the move from one country (or house) to another. Although he thoroughly enjoyed experiencing new sights and sounds, such constant travel was becoming tiresome. He had represented his country overseas on the battlefield and the sportsfield, but he had always come back to Ponsonby. Now matters of the heart took prominence.

All Saints Church c.1910. Gallaher was a member of the congregation, got married there, and lived for some years down Church Street. SIR GEORGE GREY SPECIAL COLLECTIONS, AUCKLAND LIBRARIES, I-W68

On 10 October 1906, Gallaher married Nellie Francis. The wedding ceremony naturally took place in the All Saints Anglican Church. The *Observer*'s social sphere columnist 'Muriel' devoted four lengthy paragraphs to the couple's wedding, noting that the Wednesday marriage 'occasioned a great amount of interest, and the crowded congregation was an evidence of the esteem in which the young couple are held by their many friends'. The 'young' applied more to the bride than the groom. Gallaher was by now almost 33; his new wife 11 years his junior.

Nellie's dress was described in detail, and she, on the arm of her brother Jack, was written of as 'looking winsome and charming'. Gallaher had 'Bolla' as his groomsman and clubmate DW Dunlop was his best man. Dunlop worked as an educational administrator and went on to be Secretary of the Auckland Education Board and a member of the Teachers Appeal Board.

The reception was later held 'by Mrs Francis at her residence in Church Street, where a number of friends were very hospitably entertained, and the customary toasts duly proposed and responded to. … The presents were very numerous and valuable, and included several cheques for substantial amounts.' The newly-weds departed from there to honeymoon in Rotorua, while, in their absence, friends and relations enjoyed an evening's celebration at the Ponsonby Hall.

Such was the interest in Gallaher's wedding that months later the *New Zealand Free Lance* responded to a reader's query: 'Did Davy Gallaher, the captain of the "All Blacks", marry a sister of Francis or Nicholson?'

Although no longer playing the winter code, Gallaher's sporting life continued through summers, donning his cricket whites. The *Observer* Outdoor Sports reporter 'Harrier' in October 1907 mentioned that he saw:

> … *George Gillett, the crack footballer, practising with Ponsonby on Saturday. It is said that 'Dave' Gallaher is also coming out again for Ponsonby. Cannot Francis be persuaded to come out, too? He would be a big help to the senior team. I believe he is taking on yachting again this season.*

Auckland club cricket matches of the time were played on Saturday afternoons, with the first ball being bowled at around two o'clock. In 1907, there were only six clubs, fielding a total of 22 teams across three different grade competitions. The most in-demand pitches were the three at the Auckland Domain, where cricket had to compete with cycling and athletics for space. Three other pitches were at each of the following grounds: Victoria Park, Devonport and Kingsland — site of what we now know as Eden Park. With Victoria Park functioning, cricketers such as Gallaher and his Ponsonby teammates could simply wander down College Hill to matches. The new wickets on the reclaimed shorefront did have their vagaries, and players commented that, in the early years of use, pitches played differently depending on the height of the tide.

The *NZ Truth* noted Gillett and Gallaher's presence in the local club competition, saying 'they are no mean exponents with bat and ball. The pair will strengthen the Ponsonby senior ranks this season.' Runs were hard to come by for Gallaher that season. His top score, and best example of his skills at the crease, didn't come until late February when he scored 27 against City.

Occasionally, Gallaher was known to grab an oar at the West End Rowing Club where brother Joe had been a highly regarded stroke, leading his four to a number of regatta wins, and had also been Deputy Captain in 1896 and Treasurer from 1899 to 1902.

Gallaher's interest and involvement in sport also extended to athletics. For several years he was a member of the Auckland Amateur Athletic and Cycling Association's Management Committee. He was in the company of another of his old teammates — George Tyler — who served the association for many years.

While the 1905 tour can be credited with introducing the colony's style of football to players and the public in the United Kingdom, it was also responsible for bringing back to New Zealand (and Australia)

a threat to the very game of rugby football: Northern Union — or, as it is known today, league.

George Smith and several other All Blacks, who had been approached by members of Northern Union while away, saw appeal not only in the way the game was played, but also in the financial rewards to be enjoyed from it. The All Blacks had played in front of tens of thousands of spectators without financial reward beyond the daily allowance. Smith had the mindset of a professional athlete. He had made money from his days in the saddle and there were cash incentives at some athletic meets. Now, after years of being a transient sportsman, there could be opportunities to settle into an existence that guaranteed him an income.

The ambitious Wellington club-footballer Albert Baskerville hatched a plan to try to emulate the Originals' success by taking a team of Northern Union players to England. He made himself, and his proposal, known to Yorkshire and Lancashire clubs. He also contacted Smith, who had been to Sydney with his Auckland club, City, for a series of matches. In New South Wales there was great interest in the new code. An Australian businessman committed capital, and a professional football tour became increasingly discussed by players and administrators in New Zealand.

The variant rules of the new code should not be read as the sole reason for great interest in the tour from footballers from throughout the country. There were other aspects, too, such as the stories they had read or heard first-hand from players on the 1905 tour of how they had been fêted throughout their months at 'Home'. Others wanted to travel north to see the towns and cities from where their parents and families had emigrated and where relations still resided. Plus, there was no overarching body yet set up to govern Northern Union football in New Zealand. In fact, the game itself wasn't even being played! The tour was being organized by a group who would be players as well. Selection was by application, not by recommendation or nomination from a player's union. Immediately, this widened the pool of prospective tourists. Even journeymen club players now had a chance to 'represent' their country on an overseas tour, something that was well out of their reach otherwise.

Conversely, there was one major hurdle for some to overcome. Baskerville put the cost of the tour at £50 per player. They would then receive £1 per week payment once they had arrived in Britain, and any profit from gate takings would be split evenly among the group. Mind you, £50 was no small amount. For some it was the equivalent of a year's wages. For those who couldn't raise that amount, Baskerville would allow them to deposit into the team fund whatever amount they could contribute and pay interest (of 20 per cent) on the difference.

In England, the *Observer* newspaper printed a short article in March 1907 pronouncing very confidently the end of the Northern Union game. The piece was titled 'Moribund Northern Union':

The Northern Union is apparently on its last legs. Its decline in Yorkshire has been rapid; professional 'soccer' is giving it its final kick; the revival of real Rugby in the North long ago undermined the Northern Union. Even drowning clubs will clutch at straws, and there is some talk in the North about a New Zealand side coming over to play the Northern Union clubs with the idea of rejuvenating the failure. From what Mr Stead and Mr Gallaher have laid down in their admirable book there would seem to be as much chance of help for the Northern Union from New Zealand as there is of a thaw in Zembla. The colonies are more rigid in their rugged amateurism than even the Mother Country with its rather nice definitions.

Rather than being on its last legs in New Zealand, thanks to the efforts of Baskerville and Smith, Northern Union was about to walk, crawl and then run. Duncan McGregor and Bill 'Massa' Johnston became involved as selectors of the new professional team, and fellow Original Mackrell openly expressed his desire to join the tour. The commitment of these 'stars' attracted interest from a multitude of club and provincial players from around New Zealand. Baskerville's tourists became known as the 'All Golds', due to the fact that they were receiving money to play. For many it was galling to see and hear them calling themselves the 'professional All Blacks'. Adding to that distaste, they were wearing an identical strip to that of the amateur body.

Newspapers were quick to turn on the supposed traitors to amateurism, with a key sentiment being that the man who wanted to 'make money out of the playing of rugby football is no good to the game'. The NZRFU was urged by provinces such as Hawke's Bay 'to do all possible to defeat the scheme' — whatever was necessary to keep suspected professional players off rugby fields, including banning them from their club or provincial matches until it was known just who was making the tour.

NZRFU minutes record that, as the result of information tabled by the Chairman concerning the rumoured tour, Baskerville was summoned to meet the committee. He rejected the summons and, in a rebuttal to the NZRFU, replied that as self-appointed Honorary Secretary of the New Zealand Rugby Football Club he could not divulge any information relating to the tour. He was then expelled from the union code under the rules pertaining to professionalism, and all unions were instructed to ban him from entering grounds under their control. They also wrote to the Southland union, as George Stephenson, 'a reputed professional', was apparently back playing club football in the region and steps had to be taken to stop that.

All players nominated for the June 1907 North v South match, to be played for the first time in Christchurch, were asked to sign a NZRFU declaration rejecting professionalism. The North Island players flatly refused to sign, which shocked the general public. Not only did it put the playing of the greatly awaited annual fixture in jeopardy, but for many it was a sign that rugby might actually be in danger of being usurped by the new code.

The ARFU Management Committee met with the Auckland players who were nominees at Alexandra Park. Final selection for the inter-island game rested on the players' rejection of the Northern Union approaches, if they had received any. Union representatives had in their possession a second version of the loyalty documents, this time asking players to deny links to the professional tour.

The Auckland players refused to sign the declarations, seeing them as something of an affront to their current loyalty to their clubs, provinces and the national body, as well as to their ability to freely make their own choices about their playing futures, should they consider changing their status. There was an impasse.

The North v South match went ahead with no players from the provincial champions, Auckland, appearing. This led some to think that the professional tour was not something put together in Wellington, but in Auckland. Gallaher, as a North Island selector, acknowledged as much when spoken to by a reporter on his way back to Auckland from Christchurch. He agreed that:

... the opinion generally in the South appeared to be that the movement was being engineered in Auckland and when the 12 Auckland players nominated for the North Island team refused at first to sign the declaration, additional colour was lent to the suspicion.

Gallaher further asserted that, from what he knew, 'there would be no professional tour':

The majority of the players who would be a sufficient draw had definitely announced that they were not going, and, that being so, where was the team to come from? A good forward team, however, might be secured, but where were the backs coming from? It was possible, however, that the promoters would proceed with the best team that could be secured.

The majority of Auckland players did eventually sign the documents. It was announced that the hesitation of those who had been All Blacks was because they had received a *per diem* while in Britain and were unsure whether that affected their status. Teammates said they had withheld out of support for them.

Ponsonby lost only one player to the All Golds: Charles Dunning. Apparently, George Gillett was intending to join the ranks, but changed his mind. It is not too long a bow to draw to assert that one reason for that was Gallaher's influence on the playing members of the club. He had experienced his own issues with the NZRFU but had remained loyal to it. He and others at the Ponsonby club would have expected the same of their men.

The All Golds played 49 matches in Australia, England, Wales and Ceylon between August 1907 and June 1908. Five of these games were under rugby union rules. There were three draws and 17 losses, including a run of five in a row in January 1908. On 20 May 1908, with four games left to play in Australia, Baskerville died of pneumonia following a bad case of influenza, aged just 28. Two months later, an exhibition match, involving teams called the 'Reds' and the 'Blacks', was played under Northern Union rules at Athletic Park as a fundraiser for Baskerville's mother. Eight thousand turned out to watch what is now known as the first game of 'rugby league' played in this country, which had a scoreline of 55–20. Some reporters liked what they saw. A Press Association reporter wrote:

> *The general opinion was that the play was far more spectacular, and some of the alterations at least must be introduced into Rugby sooner rather than later if the game is to hold its own. The main fact that struck everyone was the abolition of much senseless scrumming …which in itself is a vast improvement.*

Other observers declared that the game posed no threat to the popularity of 'the national game'.

The New Zealand Rugby Union had no success over a number of years with overtures to their South African counterparts for a tour. The Africans did, however, make a tour of Great Britain in 1906; one Gallaher is said to have followed with great interest, particularly as they approached their encounter with Wales. South Africa won the match 11–0. Several weeks later a humorous mourning card arrived in the mail from England for Gallaher:

> *In loving memory of poor old Wales, who succumbed at the hands of the South Africans at Swansea, December 1st, 1906. With courage bold the Welshmen came/ And played right well to win the game/ Alas! Their spirits fell complete/ When 'Springbok's' team they failed to beat.*

Selection Difficulties

*'The selectors be requested to select a team
for the third test as speedily as possible.'*

In 1907, an All Black side had to be selected to tour Australia for the first time in four years. The seven-match tour included three tests against Australia and double clashes with New South Wales and Queensland. Gallaher put his name forward to be one of the four selectors, and was appointed at a meeting of the NZRFU Management Committee on 7 May 1907. Also appointed were 'Dutchy' Evans (who had refereed the 1904 test against Great Britain), Henry Harris (Otago) and HW Kelly (Wellington).

A dozen Originals were chosen in the 22-man squad. It was captained by Jimmy Hunter as he had done in 1905, with George Nicholson (who was on holiday in Australia) being called into the team once on tour. The tour began successfully, for once, with a large win over Wellington Province before the team sailed for Sydney. Once ashore in Australia there was much talk about the proposed professional tour, but it was a series of injuries and influenza that blighted the tour.

The first match against New South Wales at the Sydney Cricket Ground drew a crowd of 49,327, which remained the highest number of patrons through the gates to a game of provincial rugby in Australia until the 2011 Super 15 final between the Queensland Reds and the Canterbury Crusaders. The home side played with great verve, but was overwhelmed by the All Blacks in the second half, who ran out 11–3 winners. The return match four days later was a complete reversal, with the New South Welshmen keeping the men in black scoreless while they ran up 14 points. That result gave local supporters heart and hope that the Australian side, wearing a jersey whose colours combined the maroon of Queensland and the blue of NSW, could do the same. It was not to be: they were soundly beaten 26–6, a winning margin that wasn't surpassed for some years. The next three matches were all convincing wins, but the final test against Australia was a 5–5 draw, a disappointment to both sides and to the New Zealand selectors.

Back in Auckland, the blue-and-whites faced the most demanding domestic calendar in their history. Twelve representative matches were played in a little over two months, including shield challenges from Buller and Hawke's Bay. Gallaher also had to select sides for eight inter-union games, a task made harder by the loss of some players to the All Golds tour. There were five losses and a draw for Gallaher's sides. Notable among the losses was an 8–11 defeat to a spirited South Canterbury side in Timaru.

That result didn't please Auckland football observers, following losses to Taranaki and Wellington. An *Observer* journalist opined that some of the players new to the team were not of the quality of their predecessors. Under the title of 'A Faded Glory — A Barracker's

Lament', there was a column-long mournful ode to the great players of Auckland rugby, including Gallaher.

If Davie Gallaher came out,
As in the days of old,
He'd put opposing force to rout,
Would Gallaher the bold.
Tho' Davie's not an angel yet,
'Tis plain as anything,
Though cast I'm told in mortal mould,
He's quite an angelic wing!

The ode concluded with:

Altho' our team was licked this year,
And fairly beaten, too.
Remember what a short career
Had fallen to that crew.
So when next year comes round apace,
'Twill be our brightest dream
To make our name at football fame
Once more o'er all supreme.

Following publication of the lament, Auckland lost only one of their final seven games and defended the Ranfurly Shield.

The annual April meeting of the Auckland Rugby Union was always well attended by club delegates and members of the general public who had an interest in the workings of the union. At a rather boisterous Friday-night assembly in 1908, Gallaher, as a Ponsonby delegate and sole selector, put forward a motion that 'the press be admitted to the meetings of the Management Committee'. Principal opposition to the proposal came from Parnell delegates, but a majority of those who rose to speak to the motion saw it as of benefit to both football supporters and the workings of the committee. One area where this motion was most applicable and relevant was in the dealings with players who were joining the professional ranks. Decisions suspending players for links to pay-for-play made behind closed doors, while procedurally correct, created a further impression of draconianism on the part of the union committee. Gallaher was concerned that such a lack of openness could create sympathy for those who were turning their back on the amateur game, and as such indirectly encourage more of an interest in Northern Union football.

The 1908 Anglo-Welsh tour, comprising 17 matches, had not been organized specifically to combat the rising interest from players and spectators in Northern Union football. In 1905, even before the Originals final selection had been made, local unions had applauded the fact that plans were under way for an English side to tour. Later that year, the NZRFU had cabled George Dixon in England to 'enter into preliminary negotiations with ERU for that body to send a team to tour NZ in 1908'. That tour did not eventuate, but the momentum being gained by Northern Union enterprises — and the All Golds trip 'Home' — was a uniting spur to finally get another side to the Antipodes, one made up of English and Welsh players. The Scottish and Irish unions did not allow the participation of their players in the tour for reasons unknown. English rugby writers thus dismissed the team as one that stood no show of competing with the All Blacks (selected by Gallaher, Harris, Kelly, and Canterbury's Samuel Wilson) and the stronger provincial sides. Talk of that did not dampen excitement in New Zealand around the team's arrival. Leading the tourists was Arthur Harding, who had been a member of the 1905 Welsh side that defeated Gallaher's men. He was of a much more pleasant disposition as a tour captain than Bedell-Sivright had been four years earlier, which contributed greatly to the popularity of the side.

In their comprehensive history of touring international rugby teams, *The Visitors*, rugby historians Rod Chester and Neville McMillan pointed out that, for the opening match of the tour against Wairarapa Bush:

> ... [a]lthough the population of Masterton was about 4000 in 1908, over 6000 people saw the game, for all roads seemed to lead to the little town. People came from every outlying district, travelling in a variety of ways — by horseback, trap, car, rail and foot. A packed train came up from Wellington, and some 30 reporters arrived from all over New Zealand. Whatever effect the new rugby code was having on the sporting public, interest in the old code was certainly not diminishing.

The first test was played in Dunedin on 6 June 1908, and the city was in a frenzy as the time for kick-off approached. Several hundred people stormed through corrugated-iron fencing at the ground, apparently angered at the expensive gate price of two shillings.

Billy Stead was reinstalled as captain of an All Black side that contained eight other players from the 1905 team. (Bob Deans was unavailable due to injury.) Gallaher was watching from the grandstand as Stead's side made a furious start to the game. Four tries were scored in quick succession, and by halftime it was 21–0. The Anglo-Welsh did get across the line for a well-taken try in the second half, but three more tries were added by the All Blacks. The final score was 32–5.

Seven changes were made for the second test three weeks later. With the home team expected to win comfortably after the result in the first test, the opportunity was taken to introduce six new players to the All Black environment. The tourists, meanwhile, had trouble in their ranks when Fred Jackson, a giant of a forward and able goal-kicker, was sent home, accused by the RFU of professionalism. (Within two years he was representing New Zealand at league, having returned to be with a woman he had fallen in love with while on tour. He later became an East Coast rugby selector.)

Come match-day, that supreme leveller arrived — rain. Great squalls and heavy showers pelted the players and spectators. The ball became slippery with a coating of mud, and was much heavier to hold as water soaked into it. It was also hard to kick off the ground. Billy Wallace was one of those brought back into the All Blacks, and not even he could goal in a first half that left the backs largely unemployed, watching the forwards wrestle and slop around, toeing the ball in dribbling rushes. At halftime the score was 0–0.

The ball was getting heavier, so when a chance came for the home side to take a penalty, big 'Bolla' Francis stepped up and managed to kick the goal to give the All Blacks a 3–0 lead. (Francis was an impressive goal-kicker. In one match, possibly against Australia in 1905, he took a kick at goal from near halfway and close to the touchline. The ball flew from the toe of his large boot, low and fast, smacking into the cross-bar with a thud that could be heard all around the ground, then it bounced over for the goal, leaving the goalposts shaking in their holes.)

The lead was short-lived and, after some industrious play, the Anglo-

Welsh scored a try right under the posts. The conversion would give them the match. So heavy with mud and water was the ball now, the kicker, Harding, couldn't even get it off the ground, let alone over the bar. The All Blacks had escaped with a 3–3 draw.

The result did not go down well with the football followers, and tensions appeared in the selectorial ranks. Gallaher attempted to distance himself from the changes made to the team by claiming that he had not been consulted over the make-up of the team for the Wellington test.

The issue highlighted the difficulties faced by selectors in having to juggle the time and travel demands of their role with their regular employment. The playing XV for Wellington was to be finalized by a meeting of the selectors, following the North v South game, three days before the second test. Gallaher was informed by his boss at the Freezing Company that he would be unable to get time off work for the trip. He sent a cable to fellow North Island selector Kelly, proposing that a Taranaki delegate, Humphries, take his place. Humphries was not available, so Gallaher then suggested former Auckland selector Fred Murray. He, too, was unavailable at short notice. Kelly, on behalf of the other selectors, apparently sent a cable to Gallaher stressing the importance of him making his way to Wellington. With his attendance out of the question, he sent a cable confirming his absence along with a suggested playing side. Gallaher claimed that he received no response from the three other members of the panel, considering their behaviour to be 'very discourteous', and told one reporter that the side he had chosen was 'superior' to the one which was flattered with a draw in the test.

The impasse remained when it came time to select the third test team. Gallaher dug his heels into the ground, insisting that the national selectors should meet in Auckland to make their selection. He had travelled south for a prior test, so why should his fellow selectors not travel to the venue of the third?

The NZRFU Management Committee was unimpressed with the suggestion. A special meeting chaired by George Dixon was convened to:

> *consider position caused by Mr Gallaher, N.Z. Selector, objecting to selection of team for third test by correspondence, and submitting that selectors should meet in Auckland. It was resolved, 'That a telegram be sent to Mr Gallaher as follows — Decided selectors meet at Wgton Saturday night. Can you arrange be here mail train that day. Impracticable selectors meet Auckland.'*

One of the difficulties of the situation was that Gallaher, as sole selector for Auckland, did not have to spend time in consultation and negotiation when choosing players, in the way that he did as a national selector. Plus, also at issue for him was fairness and consistency — what was appropriate for one or two selectors should be applicable for all.

The ARFU backed Gallaher and made known their dissatisfaction with the decision, deeming it 'equitable and reasonable' that the selection be made in Auckland. At a NZRFU Management Committee meeting two days after the special meeting, a motion insisting that the selectors meet in the capital because it was central was defeated. Instead, it was resolved, 'That the selectors be requested to select a team for the third test as speedily as possible, further that they be asked to arrange that the members of the team arrive in Auckland, Saturday, 18 July.' So, the answer from the NZRFU was, essentially, sort it out among yourselves but get the team chosen, please.

Gallaher not only had to deal with the national public's expectation of their side against the Anglo-Welsh. Hopes were high among the Auckland public that when their local boys played the visitors on 18 July there would be a repeat of the success of the 1904 team that had defeated the Great Britain side. The Auckland forward pack was, arguably, even better than that of four years previous, featuring Gillett, Cunningham, Francis, Seeling and Nicholson. Plus, they were being drilled by coach Gallaher.

Over 20,000 excited spectators piled into Alexandra Park for the match, following a rush for tickets earlier in the week at Partridge's and Cleal's, Queen Street tobacconists.

From the kick-off, the outcome was never really in doubt. The Auckland XV attacked and defended well, while their guests did just enough of the latter and little of the former, losing 0–11. Following the win, the *Observer*'s 'Frenzied Barracker' was in raptures, urging in a piece called 'An Ode to the Conquerors':

Arise, ye giddy Aucklanders,
And sing a gladsome song,
And wave your heels like pickled eels
And biff the warlike gong!
Fly round and flute, ye Aucklanders,
All rivals you can squelch,
Let others note how hard you smote
Poor Harding's Anglo-Welsh!

On it went parochially for five more verses before praising, in five-line limericks, each of Auckland's 15 players, the union secretary and Gallaher.

Davie Gallaher's football director,
Of players a mighty collector.
So here's to good health
And long life — stacks of wealth
To our Davie, the champion selector.

The man on the sidelines: Gallaher,
Auckland coach and sole selector.
AUCKLAND RUGBY UNION

A week later the tourists had to play the final match of their tour, the third test against the All Blacks. When the selections were finally made, 10 of the side who had played in the first-test rout lined up again, along with the recalled Deans and Frank Glasgow. In a further twist to the selection dispute, the appointed team manager, Laughton, was unable to make it to Auckland for the match. So who did the Management Committee turn to? 'It was resolved that Mr Gallaher be appointed manager with powers to make any necessary arrangements for training the team.' Then that decision was rescinded, probably because Gallaher couldn't commit the time to additional duties.

The crowd was a little over half the size of that which had witnessed the Auckland win the week before. After two months in New Zealand, the tourists were a tired bunch with numerous injuries, but they were set upon by a team that was out to make amends for the draw of a month previous. In the week before the match, Gallaher had taken a number of practices, honing the All Blacks' scrummaging and ball-handling skills.

Match-day brought bad weather, but the result was 29–0 in favour of the All Blacks and could have been greater had not the All Black kickers somehow conspired to miss all but one of their nine conversions. The star of the series, Wellington centre and wing Frank Mitchinson, scored two tries to give him five in the three matches.

Following the Anglo-Welsh tour, focus turned to the performance of local provincial teams. Auckland accepted and repelled four challenges for the Ranfurly Shield. They scored 76 points and conceded only eight.

Two weeks after the final match of the season, on 28 September 1908, there was a greater thrill for Gallaher than anything he had experienced on the football field. At the age of 34, Gallaher became a father when Nellie gave birth to a healthy baby girl. They named her Nora Tahatu Gallaher. While the daughter's first name was that of her maternal grandmother, the origin of Tahatu remains a mystery to family members. There was great delight and celebration among family and friends.

Two days later, contrasting that private delight, Gallaher shared in a more public sadness. Bob Deans died suddenly. He went into hospital for a routine appendix operation but complications set in and he passed away on 30 September 1908. He was only 24. It was hard for those who had played with him, or seen him in action on the field, to fathom how a strapping young man like him could suffer such a fate. Among the tributes to the young Canterbury farmer, and the man at the centre of rugby's greatest controversy, the *NZ Truth* described him as 'a brilliant athlete and citizen' and 'the touching remarks made at his graveside caused tears to come from the large assembly round, and strong men were not ashamed to weep at the loss of a beloved comrade'. The first of the Originals had died, less than three years since their celebrated return, and it was their youngest member.

Back on the Field

Gone were the days of punishing tackles,
fast breaks and rapid dribbling rushes.

At the end of July 1909, 21 players from the Ponsonby club, captained by 'Bolla' Francis, were farewelled by Gallaher and other club members as they sailed to Sydney for four matches. George Gillett travelled with the team in a non-playing capacity. The team won two and lost one before the feature match of their visit, a clash with Newtown, billed as the 'Australasian Club Championship'. On a wet afternoon, in front of 8,000 spectators, Ponsonby overran their hosts 14–6. It was a bruising encounter, with Ponsonby getting the upper hand through powerful scrummaging and repeated rushes by the forwards, helped by the inclusion of Gillett in the pack. The backs benefited from this dominance, with Duncan McGregor bagging two tries.

Keenly interested in the trip was the NZRFU, who wanted to inspect the NSWRU balance sheets of the Ponsonby visit and be advised of how the £400 credit balance was disposed of.

George Gillett had turned down his position with the All Golds, but it becomes clear that his intention to commit to the side was done purely for money. Although he had been convinced to stay with the amateur code, at the end of July 1909 while their senior players were in Australia, the Ponsonby club committee was trying to get permission from the ARFU, who in turn had to consult the NZRFU, to hold a 'benefit' match for Gillett. The intention was that Ponsonby would play Wellington's Poneke (who had got the go-ahead from their union) with proceeds to go to Gillett, who was said to be 'suffering from effects of football' and had reportedly retired due to an accident. (The effects were financial rather than physical.) The NZRFU advised that it had no power to grant such permission.

Gallaher was overseeing a busy calendar of inter-provincial and sub-union clashes through the month of August. At the same time as the 'A' side was playing Rotorua in the thermal town on 21 August 1909, there was a curtain-raiser to the Auckland 'B' v Thames match at Alexandra Park, a schoolboy match that Gallaher was keen to hear the result of. The *Observer* reported that:

The final game between Kings College and Grammar School for the Secondary Schools Championship was brimful of interest. The colours of the two teams could be seen everywhere, and it is a long time since so much interest was centred in a local Rugby game. Both teams had been well-trained, having profited by the aid of such experienced coaches as Messrs D. Gallaher and G. Gillet [sic], and their play was of a high standard.

Kings won the match 8–6, 'but looking at the play, Grammar School had a little better of the deal'. Looking through twenty-first-century eyes, it seems remarkable that an All Black selector and Auckland selector/coach would also help coach a school team. The Francis family had a proud association with Auckland Grammar School, and Gallaher was now very much part of that family. It is also indicative of the part Gallaher played in numerous voluntary activities. Could there be any better introduction for young men to the possibilities of the game than from the mouth of one of the game's great players and thinkers? Sadly, no photographs or other ephemera exist in the Auckland Grammar School archives from the several seasons Gallaher was instructing the young charges.

Having been retired from football for four years, Gallaher got back on the paddock for one final inter-provincial game for Auckland, 13 years after his first, on 26 August 1909. The Auckland team was on an intensive 10-day tour that involved five matches against Marlborough, Wellington, Wanganui, Taranaki and Maniapoto. The side was depleted before they left Auckland with the loss of the travelling Ponsonby players, and for the first match in Blenheim it didn't have a full complement of fit players. So Gallaher pulled on his boots and the Auckland kit and walked out to play alongside his old teammates Seeling and Nicholson. It was a measure of Gallaher's commitment to the team, and his fitness, that when almost 36 years old he could still take the field and be competitive.

It wasn't a good afternoon for Gallaher, as his team lost 3–8 in a very physical game. Match reports note that, while he was still a presence on the field, it wasn't with the same dominance as at his peak. He was capable on attack and defence, but gone were the days of punishing tackles, fast breaks and rapid dribbling rushes. That is not to say he was a passenger on the field. The wise head was now much more of a tactician, and his play was punctuated by a number of clever centring kicks for his players to call marks from, but Marlborough were much the better side on the day.

In a game that was all shoulders, elbows and knees from the hosts, Gallaher suffered a bad knock on his right hand. He was still feeling the effects of it two days later, and it ruled him out of the match against Wellington. Seeling also missed that game after copping some questionable attention from the Marlborough forwards. Play had to be held up for several minutes as a doctor examined the prone forward, who spent the rest of the match among the backs.

In Wellington, heavy rain fell for much of the match. Large pools of water lay in parts of the soft, muddy field. Gallaher ran one of the touchlines and was a busy man as the greasy ball was regularly kicked out of play. By the time referee Jimmy Duncan blew the final whistle, Gallaher's ears were ringing with taunts from Wellington supporters. Throughout the match, won 3–0 by Auckland, many accused him of favouring his team. Some newspaper reports criticized the behaviour of the crowd, and the *Observer* was bemused by the abuse, describing Gallaher as 'one of those sports who would be the last to take advantage for his side'. The *NZ Truth* rugby writer took the opposing stance, lambasting Gallaher:

It has been my lot to witness some 'tough' things from line-umpires, but after Saturday's exhibition Dave Gallaher goes up to the top of the class. Some bare-faced cribbing — yards, not feet — in favour of the Northerners came off Davie's bat in the first spell, but it was a fool circumstance to what followed after the teams had exchanged ends. Not only were the homers robbed of territory, but not infrequently up went his flag for 'Auckland ball', when as a matter of fact the other side should have had the option of throw-out. The 'bankers' are no mugs; they watch developments very closely, and as critics are mostly competent to express an expert opinion on Rugby happenings. They sized up Gallaher when he unloaded his tricks, and the result was the uncommon experience in Wellington of a line-umpire being persistently hooted for his unfairness. If Jimmy Duncan had been doing his duty on Saturday he would have applied the restful cure to the Northerner, and given someone else a chance of giving decisions as they should be given.

This was water off a duck's back to Gallaher. The team left the capital and headed to Wanganui. The game there was the last Charlie Seeling played for Auckland, and it was against the union from whence he had come. Three months later he signed to play Northern Union football for Wigan.

On Saturday, 4 September, Auckland stopped in Te Kuiti to play against sub-union Maniapoto. Auckland was still struggling to field a fit XV, so Dave again pulled on his boots, and the blue-and-white hoops, and took to the field for the very last time. The man who had led the All Blacks and played in front of tens of thousands at the Sydney Cricket Ground and Crystal Palace, and who had felt Welsh fervour in Cardiff on that fateful December day in 1905, finished his playing days as part of an inter-union match in the middle of the North Island. There were several hundred spectators and the small-town field was described as being 'like a billiard table but with too many holes in it'. After the match, won by Auckland 16–0, the visitors were guests of honour at a large dinner and wearily returned home the next morning.

The summer provided respite from the demands of travel, coaching and selections. Gallaher could settle into spending more time at home with Nellie and young Nora. Sport wasn't sidelined completely, however, as he donned his whites to play leisurely Saturday afternoons of cricket for Ponsonby. In his first match of the season, against Grafton, he top-scored with 43.

A curious item appeared in the *Evening Post* late that summer regarding the Auckland Freezing Company's Easter picnic:

While proceeding, by the steamer Eagle, to a picnic at Motutapu on Saturday last, Mr D Gallaher, of 'All Blacks' fame, met with an accident. He was ascending the sponson steps, when he slipped on a banana skin, and, being unable to regain his balance, made a spring and jumped well clear of the revolving paddle wheels. The steamer was immediately stopped and a boat put out to Mr Gallaher's rescue. The ex-footballer proved himself a powerful swimmer, and after recovering his hat, which he had lost, swam to the boat and was taken on board the steamer. He appeared none the worse for his experience.

Further reports of the incident, published around the country in the days after that first posting, made the scene much more comic.

The All Blacks had no commitments in 1909, but the following year, a seven-match tour of Australia took place. For the first time, the three test matches were to be played on consecutive weeks as the last stanza of the visit.

The tour took place before the annual inter-island match, so the selectors had no real guide to form. They called for nominations, with Gallaher and his cohorts having to base their selections largely on what they knew of players from the previous season. Thus, several old hands became important figures in the side: Originals Mynott (now 34) and Freddy Roberts, who captained the side, as well as 'Bolla' Francis. In something of a gamble, there were 15 newcomers.

The selections won praise from the newspaper scribes. The *Evening Post* was most effusive in their scrutiny of the 1910 All Blacks team: 'Messrs. Gallaher, Meredith, Wilson and Harris are to be congratulated on the team they have selected to do battle for New Zealand in Australia.' Furthermore, the paper considered, 'probably no better forward team has ever represented the Dominion — the men are fast, weighty, and — best of all — clever.'

The tourists left New Zealand having defeated Wellington, then had double victories over New South Wales and Queensland before the Australian tests. The first was a real arm-wrestle won 6–0 by the All Blacks. In the second test, played two days after the first and thus on a Monday, New Zealand was completely outplayed and lost 0–11. The third test, played the following Saturday, was won 28–13 by the All Blacks. Their forwards dominated, meaning the backs could flourish, and it was the two veterans of the side — Mynott and Roberts — who won all the post-match plaudits.

The first New Zealand Native team (known today as New Zealand Maori) was selected in 1910, and they played two matches against Auckland: one on 25 May, prior to their departure for matches in Australia, and the other on their return at the end of July. This was a chance for Gallaher to catch up with his dear friend Billy Stead, who was part of the Native side, having come out of retirement at the age of 32. The party was also bolstered by the presence of Bill Cunningham, and Ponsonby and Auckland forward George Sellars. Auckland won the first match and the Natives the second.

Other opposition that wasn't from one of the usual provincial teams was an American Universities side, largely made up of players from universities in California. Gallaher, with his interest in encouraging new players and expanding rugby's territories, coached the Americans for several days, drilling the forwards and explaining subtleties of play to the backs. The lessons learnt from the All Black legend enthused the visitors, and the result of the match was a 13-all draw. Just who held who to the draw was the source of some debate in the days after the match!

In 1911, Nellie's mother and the Gallahers moved from Church Street (with Nora Francis selling the property), to 43 Lawrence Street, Herne Bay. While technically in another suburb, it was only 10 minutes' walk from their previous residence and still close to the Ponsonby Football Club.

In May of that year, two of the men in football's ranks closest to Gallaher turned their backs on the 15-a-side game. Both George Gillett and 'Bolla' Francis announced that they were switching to the Northern Union game for an upcoming Australian tour. It should be read as no coincidence that they both made their announcements at the same time. Undoubtedly, they consulted Gallaher before doing so. He had no reasons to try to persuade them to stay in the amateur ranks. Gillett was aged 34, had missed selection for the All Blacks that year, was no longer an Auckland rep, and was struggling financially. Brother-in-law Francis was tipping 30. He had played for the All Blacks that year, but his days in the black jersey were essentially behind him, especially considering that the international calendar for the next two or three years was quite sparse. There was no point him waiting to add to his 10 test caps if money could be made from a game that had less physicality come scrum-time and at the breakdown.

The North *v* South match was played at the end of the 1911 season, three weeks after Auckland's provincial programme had ended. Although his North side won 19–9, Gallaher again objected to the way the selection of the side was conducted, and wrote to the NZRFU expressing such. A meeting of the Management Committee felt that the methods used had been properly understood by Gallaher, and there was little more that could be done than convey that to him.

While Auckland's Ranfurly Shield reign continued in spite of the departure of two of Gallaher's constant forward selections, they had their fair share of close calls. Wellington and Otago had drawn matches in 1910 and 1912, respectively. A last-minute try had seen Auckland hold off Canterbury by one point in a real cliff-hanger in 1910.

Between 3 August 1910 and 16 August 1913, Auckland went unbeaten for 19 matches. Admittedly, they played only five away games and had three draws, but it was a remarkable record. That was, until a strong Taranaki side (which featured seven players who would become All Blacks later that year) made their way to Alexandra Park for their sixth shield challenge. It was Auckland's twenty-fourth defence. Even though playing conditions were greasy, 16 August 1913 was to be Taranaki's day in a match described by newspapers as 'sensational'. At halftime Auckland were ahead 5–3. From the commencement of the second spell, the Taranaki forwards became more dominant and their backs could do little wrong. Two tries had them ahead 9–5. Their lead could have been more had the conversions been made, and had Auckland's defence not been so committed. But Gallaher's boys were far from done. They replied with two well-taken tries which had home fans in raptures, but fullback O'Leary couldn't convert either. So, the holders led 11–9 with time running out. Four minutes from time Taranaki scored a try to take them to a one-point lead, and the conversion made the score 14–11 in their favour, which was how the match finished. The Taranaki players were jubilant and the Auckland players gracious in defeat. The first great shield reign had come to an end after eight seasons of repelling all comers.

Gallaher had used 86 players during the years Auckland held the shield. 'Bolla' Francis had played in 13 of the defences, George Sellars in 11, and Georges Gillett and Nicholson appeared nine times each. Trusty old Bill Cunningham, who had played in 16 shield matches, retired at the end of the 1913 provincial season. He was by then 39, and had played 103 first-class matches (plus many more inter-union games) since 1899; 39 of those for New Zealand. He kicked goals and, in an age where no thought was given to leaving the field because of fatigue, played as enthusiastically at the end of a game as he did at the beginning. In a match for Auckland, an opponent raced away to score and the only Auckland player chasing him was Cunningham. He was asked why he had kept up his chase even though it was futile. Cunningham replied, 'He might have dropped dead.'

No international matches had been played in 1911 or 1912, but the calendar for 1913 was a busy one. With three tests to play against Australia in September, the national selectors made their picks for the inter-island match, which was played in Christchurch at the end of July. The *NZ Truth* cast its eye over the North Island team, which was dominated by seven Wellington and four Taranaki players, and felt that it 'on the whole looks a pretty formidable combination. One expected Wylie, the Auckland University forward, to find a place. Evidently, Dave Gallaher has not dominated the situation on the selection committee, as he has in previous seasons.' While the side might have looked formidable, it did not perform as such. The northerners took a towelling: they couldn't even register a point, while the South kept the scoreboard attendants busy as they rattled up 25 points.

Australia arrived for a nine-match tour at the end of August. Early appraisals of the touring party were that they were not a great side, suffering it seemed from the growth of Northern Union football in New South Wales. In some ways, the weakness of the tourists was fortunate for the national selectors, as an All Black side had to leave for a 16-match tour of North America before the test series against Australia was completed.

Gallaher and his fellow selectors had their work cut out selecting players for the touring party and the domestic tests. Gallaher, on behalf of his fellow selectors, recommended that the touring players totalled 23, which was agreed to by the NZRFU. When they announced the players to tour, all hell broke loose throughout the country as province after province attacked the selectors for not picking the players they considered good enough to tour and defended the selectors over some of their choices. The NZRFU was attacked for lacking fair representation on the selection panel. The *NZ Truth* carried a scathing piece on the selections, writing that 'one cannot honestly congratulate the selectors on their work; in fact, they have proved their unfitness for the positions which they occupy'. The Wellington Rugby Union's sole selector and former national selector, Vincent Meredith, was particularly vocal in his dissatisfaction with the selectors' choices. Rugby union Chairman Neil Galbraith spoke to the *Evening Post* in an attempt to defend the selectors' decisions and explain the processes and timings for player nominations.

Several days later, Gallaher unwittingly was doing the same, when a letter he had sent to the NZRFU Management Committee was reproduced in the *Evening Post*:

I am in receipt of your letter of 2nd August, and am quite at a loss to understand the attitude taken up by Mr Meredith. In the first place, he says that there appears to be some question as to whether Mitchinson's name was brought under the notice of the selectors by him or not. Now, sir, in referring to the copy of his letter sent by you, I wish to emphatically state that never at any time has Mitchinson's name been ever mentioned by Mr Meredith, and certainly no wire from him was tabled when the selectors met in Christchurch. Surely he had ample time to acquaint the selection committee, without leaving the matter till the last minute, and he must have been aware of the form displayed by Mitchinson in the Auckland–Wellington match sufficiently to justify his inclusion in any New Zealand team. Under the circumstances there is no excuse for Mr Meredith's action, unless it is pure laziness, for I personally told the manager of the team, Mr Weir, that I could not understand the omission of his (Mitchinson's) name in the Wellington nominations. If Mr Meredith was so anxious, why did he not take the opportunity of seeing Mr Mynott and myself on the Friday evening as we passed through Wellington instead of waiting till the Saturday night to wire, and then privately? Now, in regard to Ramsden's case, the committee considered the matter thoroughly and could not see their way clear to send a man who might be permanently injured in his first game, and consequently of no further use during the rest of the tour. Fit and well there would have been no question as to his inclusion. Now, in justice to myself and co-selectors, I think your executive should certainly make known the true facts of the case, considering the publicity that has been given Mr Meredith's misrepresentation of what actually took place, as I do not consider it would be advisable for any one of the selectors to enter into a newspaper controversy on the subject.

The Auckland side was the first to meet the touring Australians. It was a tough first-up assignment for the visitors. Their captain, Larry Dwyer, was a stand-out: fearless on defence, and he wowed the Alexandra Park crowd with his prodigious punting of the ball. There were even claims he could kick the leather the length of the field! In the midweek match, refereed by George Nicholson, the home side ran in four thrilling tries to defeat the tourists 15–13.

Two weeks later the first test was played at Athletic Park. The weather was dreadful, and accordingly the crowd numbered only several thousand. The All Blacks made light of the conditions and trounced the Australians 30–5, scoring eight tries to one. Three were scored by South Canterbury's centre Tom 'Tiger' Lynch. Mr Meredith must have been delighted, too, when Mitchinson came on as a replacement.

By the time of the second test a week later, an All Black touring party had sailed for North America. Thus, not one player from the first test was in the XV for the Dunedin match. The most notable aspect of the team was the bestowing of the captaincy on Ponsonby and Auckland fullback, Joe O'Leary. The personnel changes meant that there was a somewhat less one-sided match; although the All Blacks still scored five tries, they conceded three in winning 25–13. More changes were made for the third test in Christchurch, and, for the only time in Australia–New Zealand test matches, both sides were captained by players at fullback. The visitors played exceptionally well and salvaged some pride with a 16–5 win.

Meanwhile, those who had gone to North America to spread the gospel of rugby, by lining up against university teams in California and regional teams in Canada, were undefeated in their 16 outings. They scored 610 points and conceded just six!

A 10-match tour of Australia took place in 1914, and once again the selectors were in the firing line over their selections. This was exacerbated when the All Blacks lost their farewell match against Wellington, 14–19. However, they won all 10 of their Australian matches, including the three tests against Australia. They even kept the Australians scoreless in the first two.

With three matches remaining on the tour, other matters became more prominent and match-day crowds dwindled. Britain declared war on Germany. By the time the tour party arrived back in New Zealand, Kiwi soldiers had already captured German-occupied Samoa.

First World War

'The flower of Rugby had enlisted.'

Three-quarters of the 23 All Blacks of 1914 volunteered to fight at some stage of the First World War. In London's Whitechapel, home of government departments and offices, the Publicity Department of the Central London Recruiting Depot published a challenge to British sportspeople to lead by example and join the war effort. A poster was distributed boldly proclaiming that 'Rugby Union footballers are doing their duty — over 90% have enlisted. British athletes! Will you follow this glorious example?' It quoted a *Times* newspaper item which reported: 'Every player who represented England in Rugby international matches last year [1913] has joined the colours'.

Gallaher watched the progress of the war, and the participation of those he knew well, with as keen an eye as when on the sidelines of a football field. But this was an all-enveloping conflict. Its escalation dominated the newspapers and, thus, general conversation. At work, at church, on the streets of Ponsonby, there were noticeable absentees. People had gaps in their lives — and an increasing number of those gaps were permanent. All talk was of those who had left to serve their country, and their bravery, their patriotism.

A 1914 English recruiting poster targeting footballers.
MATT ELLIOTT COLLECTION

The excitement of the country's sons being part of a great adventure turned to despair for those still at home as news came back of the horror that was the disastrous Gallipoli campaign. Among the casualties was 'Doolan' Downing, the big Auckland lock forward who had played in the New Zealand team in 1913 and 1914. He was the first All Black war casualty. Ten days after his death, another from the 1913 side, back-rower 'Norkey' Dewar, was killed at Chunuk Bair.

The Auckland union, after several years' negotiation, took up its lease on a new venue — Eden Park. Gallaher was there to watch the first game on the new ground when his Ponsonby club faced off against City. The domestic provincial competition continued, but football was no longer the be-all and end-all. Around the country the sport was marked by the departures of players taking up arms. The North v South match was cancelled and the domestic competition suspended. There was still a hope that the war would be short-lived, so some matches — organized by the provincial unions themselves — were played in 1915. Auckland had a mixed season, playing Taranaki and Wellington home and away, as well as a Trentham Army Camp side.

Gallaher's final match in charge of an Auckland side was against the old foe Wellington at Athletic Park on 28 August 1915. The blue-and-whites were thumped 22–8. At the end of the season, perhaps with thoughts in mind of volunteering for service if necessary the following year, Gallaher relinquished the role of selector. George Nicholson took over in 1916 (although only one rep game was played, against a team from Trentham Army Camp's 17th Reinforcements). The domestic competition was then suspended as the war worsened. This was a move inspired by the patriotic mindset that if men were healthy enough to play football, they were healthy enough to fight, so the only organized football being played was by young men under the age of 20.

By May 1915, the NZRFU estimated that over 2,000 rugby players had enlisted to serve. Volunteers from Wellington club football were approximately 400. Wanganui had sent 120 men. Rugby officers from the Otago Province believed they had farewelled 800 players and ex-players. The relatively new South Auckland union saw off 170 players, while 240 sons of Canterbury were fighting or preparing to fight. Outgoing NZRFU President John Arneil said that 'all would be glad that the union had such a fine lot of men who were ready to offer their services for the honour of the Empire. ... It is without question that we are all under a great debt of gratitude to those who have given their lives at the front.' He also wondered if the new committee could 'devise some scheme of co-operating with the Defence Office for the further stimulation of recruiting amongst Rugby men'. Management Committee member George Fache added: 'Every man who went to the front gave his life, or did what was equal to that — offered his life. The flower of Rugby had enlisted.'

Away from football grounds, the All Saints Church is representative of how small communities lost many of their number during the Great War. Churchgoers on Sunday mornings, or at other prayer services during the week, prayed for the safe return of those whose usual place in the pews was empty. The names of the wounded and dead were a constant. In total, All Saints Church lost nearly 80 members of its congregation. Some families lost two or, in the case of the McKinstry family, three of their men.

While Gallaher was naturally saddened by the loss of young men whose abilities on the rugby field he had recognized, the mayhem half a world away on the Turkish peninsula had a more personal impact on him. Younger brothers Charles and Douglas had taken up arms as Australian troops with the 11th Infantry Battalion. Both fought and were wounded on the bloody slopes of Gallipoli. Charles — the more serious casualty, with shrapnel lodged dangerously close to his spinal cord — was sent back to Australia, taking no further part in the war. Douglas spent time recovering in Egypt from a series of wounds before being sent to the Western Front. Promoted to the rank of Company Sergeant Major, he was killed in action on 3 June 1916, amid the horror that was the battle of the Somme.

The *Evening Post*, 28 June 1916, reported, as did a number of papers, that:

Mr David Gallaher, captain of the famous All Black Rugby team that toured England, has enlisted at Auckland. He had just received advice that his youngest brother was killed in action in France, and he is desirous of filling up his blank. Mr Gallaher has had previous military experience, having served in the Boer War, from which he returned with the rank of sergeant-major.

From here the myth grew that Gallaher's reason for enlisting to serve was his brother's death. His motivation was, according to this item, one of revenge. It would have been a curious reaction for a man who so often was seen as one for whom logic and sound judgement, rather than great emotion, were the keys to his decision-making. Certainly, if one were to find oneself in the position of having a sibling seriously wounded or killed in combat, there would be grief laced with anger. But Gallaher was over the age of men required for service. He had already seen active service a decade and a half previously. He was married with a young child, a further disqualifier from service. For a man who had seen the futility of forces outnumbered on the veldt in South Africa, to seek revenge on the entire German forces seems senseless. His enlistment was surely more a question of loyalty and duty, but 'spin' turned it into something else.

At a time of concentrated marketing of the war by governments in the British Empire to new recruits, Gallaher possibly questioned why his brothers (and others he knew well) should be serving and risking their lives when he, still capable of doing so, was not. What part, too, might his ongoing friendship and correspondence with the former French captain Henri Armand have played in his decision, as he followed the decimation of the northern part of the country that had shown him and his teammates such warmth and hospitality? Gallaher was a team man and he had been on the sidelines for long enough.

Closer examination of Gallaher's army personnel file shows that he had, in fact, already put himself forward for service before Douglas was killed. A medical officer by the name of Talbot examined him on 23 May 1916. It was while he was waiting for his call-up to training at Trentham Army Camp that Douglas died. While the loss might have strengthened his resolve, it most certainly caused greater consternation and worry for Nellie. A widow with a young daughter she would not want to be. One can only imagine their conversations on the matter, echoing those of so many who had brave public faces but cheeks lined with tears behind closed doors.

A fortnight later, the *Evening Post* ran another item about the captain of the rugby team 'which made such a successful tour of Great Britain in 1905':

Mr Gallaher, who is connected with the export trade in Auckland, received a presentation of a purse of sovereigns from his business friends in that city last week, and Capt. Beck DSO handed him the pair of binoculars which he had used at Gallipoli.

Beck had been awarded his DSO in November 1915 for 'distinguished service in the field during the operations in the Dardanelles'. Shortly after, he was invalided back to New Zealand.

It was one of a number of formal community farewells for Gallaher before he travelled by train to Trentham. On 25 July 1916, for the second time in his life, this time aged 42, he took part in basic army training, as part of the 21st NCO's (Non-Commissioned Officers) Infantry Reinforcements. A month later he was allocated to the 21st Reinforcements 'A' Company, then the corresponding company for the 22nd Reinforcements. His charges were the 2nd Platoon, which consisted of the following:

Company Sergeant-Major: D Gallaher (32513)

Sergeants: AP Harvey (29339), ME Ward (32553)

Lance-Sergeant: MH Carroll (6/1482)

Corporals: C Angrove (12/884), RJ Campbell (5/220)

Lance-Corporals: FA Butterfield (21203), V Moon (12/179), AM Spencer (38453), EE Trethaway (38460), GH Whyte (33639)

Privates: RH Ashcroft (40478), WJ Bell (40489), FJ Colebrook (38352), J Currie (38355), JJ Daly (38356), W Daly (38357), J Fletcher (40536), EG Fox (40537), R Gore (38376), RJ Hamilton (38381), SAH Hammond (40558), PJ Handley (38383), R Hayes (39659), EJ Hothersall (3966), LJ Hunter (39661), AE Innis (38395), EJJ Jones (38401), HG Lang (38412), WL McCready (41246), F McKeown (38431), N Nelson (40615), A Noble (38435), CJ Palmer (38581), EA Phillips (38440), J Ross (38445), FJ Schischka (38449), GP Smith (40654), WA Smith (39675), HB Sommerville (40656), AW Thompson (38458), J Whiteside (38465), JH Williams (3847), RJ Wilson (38475), AR Wooldridge (38476).

Gallaher of the 22nd Reinforcements, 1917. Sir George Grey Special Collections, Auckland Libraries, 31-G2779

His men were from a variety of backgrounds and trades. There was an orchardist, a stone polisher, a secretary, several farmers, a waterside worker, a buttermaker, a rabbiter, a fitter, a cheesemaker, a bushman, a letter-carrier and a mill-hand among them. For many of his charges, he was by reputation the famous footballer, former leader of the country's most important sporting side. Gallaher could unite such a disparate group and at the same time give them the confidence to follow him into whatever action lay ahead. He expected loyalty from his boys, and reciprocated that by having their best interests at heart in the large, bureaucratic machine that is the army.

While in camp, Gallaher received news that Second-Lieutenant Frank Wilson had been killed at the Western Front. He had died as the result of wounds suffered at the Somme. The amiable 31-year-old unmarried teacher at Newton School West, whom Gallaher had brought into his Auckland side in 1906 and into the All Blacks in 1910, was part of the weekly congregation at All Saints and had played cricket for the Ponsonby Cricket Club. In fact, Wilson had captained the side to their first Auckland Championship win in 1915. At Gallipoli, Wilson had apparently been one of the dozen sergeants left to hold their station as the evacuation was carried out. While all who lost their lives were mourned, Wilson's death deeply affected those in Ponsonby who knew him.

Army training continued through a miserable winter. The new recruits' first two weeks were spent training without arms before learning basic drills and musketry, which included lessons in bayonet fighting. From there they advanced to firing and to night drills such as sentry duty and patrols.

Trentham Camp Routine Orders No. 607 of 16 November 1916 noted that 'The Camp Commandant desires to express his appreciation of the

excellent manner and neatness of the lines of the 22nd Reinforcements',
who were then entrained to the Wairarapa canvas camps of Featherston
and Tauherenikau. One month later there was extended leave for the
recruits from 19 December 1916 to 7 January 1917, meaning Christmas
gatherings had an added poignancy in the homes of many soldiers.

Once back at Tauherenikau camp, Gallaher and his platoon took
part in a large company training, marching over the Rimutakas to
Trentham camp. There were exercises involving day and night
outposts, setting up camp for the night, a night march and a dawn
attack. The arduous journey, in the summer heat, was perfect
preparation for what they could expect once mobilized in France. The
final days in camp were spent on administrative duties, firing exercises,
trench warfare and practising ceremonial routines.

Departure drew near for the Auckland boys, and they left camp for
their final leave. As was the norm for those who could afford it, Dave,
Nellie and eight-year-old Nora had family photograph portraits taken;
to this day treasured family possessions.

The final day of leave was often a torturous one for soldiers and
their families. Well-intentioned friends and family would call to say
their goodbyes, but often this led to emotional partings. Men tried
to part with firm handshakes, slightly solemn wishes of 'Good luck,
boy', sporting encouragement to 'Give Fritz what-oh', requests for
battlefield souvenirs, and reminders to say hello to a serving family
member or mutual friend if they came across them.

Nellie had to watch her husband go, as thousands of wives had in
the two and a half years since the war had begun, and as many more
would for another 18 months.

For little Nora — an only child, who remembered her father as 'a
jolly fellow' — the parting from her father must have been a particularly

upsetting one, but one in which the stock consoling assurances would have been made, that letters would be written, the war would soon be ended and her father would be home before too long. They were words that, even for the adults, were heavily distilled more with hope than anything else. Were there any parting words from her father as he crouched down to say goodbye to his girl that remained treasured in the memory of Nora as she grew older? For Nellie, how invaluable to her the presence of her own mother must have been.

On 15 February 1917, Company Sergeant-Major Gallaher once again strode up the gangway of a ship as part of a team bound for the other side of the world. Departing the following day, the *Aparima* was a 5,700-tonne transport ship owned by the Union Steam Ship Company of New Zealand. Also embarking, making up the 1,000-strong passenger list, were members of the Artillery, Tunnelling Corps, Maori details, Engineers, Specialist Company, Divisional Signallers, Army Service Corp, and Medical and Dental Corps.

The logistics of having a population the size of a small town on a ship were most tested when it came to meal times. With two sittings of 500 men, the quartermaster would name the companies in each sitting. Gallaher and his men sat at a numbered table, with the allocated seating for each being a permanent setting for the voyage. Naturally, it took some men a number of days to get used to the ship's motion, and it was joked that they were having six meals a day — three down and three up!

One contributor to the ship newspaper — *The Moa: Being the Literary Pickings of a Troopship* — described a facet of life at sea which took some of those sailing on such a vessel for the first time days, and even weeks, to get used to:

The boat sways with the swell and the room creaks and groans,
as girders and beams move in their tight sockets. The creaky noise
pervades the place, a noise such as you never get on shore except on
very windy nights and in earthquakes, and mingled with it is the
hum of a thousand men conversing, punctuated by a frequent yell of
delight as some frantic card player betokens by his antics the playing
of a 'stoush' hand.

Another contributor, using the pseudonym 'The Great White Hope', composed an acrostic: a popular exercise in composition of the time in which all the first letters of a line combine to spell a name or sentence when read down:

H *for the Homeland, we all love so well*
M *for the Maoris, sound as a bell*
N *for the nurses, there are two on this tramp*
Z *for the zeal, that they show to the camp*
T *for the Troopship, the name is below*
A's *for our Company, the best of the show*
P *is the policeman, on guard at the clink*
A *is the armlet that marks him, I think*
R *is the reveille, which makes us all swear*
I *the identity disc, we all have to wear*
M *stands for the men, whose loyalty won't swerve*
A *is the army, that were [sic] going to serve*

On Sunday mornings, as the ship made its way steadily across the ocean, there were church parades, with prayers and hymns, followed by a communion service. A contemplative Gallaher would also attend

Evensong, which was held in the mess as the day drew to a close.

Once settled aboard, Gallaher found there was a familiar face among the ship's crew. The Chief Steward was James Mackie who had travelled to the Boer War on the *Cornwall* with the Sixth Contingent. He had spent time with Kitchener's scouts, then after the war had joined the Union Steam Ship Company. Gallaher told his boys that 'he's an authority on anything relating to boxing and enjoys nothing more than a good old mill in the ring. He's a great favourite with the ladies, and the general public.' As the trip progressed, Mackie proved popular with the troops, too. Gallaher and Mackie could often be found in conversation around the boat, discussing their time in Africa, the whereabouts of old colleagues, and matters pertaining to the oval ball.

After a month at sea, a Sports Committee was established. Gallaher took his place alongside 14 others in organizing egg-and-spoon races, pillow-fighting on a spar, wrestling bouts, skipping and sack races, and even obstacle-course races which saw men climbing over and under nets and ladders and through a wind chute. In the evenings, boxing bouts would draw large, raucous crowds. Tug-of-war matches between NCOs and officers were similarly popular.

Arguably the greatest energy and debate went into organizing a football match for when the ship reached the Cape of Good Hope. Two teams were put together, with Gallaher in charge of one XV. Known on board as his 'hefty lot', the team was made up of former senior players and several who had represented their province, such as the Taranaki halfback Thurston and the Wellington and Wairarapa forward Petty. Gallaher slotted in at wing-forward (of course) and led practices that mostly involved long periods of scrummaging and backs passing with a make-do ball on the narrow decks. The ship's newspaper recorded that: 'The ruling passion of dear old Maoriland is strong.'

(Whether a game was played when the ship reached the port of call — and if so what the result was — is not known.)

The *Aparima* took nearly three months to reach Plymouth, arriving in the south of England on 2 May 1917. Here, the soldiers disembarked and then went on by train to Sling Camp, a training depot on the Salisbury Plain. In *The Chronicles of the New Zealand Expeditionary Force*, a column titled 'Mostly About the Boys' noted that 'C.S.M. Dave Gallagher [sic], of All Black fame, arrived with the 22nd Reinforcements, and is now at Sling'. Mention was made of old teammates Billy Glenn being a 'Military Cross man' with the RFA, and Ernie Booth working for the Australian YMCA.

On 6 June 1917, Gallaher — having just been confirmed in the rank of Sergeant — left with his platoon for France by train and boat. Three days after leaving Sling they marched into the New Zealand Infantry and General Base Depot at Étaples, south of Boulogne. As they were travelling, the great attack by New Zealand and Australian forces on Messines — The Big Show — was occurring. One of the casualties of that event was the Ponsonby, Auckland and All Black front-row forward George Sellars. He was killed while bravely trying to carry a fallen comrade to safety. It was several weeks before Gallaher received the news.

The bustling depot at Étaples, a mix of hospitals and reinforcement camps, was full of soldiers heading for the front, those heading away from the front — be they sick, wounded or on leave — and those recuperating before being sent back to experience further hostilities. Two weeks were spent at Étaples before Gallaher and reinforcements for the 2nd Battalion of the Auckland Regiment were given orders to join their body in the field.

Some Corner of a Foreign Field

'The snarl of shrapnel and the shrieking shell.'

The summer months of 1917 were miserable on the Western Front. When serving in Africa, conditions had been harsh, but Gallaher and his contingent had been mobile, roaming hundreds of miles on horseback in their pursuit of Boer soldiers. There had been a sense of space and even freedom. In northern France, the conflict — arrived at after marching mile upon mile on cobbled roads that jarred the feet and legs — was much more sedentary.

At times it could even be described as claustrophobic. Gains were small. Front lines advanced infrequently. Two lines of soldiers were stationed near each other, subjecting each other to relentless assaults with artillery and gas shells. Fear, hunger, boredom, lack of hygiene and the changing weather were features of trench life. When shells rained down, soldiers listened for the whistling of their trajectory, praying arriving missiles wouldn't explode on or near them. Men watched helplessly as their mates' bodies were blown apart, scattered beyond recognition over the churned-up soil. Others lost limbs, felt their lungs and eyes burning as gas entered them, had hot shrapnel or bullets puncture them, or suffered shell-shock from the jarring barrages of shells. The earth beneath them shuddered with every exploding bomb. Their ears rang from the relentless, thunderous 'boom' of artillery fire. Although shoulder to shoulder, even yelling in their nearest mate's ear was barely audible.

July and August had some hot, dry days, but they were matched by days of exceedingly heavy rain. This quickly turned the dusty roads, paths and dirt trenches to mud. Bogs formed in shell craters. When the rain fell there was little shelter. Men covered themselves as best they could, crowding dug-outs or forcing themselves against the walls of the trenches. In torrential rain they watched the water rising in the bottom of their trenches. The whale oil they had rubbed on their feet to waterproof them was of little benefit when days on end were spent sitting or plodding through pooling trenches. When the rain passed and the sun came out again, the mud began to dry. It stank to high heaven.

If the wind was blowing in the right direction, gas canisters would be opened and clouds of the choking, searing gas would waft across the lines. The soldier on gas guard would ring a bell, sending men scrambling for their rudimentary masks as their eyes began to water and the gas burned the back of their throats.

Private Richard Ashcroft, from Gallaher's platoon, wrote a moving poem titled '1914–1917', submitting it to the soldiers' newspaper New Zealand at the Front. It perfectly captured the dreadfully bleak day-to-day existence of those in the trenches, and the hope that all soldiers had — often placed in the hands of a higher power — of a safe return home.

1914—1917

SOMETHING alone I crave—a little rest;
    Rest from inhuman things conceived in Hell,
The snarl of shrapnel and the shrieking shell,
Mysterious No-man's land where dread things dwell.
So may my spirit once again be blest,
And strong to reach the heights from which it fell
Thro' listening to the War God's deadly jest
When ghouls wreaked vengeance on the tortured west.

Soon may I see the white-sailed yachts come home
At eve across the Waitemata's tide,
    Its placid azure cleft to sparkling foam,
    And hear the sound of laughter as they glide—
Fair women's laughter, sweet to those who roam
    Thro' stricken fields, shall bring me back my
      pride,
        And in that Land where God has built His
          shrine
        There will be peace at last for me and mine.

R. H. ASHCROFT.

Messines.

The 1917 poem written in France by one of Gallaher's platoon, Richard Ashcroft. MATT ELLIOTT COLLECTION

During hours of inactivity, which were many, Gallaher's men smoked, wrote letters to loved ones at home, or picked lice from the seams of their uniform. They waited for new mail and meals to arrive, but most of all they waited to be relieved by other units. Even though they wouldn't admit it, for fear of letting down their cobbers, the men wanted away from the front lines. They wanted a bath, clean clothes, a shave. They wanted to be cleansed of the mud, the dirt and the blood ... theirs and their mates'. They craved a decent hot meal and to feel slowly invigorated by it. They wanted silence and to sleep unfurled and uninterrupted for as long as possible, without having to brace themselves against every noise. Lying in a barn, sleeping deep on a makeshift bed, in a bivvy — anywhere, so long as it was free of lice.

When they had served their rotation away from danger, well behind the lines, Gallaher would then have to tell his platoon, 'We're going up the line again, boys.'

Following the success of the attack on Messines, preparations were being made for the New Zealand Division to be part of another 'big push'. This time they would concentrate their assault on two small hills, known as the Gravenstafel and Bellevue spurs, that run up to the Passchendaele Ridge. Gallaher found himself (indirectly) once more under the command of Herbert Plumer, now a 60-year-old general. The carnage of the Western Front was a very different campaign from that of southern Africa, and the stress felt by Plumer was best illustrated by the fact that his hair had gone completely white in two years.

September 1917 was largely spent training near St Omer, miles away from the front. Then the New Zealand Division began to move forward to reach the lines. They marched for several days, passing through the ruined medieval town of Ypres, their boots pounding on the cobbled streets. Soldiers marvelled at the destruction of the town.

Not one building was left standing. All that remained of the once glorious city cathedral was a ghoulish shell.

When they arrived at the front, there was little time to settle in and prepare for the next push, which was scheduled for 4 October 1917. They had to be ready to go in quick time.

On 3 October, the enemy had been silent during the day, but that changed as night fell and sporadic barrages fell around the New Zealand and Australian troops. The pre-dawn hours awaiting orders in the trenches are best described by Ormond Burton, who wrote of his time with the Auckland Regiment in the book *The Silent Division* that:

> ... *during the night a drizzling rain commenced to fall. Through the miserable hours of waiting, men huddled together in the shell-holes, without overcoats, shivering under their oilsheets. All night the German guns searched the slopes, and towards morning their fire became very intense. In the darkness officers and NCOs moved around seeing that all was in place and giving the last instructions. Breakfast was an unappetizing meal of bully beef, dry bread and water, nerves on edge after the ordeal of the night, very tired, counting off the moments until the barrage, half-eager for it to come, yet fearful of the coming, for all know that many must die when the hour strikes. On the other side German soldiers were also waiting to attack ...*

At 5.30 in the morning, German artillery began bombarding the Anzac lines, but fortunately much of it was misdirected and fell some distance from where the troops were readying themselves to advance.

Zero hour. As the hands on wristwatches ticked over to six o'clock — 15 minutes before sunrise — New Zealand and Australian guns opened fire, providing cover for the infantry to hop the bags and attack the German lines. This shelling decimated large numbers of German infantry. The Wellington regiment made their way through an estimated 500 casualties. But the advance was not a walkover. The Germans retaliated at 10 minutes past the hour with a determined charge of their own, one of the few times both sides met with bayonets drawn, and their guns were let loose on the lines of slowly advancing Anzac soldiers.

Burton also recalled the German barrage on the paths the Kiwi soldiers were following:

To either side and clear in view lay dead men blackened by the explosions. Shell after shell shrieked down and burst a few feet on either side, flinging columns of black mud into the air. The nervous strain was a terrible one because it was impossible to hurry and the screaming missiles fell with a machine-like regularity.

It was under this torrent of shelling that Gallaher was struck and fell. As he led his platoon over the top and towards the enemy lines, a shell exploded in front of him. He suffered severe wounds to his face and head but, like so many that day, he did not die immediately.

The two sides called a truce later in the day, allowing them to tend to their injured and attempt to clear their dead. Private Monty Ingram wrote in his diary:

Enemy Red Cross men can plainly be seen gathering in the dead and wounded on our front. All about us are our own dead and dying, lying in the mud in the drizzling rain. God knows when they will be removed as a vast sea of mud lies between us and the habitable rear from whence the stretcher bearers must come. Most of our own stretcher bearers have 'gone West' and we are physically incapable of removing them ourselves. ... A few yards behind our trench lies one of our wounded in delirium. He is on his back, his head resting in his helmet which is a basin of blood; he is making awful grimaces and appears to be choking. Someone goes over to him and discovers that his denture is stuck in his throat and he is certainly choking. The denture is relieved but not before the fingers of the Good Samaritan are severely bitten by the delirious man. We go about tending our wounded, endeavouring to make them more comfortable, though God knows our efforts are but poor relief. All we can do is lay them on a ground-sheet, cover them with another sheet and leave them in the drizzling rain and gathering darkness, alone with their thoughts and pain.

In Gallaher's case, he was carried from the battlefield to the 3rd Australian Casualty Clearing Station. These stations were nothing more than a flagged area behind the front lines where the dead and dying were lain on whatever could keep them up off the mud, and medical staff ascertained the injuries, the seriousness of the wounds and where they should next be evacuated to. Rarely was there shelter, even makeshift, so the workers and the wounded were exposed to the elements.

Gallaher's wounds were so severe that he passed away before he could be moved off to a field ambulance. The proud son of Ireland and New Zealand — father, husband, churchgoer, unflappable captain and soldier — lay dead on a foreign field.

War, as they say, has no favourites. That Gallaher had been an All Black, was the father of a nine-year-old girl, a husband, an inspiring leader, and a man of enormous loyalty to his community meant nothing in the mud and the destruction of Flanders. He was but one of millions of soldiers from a multitude of countries who fell in the 'war to end all wars'. Two other members of the 22nd Reinforcements were killed on the same day as Gallaher. Owen McLean was a young private, with family in the Auckland suburb of Epsom, who had been a men's outfitter before the war. Second Lieutenant Evan McRoberts was a married man, a former clerk, from Auckland's Mt Eden.

Eight days after Gallaher died, New Zealand suffered its darkest day. The Battle of Passchendaele was a military disaster, a slaughter. It saw over 2,500 of her sons killed or wounded in just 24 hours.

The Auckland Rugby Union's Management Committee paid tribute to Gallaher at a meeting on 24 October 1917. Committee members themselves had been touched by the fact that President John Arneil's son, a member of the New Zealand Rifle Brigade, had served and been wounded. The two sons of the Chair of the Management Committee, Mr F Ohlson, had enlisted and served in the early part of the war. Among the committee present was Gallaher's former Ponsonby, Auckland and All Black teammate George Nicholson. With great solemnity, messages of condolence to Mrs Gallaher from the Canterbury and Otago rugby unions were read. As members stood in silence, the following was also read aloud:

The Committee of this Union tender its deepest sympathy with the relatives of the late Sergeant Dave Gallaher, died of wounds received in action in France, in the service of the Empire. The late Sergeant Gallaher's long and honourable association with Rugby Football, his connection as Field Captain of the great 'All Black' team, as sole selector for many years for this Union, and as one of the selectors of the N.I. teams will not soon be forgotten, and his death will leave a gap difficult to fill.

Following Dave's death, another Gallaher brother, Henry, enlisted to fight for the Australian forces. He first saw action on 6 April 1918. Eighteen days later, during fighting around Villers-Bretonneux, he was killed. Five Gallaher brothers had proudly worn the uniforms and badges of Australian and New Zealand soldiers. Three died on the other side of the world from their adopted countries to which they had shown such a sense of duty. One who survived suffered the physical effects of the war for the rest of his life. The cruel blows inflicted by the four years of war on a family such as the Gallahers brings to mind the words of a poem called 'Waste' written by a British war chaplain, Geoffrey Studdert Kennedy (awarded the Military Cross for bravery at Messines), who wrote:

Waste of muscle, waste of brain,
Waste of patience, waste of pain,
Waste of manhood, waste of wealth,
Waste of beauty, waste of health,
Waste of blood, and waste of tears,
Waste of youth's most glorious years,
Waste of ways the saints have trod,
Waste of glory, waste of God.

Gallaher's grave, Nine Elms.
RAMELTON.NET

Afterword

O valiant hearts, who to your glory came through dust of conflict and
through battle flame, tranquil you lie, your knightly virtue proved, your
memory hallowed in the land you loved.

— All Saints Parish Roll of Honour 1914–1918

Thirteen former All Blacks lost their lives in the Great War.
Gallaher's 1905 teammate Billy Glenn was awarded the Military
Cross for bravery during the war. Great Britain players from the 1904
side — Bedell-Sivright and Swannell — lost their lives in combat. Most
of the teams who played the 1905 Originals had members of their line-
up perish during the war. Of the Cheshire XV, six of the 10 Birkenhead
Park players in the side were killed, including captain Percy Kendall.
All four of the 1905 Home nations test teams lost players. Irish captain
Basil MacLear, a captain with the Royal Dublin Fusiliers, was killed
in battle at Ypres in 1915. English internationals Edgar Mobbs and
JE Raphael lost their lives. Mobbs, who had also played for the Bedford
XV, established a Sportsman's Battalion. With the rank of lieutenant-
colonel he was awarded the DSO, but was killed near Passchendaele
nine weeks before Gallaher. Welsh forward Charlie Pritchard was also
a casualty. The list of former players who lost their lives at the Western
Front could run for several pages. Perhaps the most harrowing statistic
in relation to players connected to the Originals is to do with James
Ross, the Surrey forward, who went on to be capped for Scotland.
He was one of 100 men from the London Scottish club who were
killed during the war. In fact, an astounding 45 of the club's 60 playing
members lost their lives.

Gallaher had initially been buried by the Ypres–Menin road. At the war's end, one of the first to visit Gallaher's final resting place — in the Nine Elms cemetery, Plot 11, Row D, Number 8 — was Henri Armand, who had captained France against the Originals.

Dave and his two brothers Henry and Douglas are inscribed together, among the thousands of other names, on the walls of the Auckland War Memorial Museum's Hall of Remembrance.

Gallaher's widow Nellie, like so many of her generation who found their lives tragically changed by events half a world away, was a woman of great fortitude. One can only marvel at how thousands of wives and mothers coped with the loss of their beloved men and boys. There is a phrase that perhaps aptly sums up where they got their strength from. It is written on the headstone of Dave's great teammate Bill Cunningham, who died in 1927 and was buried in Auckland's Hillsborough cemetery. (Among Cunningham's pallbearers were Fred Murray and Georges Tyler, Nicholson and Gillett. When his coffin had been lowered into the grave, an Auckland rugby jersey was dropped onto its lid.) At the bottom of his headstone are the words: *God Knew Best.* This was the philosophy that helped so many cope with their wartime grief. Nellie suffered another blow when her mother died the year after Dave.

All Saints Church was a place for her to pray for the soul of her husband and for her to ask her God why he had taken her husband and the father of her little girl. It was also a place for her to thank God for the life of her husband, and where she was supported and comforted in the immediacy of her loss. For the rest of her life she continued to be involved in church activities, many of which were for the benefit of others. Her lifelong involvement in the parish was an example to others of a life of dedication and selflessness — something her husband would have been proud of. Nellie died in January 1969.

At a meeting of the ARFU Management Committee on 10 August 1921, it was proposed that 'at [the] annual meeting of delegates 1922 season it be a recommendation that either a Challenge Shield or Cup be given for senior competition to perpetuate the memory of the late D. Gallagher [*sic*].' So the Gallaher Shield came into being and was first played for in 1922. The Ponsonby club has won the shield more times than any other.

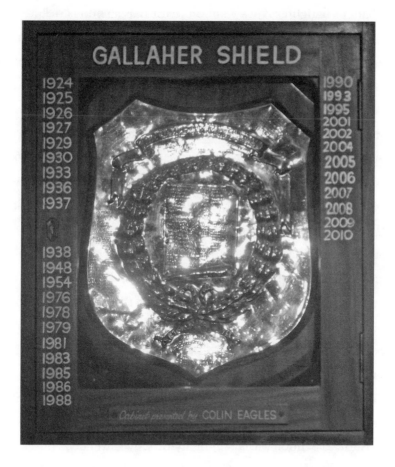

The Gallaher Shield, Auckland club rugby's most sought-after trophy. Here it resides on the wall of Gallaher's club, Ponsonby, which claimed it for an extraordinary eighth year in a row in 2011. MATT ELLIOTT COLLECTION

In 1924, Cliff Porter's All Blacks visited Gallaher's grave during their tour of Great Britain, Ireland, France and Canada, placing a wreath on behalf of the Ponsonby club. Porter's side avenged the 1905 loss against Wales (winning 19–0) and went through their 32 matches unbeaten. They became known as 'The Invincibles'. They did not play a test against Scotland on that tour.

The last of the Originals, Billy Wallace, died in 1972, aged 93.

Gallaher's daughter Nora went on to excel as a young cricketer and devoted herself to a number of voluntary organizations. She passed away aged 91, in December 1998. Her funeral service was also held in All Saints Church.

In 2000, the French and New Zealand rugby unions agreed to contest a cup named after Gallaher. When it was first played for in Paris on Armistice Day of that year, the All Blacks wore a red poppy sewn into the sleeve of their jerseys. They won 39–26.

In 2005, then-captain Tana Umaga led a contingent of All Blacks to Gallaher's birthplace, Ramelton. In his autobiography he wrote that Gallaher was 'the father of the All Blacks'. Members of the team also visited the Letterkenny Rugby Football Club and helped christen the club's ground 'Dave Gallaher Memorial Park'. The club (founded 100 years after Gallaher's birth) sports a silver fern and Gallaher's name as part of its crest. The same year, Gallaher was inducted into the New Zealand-based International Rugby Hall of Fame.

In 2010, a mural painted by Renee Te Pairi, Steve Graveson and Dena Hale featuring Maria and Dave was unveiled on the gable end of the No. 2 Katikati School Maria taught at and Dave attended.

In July 2011, the statue of Gallaher by Auckland sculptor Malcolm Evans was unveiled at Eden Park.

Malcolm Evans's bronze sculpture of Gallaher — a Ponsonby club initiative — which stands at the northern edge of Eden Park. MATT ELLIOTT COLLECTION

When Auckland Rugby committee members paid tribute to Gallaher on the news of his death in 1917, they referred to his 'long and honourable association with Rugby Football'. He gave freely of his

time, to Ponsonby, Auckland and New Zealand football, as well as to a number of other organizations. He did this because he felt he could — and wanted to — contribute something to those associations. As an athlete, he may not have been the most natural of footballers, or be remembered as the greatest to play the game, but he was a keen competitor, a stalking, disruptive adversary. While he would appeal to referees with great gusto during play, he accepted their decisions, and even one of rugby's greatest controversies could not draw a sour word from him.

Off the field, he was a man of few words; what some might describe as 'a thinker'. His chosen loyalties were unshakeable, his sense of fairness unwavering.

Over a century after he last walked off a football field, his reputation as a player and a leader have only been enhanced; not by further clouds of myth enveloping his story, but by the discovery of more details of just what a man he was. We elevate our humble heroes, and that is what Dave Gallaher was. He saw himself as but one of a unit. He did have the privilege and responsibility of having to lead others into play and into battle. At all times, he had the best interests of his companions at heart, be it to his detriment or not. The 1905 All Black tour was a crucial undertaking. Would New Zealand rugby be the same had Gallaher's team returned having suffered a series of losses? Gallaher was a person of fortitude and selflessness; a boy from the north of Ireland who became a proud New Zealand man. He played a key role in establishing the impetus for the All Blacks to become the most successful international rugby team in the history of the game. More than that, he answered the call to serve his country, not in one war but two. He was a man of his times, but his life's example remains timeless.

Appendix

Dave Gallaher's career as player, selector and coach

Positions: Hooker, Wing-forward

Club football: Parnell (Juniors), Ponsonby

Auckland Senior Grade Club Championship: Ponsonby, 1897

Auckland debut: *v* Queensland, Auckland, Saturday, 8 August 1896

Final first-class match: *v* Marlborough, Blenheim, 26 August 1909

Auckland representative: 1896–97, 1899, 1900, 1903–05, 1909: 26 matches (15 wins, 9 losses, 2 draws)

Auckland points: 6 — 2 tries: *v* Otago, Dunedin, 1899; and Great Britain, Auckland, 1904

All Black number: 97

All Black debut: *v* Wellington Province, Wellington, Saturday, 11 July 1903; aged 29 years, 254 days

Test debut: *v* Australia, Sydney, Saturday, 15 August 1903; aged 29 years, 289 days

Final test: *v* France, Paris, Monday, 1 January 1906; aged 32 years, 63 days

All Black captain number: 13

All Black tests: 6 (4 as captain)

Total All Black games: 36

Matches as All Black captain: 27 (25 won, 2 lost)

All Black points: 14 — 4 tries: *v* Wellington Province, Wellington, 1903; *v* Combined Western Districts, West Maitland, 1903; *v* New South Wales Country, Sydney, 1903; *v* Devonport Albion, Devonport, 1905; — 1 conversion: *v* British Columbia, San Francisco, 1906

Games against New Zealand: 2 for Auckland at Auckland — 7 August 1897, and 1 July 1905

North *v* South: 1903, 1905

Total first-class matches: 64

National selector: 1907–1914: All Blacks played 50, won 44, lost 4, drew 2

Auckland sole selector/coach: 1906–1915: Auckland played 65, won 48, lost 11, drew 6

Bibliography

100 Years of Auckland Rugby. Unity Press, Auckland, 1983.

Auckland Amateur Athletic and Cycle Club, *Jubilee Souvenir 1877/78 – 1927/28. Athletic Recorder and Official Programme.* AAAC, Auckland, 1928.

Auckland Cricket Association, *100 Not Out: A centennial history of the Auckland Cricket Association.* Auckland, 1983.

Barrow, Graeme, *Up Front: The story of the All Black scrum.* Heinemann, Auckland, 1985.

Baskerville, AH, *Modern Rugby Football: New Zealand methods.* Wellington, 1907.

Burton, OE, *The Silent Division: New Zealanders at the front: 1914–1919.* Angus & Robertson, Sydney, 1935.

Bush, Ernest E (ed), *The Katikati Story.* Tauranga Historical Society, 1975.

Carlyon, Jenny and Diana Morrow, *Urban Village: The story of Ponsonby, Freemans Bay and St Mary's Bay.* Random House, Auckland, 2008.

Carter, A Kay, *Maria Gallaher: Her short life and her children's stories.* Champion Associates, Paraparaumu, 2011.

Chester, RH and NAC McMillan, *Men in Black.* Moa Publications, Auckland, 1978.

—— *The Encyclopedia of New Zealand Rugby.* Moa Publications, Auckland, 1981.

—— *Centenary: 100 years of All Black rugby.* Moa Publications, Auckland, 1984.

—— *The Visitors: The history of international rugby teams in New Zealand.* Moa Publications, Auckland, 1990.

Cleave, Arthur (ed), *Cleave's Auckland Provincial, Commercial, Municipal, and General Directory.* (Various.)

Coffey, John and Bernie Wood, *Auckland, 100 Years of Rugby League 1909–2009.* Huia Publishers, Auckland, 2009.

Crawford, John and Ellen Ellis, *To Fight for the Empire: An illustrated history of New Zealand and the South African War, 1899–1902.* Reed, Auckland, 1999.

Crawford, John and Ian McGibbon (eds), *One Flag, One Queen, One Tongue: New Zealand, the British Empire and the South African War.* Auckland University Press, Auckland, 2003.

Dixon, George, *The Triumphant Tour of the New Zealand Footballers.* Geddis and Blomfield, Wellington, 1906.

Ellison, Thomas, *The Art of Rugby Football: With hints and instructions on every point of the game.* Geddis and Blomfield, Wellington, 1902.

Fagan, Sean, *The Rugby Rebellion: The divide of League and Union*. RL1908, Australia, 2005.

Fox, Dave, Bogle, Ken and Mark Hoskins. *A Century of the All Blacks in Britain and Ireland*. Tempus, Gloucestershire, 2006.

Gallaher, D and WJ Stead, *The Complete Rugby Footballer on the New Zealand System*. Methuen, London, 1906.

Gray, Arthur J, *An Ulster Plantation: The story of the KatiKati settlement*. Reed, Wellington, 1938.

Hall, DOW, *The New Zealanders in South Africa 1899–1902*. Department of Internal Affairs, Wellington, 1949.

Harper, Glyn, *Massacre at Passchendaele: The New Zealand Story*. HarperCollins, Auckland, 2000.

Haynes, John, *From All Blacks to All Golds: Rugby league's pioneers*. Ryan and Haynes, Christchurch, 1996.

Heidenstrom, Peter, *Athletes of the Century: 100 years of New Zealand track and field*. Wellington, GP Publications, 1992.

Howitt, Bob and Dianne Haworth, *All Black Magic: 100 years of New Zealand test rugby*. Harper*Sports*, Auckland, 2003.

—— *1905 Originals*. Harper*Sports*, Auckland, 2005.

Ingram, Wallie, *Legends in their Lifetime*. Reed, Wellington, 1962.

Knight, Lindsay, *They Led the All Blacks*. Rugby Press, Auckland, 1991.

—— *The Shield: A century of the Ranfurly Shield*. Celebrity Books, Auckland, 2002.

—— *The Blue and White Jersey: Celebrating 125 years of Auckland rugby*. Celebrity Books, Auckland, 2008.

Lawrence, Richard, *Unshaven Jaws: Sixty All Black test captains 1903–2007*. Richard Lawrence, Hastings, 2007.

Linklater, Joseph, *On Active Service in South Africa with the 'Silent Sixth'*. McKee and Co., Wellington, 1906.

Lovesey, Peter, *The Official Centenary History of the Amateur Athletic Association*. Guinness, UK, 1980.

Macdonald, Finlay, *The Game of Our Lives: The story of rugby and New Zealand — and how they've shaped each other*. Viking, Auckland, 1996.

Mackenzie, JM, *All Blacks in Chains*. Truth, Wellington, 1960.

Mackenzie, Morrie, *Black, Black, Black!* Minerva, Auckland, 1969.

McCarthy, Winston, *Haka! The All Blacks story*. Pelham, London, 1968.

McCrystal, John, *The Originals: 1905 All Black rugby odyssey*. Random House, Auckland, 2005.

McLean, TP, *Great Days in New Zealand Rugby*. Reed, Wellington, 1959.

—— *New Zealand Rugby Legends: 15 reflections*. Moa Publications, Auckland, 1987.

—— *The All Blacks*. Sidgwick and Jackson, London, 1991.

McMillan, Neville, *New Zealand Sporting Legends: 27 pre-war sporting heroes*. Moa Beckett, Auckland, 1993.

Mulgan, John, *Report on Experience*. Oxford University Press, London, 1947.

Neazor, Paul, *Ponsonby Rugby Club: Passion and pride*. Celebrity Books, Auckland, 1999.

New Zealand at the Front: Written and illustrated by men of the New Zealand Division. Cassell, London, 1917.

Official Souvenir of the 1905 New Zealand Team. New Zealand Rugby Union.

Palenski, Ron, *The Jersey: The pride and the passion, the guts and the glory — what it means to wear the All Black jersey*. Hodder Moa Beckett, Auckland, 2001.

—— *All Blacks Myths and Legends*. Hodder Moa, Auckland, 2008.

Palenski, Ron (ed), *All Blacks: The authorised portrait*. Hachette Livre NZ, Auckland, 2007.

—— *Between the Posts: A New Zealand rugby anthology*. Hodder and Stoughton, Auckland, 1989.

Patterson, Brad (ed), *Sport, Society and Culture in New Zealand*. Stout Research Centre, Victoria University of Wellington, 1999.

Phillips, Jock, *A Man's Country? The image of the pakeha male — a history*. Penguin, Auckland, 1996.

Reyburn, Wallace, *A History of Rugby*. Arthur Baker Ltd, Wellington, 1971.

Richards, Huw, *A Game for Hooligans: The history of rugby union*. Mainstream Publishing, Edinburgh, 2006.

Romanos, Joseph, *Famous Fullbacks*. Rugby Press Ltd, Auckland, 1989.

—— *Famous Flankers*. Rugby Press Ltd, Auckland, 1990.

Rugby in Auckland, 1883–1967: Official history of the Auckland Rugby Football Union Inc. Unity Press, Auckland, 1967.

Ryan, Greg, *Forerunners of the All Blacks: The 1888–89 New Zealand Native football team in Britain, Australia and New Zealand*. Canterbury University Press, Christchurch, 1993.

Ryan, Greg (ed), *Tackling Rugby Myths: Rugby and New Zealand society 1854–2004*. University of Otago Press, Dunedin, 2005.

Seddon, Thomas, *The Seddons: An autobiography*. Collins, Auckland, 1968.

Smith, Max, *Champion Blokes: 44 great N.Z. sportsmen then and now*. Whitcombe & Tombs Ltd, Auckland, 1964.

Stead, WJ and New Zealand Sports Hall of Fame, *Billy's Trip Home: The remarkable diary of an All Black on tour*. New Zealand Sports Hall of Fame, Dunedin, 2005.

Stewart, Adela, *My Simple Life in New Zealand*, R Banks, London, 1908.

Stewart, Col. H, *The New Zealand Division 1916–19: A popular history based on official records*. Whitcombe and Tombs, Auckland, 1921.

Stokes, Evelyn, *A History of Tauranga County*. Dunmore Press, Palmerston North, 1980.

Stone, RA, *Rugby Players Who Have Made New Zealand Famous*. Scott and Scott, Auckland, 1938.

Stone, RCJ, *Logan Campbell's Auckland: Tales from the early years*. Auckland University Press, Auckland, 2007.

Stowers, Richard, *Kiwi Versus Boer: The First New Zealand Mounted Rifles in the Anglo-Boer War 1899–1902*. Richard Stowers, Hamilton, 1992.

Swan, AC, *History of New Zealand Rugby Football, 1870–1945*. Reed, Wellington, 1948.

—— *The New Zealand Rugby Football Union, 1892–1967*. Reed, Wellington, 1967.

The Cyclopedia of New Zealand: Industrial, descriptive, historical, biographical facts, figures, illustrations. Cyclopedia Co., Wellington, 1897–1908.

The Wales Test 1905: Wales 3, All Blacks 0. Nag's Head, Christchurch, 1983.

Tobin, Christopher, *The Original All Blacks 1905–06*. Hodder Moa Beckett, Auckland, 2005.

Turley, Alan. *Rugby: The pioneer years*. HarperCollins, Auckland, 2008.

Twisleton, Corporal F, *With the New Zealanders at the Front: A story of twelve months campaigning in South Africa*. Whitcombe and Tombs, Christchurch, 1902.

Umaga, Tana with Paul Thomas, *Up Close*. Hodder Moa, Auckland, 2007.

Verdon, Paul. *Born to Lead*. Celebrity Books, Auckland, 2000.

—— *Tribute: Ranking the greatest All Blacks of all time*. Cumulus, Auckland, 2001.

—— *Heritage: Golden years of All Black rugby*. Hill-Verdon Publishing, Auckland, 2002.

Why the All Blacks Triumphed, Daily Mail, London, 1906.

Wright, Matthew, *Western Front: The New Zealand Division in the First World War 1916–1918*. Reed, Auckland, 2005.

Archives New Zealand

Allotment books (old) — Auckland Land District c.1901–1921.

Auckland Hospital Register of Patients, No. 1-1792: ZAAP-15288-2a.

New Zealand Defence Force Personnel Record — David Gallaher: AABK 18805 W5515 0001971.

Other sources

Auckland Public Library Family History e-resources and Heritage Images online.

Auckland War Memorial Museum 'Cenotaph' database.

National Archives of Australia.

New Zealand Electronic Text Centre: www.nzetc.org

New Zealand Mounted Rifles: www.nzmr.org

www.paperspast.co.nz

www.rugbymuseum.co.nz

Unpublished material

Auckland Rugby Football Union Minute books and annual reports — various.

Buchanan, Timothy, 'Missionaries of Empire: 1905 All Black Tour', extended essay, University of Canterbury, 1981.

Dixon, George, Papers relating to the 1905 All Black Tour. Auckland War Memorial Museum, MS748.

Electoral roll, Electoral district of the City of Auckland, 1893. Electoral district of the district of Parnell, 1896.

Electoral roll for the City of Auckland. H Brett printer, 1893.

Letters from Dave Gallaher to his sister Molly, Alexander Turnbull Library, MS-papers-3576.

Macauley, Samuel, Shipboard diary. Auckland War Memorial Museum Library, MS91/54.

New Zealand Rugby Football Union Minute books: 1B 27/4/1900–28/4/1905; 2 3/5/1905-20/2/1908; 3 27/2/1908-14/12/1911; 4 7/2/1912-5/2/1919.

1917 diary of Lance Corporal Cyril Elliott, New Zealand Rifle Brigade.

Sixth Contingent Magazine, 1904–1961.

The cuttings scrapbook of Auckland manager Charles Stitchbury.

Lady Jocelyn Herald, printed by Edward Morgan-Morriss, 1878.

The Moa: The journal of the Twenty Seconds on troopship 'Aparima'.

Audiovisual

'ANZAC Special: Dave Gallaher.' Sky Sport, 2005.

'Giants of the Past.' Pacific Films, 1967. Film Archive. F7856.

'New Zealand v England, 1905.' Film Archive. F27366.

'The All Blacks arrival and reception at Auckland, 1906.' Film Archive. F4361.

'The Invincible All Blacks Record Tour 1924–25.' Film Archive. F7026.